I LOVE THE
BONES OF YOU

I LOVE THE BONES OF YOU

My Father and the Making of Me

CHRISTOPHER ECCLESTON

**SIMON &
SCHUSTER**

London · New York · Sydney · Toronto · New Delhi

A CBS COMPANY

First published in Great Britain by Simon & Schuster UK Ltd, 2019
A CBS COMPANY

Copyright © Christopher Eccleston, 2019

The right of Christopher Eccleston to be identified as the author
of this work has been asserted in accordance with the
Copyright, Designs and Patents Act, 1988.

1 3 5 7 9 10 8 6 4 2

Simon & Schuster UK Ltd
1st Floor
222 Gray's Inn Road
London WC1X 8HB

www.simonandschuster.co.uk
www.simonandschuster.com.au
www.simonandschuster.co.in

Simon & Schuster Australia, Sydney
Simon & Schuster India, New Delhi

The author and publishers have made all reasonable efforts
to contact copyright-holders for permission, and apologise
for any omissions or errors in the form of credits given.
Corrections may be made to future printings.

A CIP catalogue record for this book
is available from the British Library.

Hardback ISBN: 978-1-4711-7631-9
Trade Paperback ISBN: 978-1-4711-7632-6
eBook ISBN: 978-1-4711-7633-3

Typeset in Perpetua by M Rules
Printed in the UK by CPI Group (UK) Ltd, Croydon, CR0 4YY

MIX
Paper from
responsible sources
FSC
www.fsc.org   FSC® C020471

To my mother Elsie, my son Albert
and my daughter Esme. I love you.

CONTENTS

PROLOGUE

I saw how the story ends.

My dad was eating his dinner. Every mouthful, so slowly. A labour of disinterest and disengagement as he lifted the fork to his lips.

Opposite him was an aged man of similar disposition. Like my dad he was wearing a baseball cap. Neither said a word. No acknowledgement of one another's existence. It was the first time I'd seen Dad in the home. I walked over – 'Hi, pal.' He just mumbled. Nothing remotely coherent. I sat down and looked at him, my face no more than 12 inches from his. The nose, the brow, it was all still there, same as when he peered down at me from his chair, his throne, as I lay on the carpet playing with the toy Indians, Cochise, Chief Sitting Bull, Hiawatha – 'Hiawortha' as he said it – and Crazy Horse, which he'd given me, and so perfectly named, as a kid. That was the face of Ronnie Ecc: handsome, fearsome, an eagle. Except this eagle was no longer soaring. The eyes, no more sharp and searching. The lustre had gone. The last few downward spirals of a once strong, proud and vital being.

I was struck by the sheer pathos of it. I could see that life can end like this. We lose our physical strength. Our mental capacity does diminish. What cut deeper, to the core in fact, was the absence of spirit. My dad had always been a grafter, a fighter, full of bonhomie and passion. Now he didn't know who he was, where he was. A man once so full of vigour had been slowly drained of life, replaced by mere existence. I was seeing my dad reduced to a shell.

His appearance said everything. Dad had always been so fastidious about the way he looked. Always immaculately clean. As a kid, it used to make me laugh. He'd wash his face so hard that his nose would shine, dry his hair so vigorously it stood up – the detail only a child sees. Coming in from work would be marked by a shave and a spruce-up. No way did he want to wear the factory when he wasn't in it. Looking good was hugely important to him and, when the dementia came, my mum kept up the standard. When he lived with her, he was turned out fantastic. But he wasn't getting that care in the home. And I don't blame those people. They were understaffed. And they didn't love him. You don't get cared for the same as you do by people who love the bones of you.

We used to drive past this place. 'Shoot me,' Dad would say. 'I'm not ending up in there. I tell you, shoot me. If you won't shoot me, I'll shoot myself. Nobody is looking after me. Nobody.' And now here he was.

I sat in front of him and cried. I put my arm round him, hugging him, touching him. My dad and not my dad. I was seeing him away from my mum, away from the love and the care that he'd enjoyed. And I was seeing where he was in life, where his story was ending. Here, in this home, was where his life was ending. And it did end there. That was where he died.

I'd been grieving for him for years.

I

UP THE DANCERS

I lay in bed, and as the stories washed over me, I was blessed with an overwhelming feeling of 'this is my dad'. He'd read me a chapter a night, and when the time came to finish he'd put his face on mine – a kiss and not a kiss – and we'd both be embarrassed. Other times, at the end of a long working day, he'd fall asleep on the bed next to me. The closeness was incredible. Me, my dad, and a book. Gentleness and intimacy. I saw a totally different side to this man. I don't say that with hindsight. Absolutely I felt it at the time.

Dad had to take over my bedtimes. Mum had started working too. She began her shift at 5 p.m. and Dad got in at six. It was up to him.

At first, it seemed weird – this was what my mum did – but I quickly grew to love the new arrangement. It became a bit of a routine. Dad would make me two pieces of toast at about half past eight, we'd watch TV, preferably Hannibal Heyes and 'Kid' Curry in *Alias Smith and Jones*, and then that was it – 'Come on, up the apples and pears. Up the dancers.'

What I loved most was that he read to me. I hear people say I've got a strong voice on stage and, without a doubt, Dad is where it came from. He had a beautiful tone and was very confident at reading. He coloured a story in and made it sing from the page. He read me *The Adventures of Tom Sawyer*, although I wasn't actually that interested in the title character, and I don't think he was either. We just wanted to hear about Huckleberry Finn, who was poor but extremely resourceful. I identified that character as being my dad, and I think he recognised the same — it came across in his reading. Dad liked a story about the lost, the marginalised. He also read me *Black Beauty*, Anna Sewell's novel about a horse that is badly treated, abused, an outsider, before eventually becoming treasured and loved. Both books are about being misunderstood and downtrodden and eventual triumph. Dad absolutely occupied those two books. He was a voracious reader and I wouldn't be surprised if, as a child, he'd read them himself.

One day my mum didn't go to work. When it got to bedtime, Dad looked at me. That familiar cry of 'Up the dancers!' went up.

'I want Mum to take me to bed.'

'Right, OK.' Off me and my mum went.

Next day, after school, Dad was still at work. My mum had a word: 'You know yesterday when you asked me to take you to bed?'

'Yes.'

'Your dad was a bit upset. He went to pieces.'

Inside I was thinking, *You can't say that about my dad. You can't say my dad went to pieces because of me.* But actually it wasn't her who had brought me up short; it was the notion of me having power over my dad. I was stunned. 'He was hurt by *me*? He treasured that time together?' In my head, I'd always thought he didn't want to do bedtime. This, I now realised, was actually a man who felt very tenderly towards his child, and that child had hurt him. To understand that my dad loved me, and to witness my mum's protectiveness and sensitivity to him, was a beautiful moment. It deepened my love for them both.

I really admired Mum for unveiling my dad's true feelings, and her own, and it wouldn't be the last time she did so. On another occasion, me and my mate Dave were mucking about in the garden. My mum came out. 'Eh, you two, be quiet! Chris, your dad's in bed and he's working nights.'

It didn't stop us. She came out again. 'Come in here, you!' she said to me. I stood in the kitchen. 'Your dad's in bed because he's working nights, and he's working nights to make money to look after you, so go and play somewhere else.'

Again, I took in what she said. *God, she loves him,* I thought. *She knows what he does for the family, and I'm being an idiot, and she's told me.*

Those two incidents were just huge. Mum was telling me something important: 'You understand who he is.' I'm still not sure I do. I've been trying to work out my dad since my very first memory of him, lying on that living-room carpet playing with my toy Indians as he sat in his chair. That memory, appropriately enough for a man whose character and personality I'm still trying to pin down, is ambiguous.

We were in our front room in Little Hulton, the black-and-white TV was on, and he was slightly to my left, reading his paper. We were both absorbed.

'Have you noticed anything?' I turned my head and looked up at him on his throne. His voice had taken me by surprise.

Why is he talking to me? I puzzled. *He doesn't talk much when he's got his paper.* I was always careful not to annoy Dad so I could simply have this time in his presence. Even at that age, I wanted him to be happy.

I read his face to gauge his mood, too young to truly assess his tone and expression. Was he joking? Was he angry? Which way was this going to go?

One thing I did know was I felt thrilled to be asked a direct question, like he would ask an adult. Trouble was, I didn't have the answer. Would I disappoint him? Get in trouble? I didn't want to spoil this moment. I was so happy to be in the same space.

'No.' (I had to say something.)

'I've stopped smokin'.'

He was desperate for a fag, craving nicotine, and wanted to share it with somebody, an urge born of the irritation of that need. My dad was, like me, a schizo-smoker. He'd not smoke for five years, puff through forty a day for a decade, and then stop again. Senior Service he smoked, and then Benson & Hedges, before jacking them in too. 'I'm giving them up,' he said. 'I'm only smoking cigars.' He'd smoke ten Hamlet a day and inhale them. When he slept, his chest sounded like a crying baby.

As a young lad, when Dad paid me attention it felt so special. The toy Indians were a case in point. While I had toys, I was quite destructive, wouldn't take proper care of them, but the Indians were different. They came alive because my dad was invested in them. He named them, and in so doing engaged in an imaginative game with me, so much more than just 'Here you are, play with these.' They were important.

My playing with Indians fitted in with his own love of the cowboy films. He would always side with the Native Americans, so much so that I look at his nose, and mine, and think about how those very people came to Salford in the early

1900s in a travelling Wild West show, setting up their wigwams at Trafford Park on the docks. These were Sioux Indians, otherworldly, mysterious, and, inevitably, some of the local women took a shine. There is definitely Sioux Indian blood in Salford, totally befitting the radical history of the place. The Sioux Indians were about as radical as they come. While at the docks, a Native American chief was taken seriously ill because of the cold. Eventually, he died in Hope Hospital, at which point several other Sioux broke in, carted him away, and buried him according to their own rituals. The site is now a car park, the Sioux version of Richard III in Leicester.

Are we Native Americans? I'd wonder as I looked at mine and Dad's noses. Why not? The DNA will be all across Salford. I expect, just like my dad, there were, and still are, lots of blokes in Salford deconstructing the American myth of the cowboys and Indians film. 'What's all this about? It's their bloody land. The cruel bastards, leave them alone.'

Dad was just the same with the spaghetti westerns. He loved Clint Eastwood's *The Man with No Name*, an outsider, on the side of the Mexicans. Again, that suited Dad because, if he was going to side with anyone, it would be the oppressed. If we went to the cinema, it would often be to see a spaghetti western. Often, he'd blag me in on the door. I loved those films, and love them to this day, but more than that I loved being with my dad. It felt rare. My mum was always there. I knew she would always have time for me, that I could be emotional with her and she would be emotional with me. The cinema was something I could share with my dad, to the extent I would watch him as much as I watched the film. I'd sit next to him in the darkness and, like a flower in the daylight, sense him opening up. Going to the cinema was massive. I loved it. I loved, loved, loved being with my dad.

I'd create games that would give me, and him, a chance to show our affection. With my son Albert I give him a big hug and a kiss and tell him I love him. My dad didn't do that and so, instead, when he came in from work, I'd run into the kitchen, slide on the oilcloth, and snatch his *Daily Express* from the tool pocket of his blue overalls. It's nice to walk through a door and your son to run at you. I knew he loved it.

Sometimes I'd ask, 'Dad, can we have a silly half-hour?' He did it more with my twin brothers, Alan and Keith, eight years older than me, but on occasion he'd wrestle with me and teach me a bit of boxing, lightning fast. He'd get me on the floor and rub his bristles on my face, which was just heaven. I'd be laughing and giggling. The very fact it was my dad, and his face was so close to mine, and I loved that face so much. And I loved him so much. I could feel that he was getting pleasure out of it. Just nothing like it. Even talking about it now, I get emotional. Other times my brothers would watch *Kung Fu* with John Carradine and then go upstairs and start karate-kicking each other, with my 7-year-old self joining in. We had wood-chip wallpaper and as we careered around, it would get under our nails, so painful. My dad, meanwhile, would be stood at the bottom of the stairs – 'Eh, down here now!' We'd all come down, light fittings swinging behind us. Alan and Keith would get a light clip on the head. I'd cower slightly, but he'd never hit me.

'Bloody nearly had the ceiling down!' I think actually he found it amusing.

Dad used to have this trick where he'd put his finger under

my chin — 'Get out of that without moving.' Master Kan, a character in *Kung Fu*, had something similar. 'When you can take the pebble from my hand,' he would tell a young protagonist, 'it will be time for you to leave.' My dad would do the same with me, except instead of a pebble he would have one of those little stubby pens from Ladbrokes. I'd grab for it, but his fist would always close before I got there. In all those exchanges, there was every bit as much love as him bear-hugging and kissing me. They touch me now as they did then, always in the back of my mind.

At home, there was a quirky individuality about Dad. He was the master of memes in the original sense of the word. Radio, or the wireless as he referred to it, had been massive for him growing up, as it was for that entire generation. It had enormous potency, not just in the gravity of the news it brought, but in the escapism it delivered. Dad revelled in that little box and it had a seismic impact on his love of language. His big thing was *Dick Barton — Special Agent*, which again he carried through life, especially the 'Da-da-da!' of its theme tune. Whenever a key moment happened in a film, such as the Indians appearing over the hill in a western, he'd be straight in there — 'Da-da-da!' References from old shows peppered his language. I'd ask him how he knew something and he'd say, 'I know because I am The Whistler,' and start whistling, a reference to the American radio show of the same name. He loved Frank Randle, the Lancashire comic — 'I've supped some ale toneet'.

He'd throw phrases around all the time, all lodged in his head from time spent in front of the speaker. 'A shot rang out, the lights went out, the cat ran out, I ran out . . . I'm not staying in there it's bloody dangerous.' 'Stand and deliver, your money or your life.' 'The Lord said to Moses "Come forth!", and he came fifth and won a teapot.' 'If a fella met a fella in a field of fitches, could a fella tell a fella if his belly itches.' 'Spring is sprung, the grass is ris. I wonders where the birdies is.' 'I see no ships, only fish and chips.'

He had another one that only came out when Mum wasn't there. 'Sergeant Major, is the soup ready?' 'Fuck the soup. Right, marker, steady!' That wasn't a radio meme but a hangover from his National Service days, driving a tank carrier over Salisbury Plain chasing rabbits and foxes.

Those things are amazing as a child, an instant insight into a parent's more playful side, a hint that actually they are more like yourself than you might ever have imagined. When Dad came up with those limericks and phrases he'd heard on the radio, he was softening, and it allowed me to get closer to him. I'd then go off and expand those words and images in my own imagination, to the extent it's not too big a stretch to say Dad's relationship with radio fed into me going to drama school. Maybe one day they'll do the same with someone else. Dad may be gone but those favourite sayings, plucked from the airwaves, have travelled through the family. His grandchildren and even his great-grandchildren are now familiar with some of his verbal tropes.

Clearly, there was fun and stability in the house and yet all the time I had a nagging insecurity about the twins' relationship. My brothers were patient, loving and generous with me. Alan, the slightly more demonstrative of the pair, bought me a yellow shovel-nosed car once, which I still think of, and we would play with cap and spud guns. In fact, Alan once gave Keith a detached retina with a dried pea fired from a Gat gun – he'd stuck his head round a corner at an inopportune moment. I dogged them terribly to play with me and, where they could, they would do just that – but I envied what they'd got, what they shared, to the extent I even split them up. They shared the larger bedroom while I was in the box room. Eventually, by sheer virtue of moaning, nagging and making a fuss, they gave into my selfishness and babyishness and Alan had the box room while I went in with Keith. It didn't last long. It was obvious they should share the bigger room and Mum reversed the decision. This was about more than rooms, though. It was me trying to create a symbolic relationship as a twin. But I wasn't a twin and there was no use pretending otherwise. The situation was indicative of a general paranoia about Alan and Keith. I was needy and there were periods when I felt left out. Often that was simply because they were older than me so they could do stuff like stay up later watching telly. But a good deal of it was the pop psychology of 'Where's my twin?' My brothers had a special bond, my mum and dad had a special bond – what did I have?

To be fair, Mum and Dad never made a special thing of my brothers being twins. For instance, they only ever dressed my brothers the same out of necessity. There was too much common sense in them for it to be any other way. Their clothes did affect me, though. I'd get all their hand-me-downs, which, because eight years had elapsed until they fitted me, were totally out of sync with the times. I was profoundly self-conscious about this. In the late '60s and early '70s, boys at junior school were starting to wear long pants all the time, but my mum would insist that I wore shorts, always shorts that our kid had worn, that were, thanks to changing fashions, by now ridiculously long. There was a kids' programme on the telly at the time called *Sam*. It was set in the '30s and Sam was an old-fashioned kid with old-fashioned shorts – long shorts. It caused me issues at Bridgewater Primary School, where other kids would make comments. It made me profoundly self-conscious, not because I was scruffy – Mum would have never had me scruffy – but because I looked different. I was bullied in the infants by one girl in particular. Looking back, I can see she probably had issues of her own. She looked unwashed, was bigger than her age, and was bullying a male child, so who knows what was going on? Whatever the underlying reasons, I was absolutely petrified. I cannot claim virtuousness on this count. I bullied a lad when I moved up into the juniors. I used to make him give me his crisps. I'll carry the absolute shame of that to my grave. I picked on the weakest, most vulnerable kid, and I bullied him. There's no excuse for it. I'd like to find him and say sorry, but what's the use of apologising now?

As a kid, I found myself mentally split over my brothers. I was proud of the fact there were twins in the family. People would say to me, 'What's it like to grow up with identical twin brothers?' and I would say, 'What's it like not to?' It was my only framework and I liked it because it made us special, and I wanted to be special. I still to this day have the same enthusiasm when I tell people about them – 'My brothers are twins!' It's also a bit sci-fi – 'Morning,' coming from two people who look exactly the same. But the feeling that there were two pairs in the house, Mum and Dad, Alan and Keith, and then me, at once part of them and part removed, on the outside observing, absorbing, was overwhelming.

That sense of being different drove a competitiveness in me.

I'd get them on the squash court when I was fourteen and they were twenty-two and my attitude was always 'I'll beat you'. Which I did. I'd inherited my dad's hand–eye coordination, whereas Alan and Keith weren't particularly sporting. But this was a gulf, in age, attitude, reference and experience, that could never be bridged with a little green ball. No matter how much I tried to see the world as they saw it, I never found it any easier than trying to recapture a dream after waking in my sleep. But maybe that's forever the fate of the youngest. The age difference never seems to go away. George Harrison once noted of Paul McCartney: 'When I met Paul, I was five years younger than him, and I'm still five years younger than him now.' I'm still eight years younger than my brothers, even though I'm fifty-five.

It wasn't just inside the family I would fixate on people; it happened outside our four walls too. At school one day, I was watching a mate called Mark Kavanagh walking along. *Isn't Mark Kavanagh amazing?* I was thinking. *There is nobody more Mark Kavanagh than him. Mark Kavanagh? I can't believe he even exists, he's so original.* I did that to few people, not because I was close to them or they were girls I was in love with, but because I was experiencing people in a way that was slightly unusual – as if I had a filter out on me. Maybe that's where some of the fascination about character, being amazed at the idiosyncrasies of another person, comes from. The basic fact that they are experiencing reality in an entirely different manner, and yet we are coexisting. Seeing the world through others' eyes – think about it too much and at some point you end up not knowing where they end and you begin.

Having twins meant an unusual experience for Mum, too.

Twins weren't as common as they are now with the advent of fertility drugs. When they did come, it presented a strange dynamic, one in which a mother could be forgiven for feeling excluded. Some might think with twins a mother gets twice as much, but Alan and Keith always looked to each other first. When I came along, it was her first one on one. I asked her once about the eight-year gap between myself and the twins and she said my dad was careful but she wanted another child. She was a fair bit older at that point and was perhaps aware of how the clock was running against her. They had been hoping for a girl and then I came along. I was going to be Alison.

I was twenty-one when Mum told me, quite casually, that she'd had a miscarriage after me. Her revelation stayed with me. As with all kids, it never occurred to me that I might have had other siblings who never made it. I thought how I could have had a younger brother or sister, someone I could have looked after and played with. Even now I know that, if that child had survived, it would have changed the course of my life, because whatever I have done was forged in the crucible of that home and those relationships. Two pairs and me. If I'd had a sibling near my age, I'd have been very much involved with them. Instead, I had a sense of being alone, an only child in a family set-up. I was sat on the outside, being novelistic, freezing moments, cataloguing. I was a difficult kid who spent a lot of time in his own company, joined only by a secret cast of characters. 'Old Man in the Rain' entailed me sitting on a fishing basket, half in, half out our back door, being just that, an old man in the rain. 'The Woman on the Landing' had a slightly more ghostly presence, while for 'The Mad Professor', who resided in my bedroom, I'd get little tubes of glitter and spray aerosols into them. The glitter would go everywhere and the professor would be blown up. My characters weren't just confined to the house. Morbidly, when I went to the swimming baths, I used to play 'Dead Man on the Rocks'. I'd lie on the steps, semi-immersed in the water as if I was a corpse. Whenever there was even the lightest dusting of snow, meanwhile, I used to be 'Scott of the Antarctic'. I'd walk a spiral in our front garden until I got to the centre, where I'd die – because, according to me, that's what Scott did.

The massive obsession was Sean Connery as James Bond. When I got home from school, I'd get changed into a suitable outfit – pair of blue flares, an odd material with protruding seams and white elastic that had come away from the waistband, and a blue polo neck. Once in my costume, from then on whatever I did was as James Bond – James Bond Makes His Toast, James Bond Goes For A Pee – culminating in me taking a toy gun, with the look of a Walther PPK, and putting my dad's vinyl album of John Barrie's greatest hits on a loop. It would reach a finale of me taking a powerful industrial lamp of my dad's and positioning it so it created a spotlight on the privet hedge. At that point, I'd replicate the iconic gun pose of the Bond opening credits. Or I'd run into the glare as if I'd been spotted in a searchlight. I'd do that for hours. I used to sign my name 'Chris Eccleston 007'. So embarrassing.

I was obsessed with Sean Connery's Bond because to me he was the archetype of masculinity. I thought that's what a man should be. I had all the James Bond annuals and in one picture Connery was knocked out on the floor. Even the way he lay was virile and macho and cool. I'd be on the floor myself, twisting, turning, trying exactly to replicate the body position. Later I'd hear the famous story about Bond producers Albert 'Cubby' Broccoli and Harry Saltzman interviewing Connery for the role, watching afterwards from the window as he disappeared down the street. He got the part, they said, because he walked like a cat.

The guises I'd adopt were for nobody's benefit but mine. I'd do a lot of things on my own. I'd spend hours in bed reading. If I went outside, I'd be kicking a football, commentating like I was on *Match of the Day*. I would lose myself so thoroughly in my own imagination that I experienced what I can only describe as a series of petit mal seizures. It happened a few times, like I'd hypnotised myself, convinced myself I was that character, which I think all children are capable of doing – I see it in my daughter Esme, chattering away to herself – until something snapped me out of what I was doing. On one occasion, I went down the stairs and into the living room while in such a state.

'There's a rhythm,' I told my mum and brothers.

They were watching telly and looked at me, confused. 'What?'

'Can you not hear it?' I was going round touching the furniture as if I could feel something. 'It's all the same rhythm.'

I'd got so deeply into play that I'd altered my own mental state and was hearing this definite rhythm. Like I was going the way that madness lies. I don't understand it myself, so who knows what they made of that situation.

Another time, I was convinced there was a Greek statue staring at me through the window. I went downstairs, got Mum and Alan, and took them up to my bedroom.

'Look! Look at that! There!' Again, one can only imagine

what they were thinking. The only logical explanation is I dreamed the statue so vividly that I could still see it when I woke up.

You could look at this period as the beginning of a third eye, an altered state of consciousness and perception. I wonder also if it was the beginning of what has been branded as my intensity, like a pre-stutter, connected similarly to my power of concentration. Believe me, I can really concentrate hard. When I'm doing takes, or I'm on stage, the concentration is solely on the acting. It has to be, that's the job. And that is effectively changing my mental state.

It's not just me who says that. Peter Vaughan acknowledged as much about himself during filming for *Our Friends in the North*. We were doing a take, me as Nicky Hutchinson, he as Nicky's dad Felix, in a typical TV studio where somebody drops a matchstick and it sounds like a bomb's gone off. There was this tiny noise.

Peter halted. 'Ah, can we go again please?' He was slightly angry and embarrassed because he thought he was being indulgent.

'Do you feel all right, Peter?' I asked.

'Yes,' he said, 'but all the antennae are out.' He meant he had entered a very externalised state. That's not easy to do. You can't just flick a switch and go, 'I'm in character now!' It needs to happen more naturally. Often it never does. The frustration of being an actor is that so often you are trying to capture something that is completely illusive. A child's mind, uncluttered by extraneous thoughts, is perhaps in a better position to achieve that disconnection from reality. The point is, with me, I seem to have felt shadows of other characters, real and imagined, all my life.

When I was seven, I went round next door to Lily and Charlie Donegan's.

'My Great Auntie Annie's dead,' I told them.

Great Auntie Annie had come to live with us as a grey-haired old lady in ill health. She was a matter-of-fact woman who I always found slightly unnerving. Once, I arranged my toy cars on a stool.

'I've parked them up,' I told her.

'No, you haven't,' she said. 'They're all touching, and when cars park there's always a space.' You see? Matter of fact.

With Annie in the house, it felt like death was around, purely because she was so ancient. Her presence placed a veil of morbidity over my head. Lily and Charlie came round.

'She's not dead, love, she's asleep.'

Death wasn't long, however, in manifesting itself. One day she was there, one day she wasn't, and I've since come to realise the event traumatised me. For years afterwards, on a Sunday night when I used to have to go up for a bath, right up to when I was sixteen, I would be terrified that when I came out of the bathroom there'd be a woman in a nightdress with very grey hair staring at me. I know that's a cliché – the classic grey-haired lady of practically every ghost story ever written – but it was reinforced by the TV of the time. I loved the ITV series *Thriller*, which presented a different, often haunting, drama each week, and had seen an episode about just this sort of ghostly old lady and another featuring a nun. My fear of a malevolent presence in my house was very potent to me, but because I was sixteen and living in a very macho culture, I was deeply embarrassed that my imagination was so active. No way was I going to tell anyone. Another little oddity kept locked in my head allowed a glimpse of daylight only recently when I used my dread fear of the ghost of Auntie Annie to inform my emotion when I encountered the witches in *Macbeth*.

There's part of me that thinks I've used my own 'third eye' experiences to tell myself how special I am. Nowadays, I would imagine my parents, if asked, would describe me as an imaginative, sensitive child, but there was no language of that back then. I was just Chris being Chris. 'Eh up – he's off again.' You didn't dwell, you just got on with things. I do know, though, that my house, my box room, my family, played a huge part in who I am.

A crucible for a little boy.

2

SALFORD

*'My function is not to reassure people. I want
to make them uncomfortable. To send them out of
the place arguing and talking.'*
Ewan MacColl

There was another cauldron bubbling away in the background.
As much as my heightened imagination was piqued within those
four walls in Little Hulton, the overarching influence in my life
was 6 miles away down the road.

I came to being in 59 Blodwell Street, Salford, a classic two-
up-two-down council property where you stepped straight
out onto the street. Not any more – it's been knocked down.
It was unusual to be born at home in the mid-'60s, but Mum
had already given birth once – well, twice really – and the
rules allowed for the second child, in her case the third, to be
born domestically. I didn't make it easy. I started on the Friday
afternoon and didn't deign to emerge until the Sunday night at
five to six. I was 9lb 4oz. My Uncle Joe used to call me Garth
after the outsized adventure hero from the *Daily Mirror* cartoon
strip. I'm not sure if Garth was the same, but I remained bald
as a coot until I was three.

While there were plenty of slum clearances going on in Salford in the '60s, Blodwell Street wasn't one of them. It was simply a row of old terraced houses, outside toilet, bath in front of the fire, the same sort of homes that other cities have regenerated and reinvigorated for new generations. The seed of a move away was only planted in my mum's head when a neighbour knocked on the door.

'Would you ever consider moving out of Salford?' she asked. The woman's sister was living in Little Hulton and wanted to come back to Salford because she missed it. Essentially, it was an unofficial council swap. My mum was keen, seduced by the inviting prospect of clean air, more room, and the fear that in Salford my brothers were starting to run wild. My dad was completely against it. He would have stayed in Salford, but Mum was from a more aspirant background. She was posh working-class, put in a blue dress as a little girl on election day, not an uncommon occurrence among a good proportion of the working class who'd rejected socialism – 'We know who we are, we know the king's the king, and they know what's best.'

The Conservatives at that time, laughably, embodied morality, whereas support the Labour Party and you were a communist – or a 'commonist' as my dad got called when he went to pick my mum up from my Grandma Elliott's house wearing a red shirt on their first date. Red shirt, suit, fags – that was my dad all over. He was a bit rough while Mum was genteel working-class. Her grandma looked like Queen Victoria, and it was her who put Mum in that little blue dress. Mum's mum had died when she was four. She wasn't allowed to go to the funeral. It was deemed not to be proper (I disagree with that – I believe children should not be denied the ritual).

Instead she went to the cinema. Afterwards, she was looked after by her dad, Joe. He wasn't a rough Salford bloke in the way that my Grandad Pop, my dad's dad, was, but he was still a tough man, with a look of Robert Mitchum I always thought. To be on your own with no wife and a small child, particularly if that child was female, was deemed unmanly, and Joe, still a young man, didn't bother about Elsie as he should. At one stage, Grandma Elliott came to Salford to see them only to find the little girl in the house on her own. She went to the nearest pub and there was Joe. She went back to the house, took Elsie by the hand, strolled into the pub, and told Joe, 'She's coming with me.' That was it – and I think that's what he wanted. It didn't mean the end for their relationship, though. Over time they got to know each other and grew close in later life.

My mum, when she developed her own mind, would also reject the political overtones of the blue dress. That's not to say she didn't defer – she and Dad saw the middle class as their betters – but if it came to it and anyone tried to use or trample them, they'd have 'em. She and Dad were Labour. My mum did vote Liberal on occasion, because she would really think about what was being offered; she would see the nuance and still does to this day. My dad never thought about it. He'd have voted for Blair post-Iraq even when we knew the liar he was (actually, by that time dad was too far gone with dementia to notice). For him, politics was very meat and potatoes – 'You vote for Labour, the party of the working man.' The Conservatives were 'bastards – Tory bastards'. We stopped at a service station once and Ted Heath pulled up in the car next to us. My mum was nervous.

'Ronnie,' she said, 'don't say anything.' He didn't. He feared my mum's ire more than he hated Ted Heath.

Mum definitely had influence over Dad. He respected her and she was never the 'little woman' of the relationship. For her part, she knew he lacked the confidence to try something new — if my dad had taken the lead, they'd never have had a holiday, let alone moved home, so she wouldn't hold back on being direct. I'm still on the end of that now. 'Buck your ideas up, Christopher! Maurice isn't an idiot,' she told me recently when I was reading my lines to *The A Word* with her.

Inevitable then that, despite Dad's initial misgivings over the house in Little Hulton, she got him to go and have a look. What they found was a much bigger home, 1930s, two bedrooms and a box room, semi-detached, garden front and back, on a council estate almost in the countryside, the latter being massive to two people for whom openness and nature meant so much. We're not talking abject luxury here. The house had no central heating, we had an open fire that heated the water via a back boiler, and oilcloth because Mum and Dad couldn't afford carpets, but it was definitely a step up from Blodwell Street, the better environment to raise her family for which Mum yearned. In order to pay the rent for the new house, for a while my dad did his shift at Colgate from eight 'til five, came home, had his tea, and then, five days a week, from six 'til ten, worked at Bulmers, the cider brewery, again driving a stacker truck.

I was seven months old when we made that move. Clearly, I have no memory of the time I spent in that terrace, but what I do know is I came to consciousness in Little Hulton thinking, *I don't come from here*, a mental default I would carry with me for ever. I've spent my life enjoying being a stranger in places. It's one of the main things I love about acting, being an outsider in a town. I've done it in Los Angeles, I've done it in Austin, I've done it in Melbourne, Leicester, Nottingham, Glasgow. I never to this day say I'm from Little Hulton. Salford overrode any time-hewn attachment to LH. I grew up hearing conversations about how 'we're not from here', reinforced by the fact that anybody visiting us came from Salford and if we visited anyone we went the other way. All the tales, all the anecdotes, were about Salford. I'd hear about my mum's sister Olive, attractive, busty and red-headed, who worked in the ticket booth at the Ambassador Cinema, known as 'The Ambass', and how, before Ronnie met my mum, all the lads used to try it on with her. 'We couldn't get a smile out of her,' my dad said. My mum later explained it to me – 'Olive just thought they were all common.'

For all its distress and dirt, Salford, to me, had a sense, and still does, of being Camelot. All my values, all the stories, all the honesty I saw in Mum and Dad's work ethic, come from there, passed on to new generations. There was a story oft told about my Uncle Bill, made unemployed, like so many others in the Great Depression of the 1930s, and not coming home, the family sending out search parties before he was found crying in a doorway. I first heard that story as a 6-year-old. It gave me a value, so when, ten years on, I was watching *Boys from the Blackstuff*, and making the connection, '1930s, 1981 – hang on', I knew exactly who I was from. In our house, we had a shared ethos of 'This is who we are'. Salford was my domain, and maybe, when I got older, that was why it was so easy to leave Little Hulton – I never really felt like I belonged there. Yes, there was a real sense we'd moved up in the world because we were in a better house, more room, but at the same time it felt as if the people in Little Hulton were very different, rural in a sense, far less inner-city. It seemed they felt it too. There was a bit of a class thing going on. Even though everyone was in council houses, Salford, as it always has been and always will be, was seen as rough. So our family was seen as rough. To add to the interloper feel, the families that came to Little Hulton from Salford were officially called overspill – a charming phrase. That same term was used again when there was another wave of newcomers in the '80s, except this new influx were much more socially challenged in terms of employment and drugs after several years of Margaret Thatcher. There was more criminal activity. That dignity and sense of morality that comes from having a job wasn't there; the old thing about people keeping their gardens right, and then, before you know it, they're full of fridges and broken-down vans. All of a sudden there were lads in baseball caps hanging about on the streets. Thanks to the Tories' social and economic policies, people were skint and they started nicking. Having never had any problems in twenty years, my mum and dad were broken into four times in a decade. They shared a sense of bemusement that somebody of their own could come and rob them. Hurt pre-empted anger – 'We don't do that to each other.'

That's not to say Little Hulton was previously an idyll. It was a typical working-class estate. When I was a kid, I was frightened of the skinheads. A load of them used to go out in a white Bedford van and jump out and batter people. It was possibly an urban myth, but there was a story that one bonfire night some skinheads had stabbed a Guy Fawkes dummy, only to discover there was somebody in the disguise. But Little Hulton had never been a place where people turned on one another. In the end, lack of opportunity and austerity in a decade, the '80s, where others were making an obscene display of their wealth eroded natural working-class pride.

We were never overwhelmed with visitors in Little Hulton, but New Year's Eve was always a big get-together. Mum and Dad wanted it to be all-encompassing, not something owned by one age group, and so my brothers would bring all their mates. Mum and Dad adored the twins' friends and the liveliness they brought to the house. They didn't want everyone sitting around on chairs; they wanted a proper do, a good old-fashioned knees-up. While my mum piloted the cooker, doling out pies – beef and mince, steak and kidney, cheese and onion – as well as potato hash and beetroots that she did in their juice with sugar, and my dad cut open another Watney's Party Seven, my brothers and their girlfriends would be dancing away in the front room watching Rod Stewart's Hogmanay special. Younger than anyone else by some distance, I'd stay up, observing, taking it all in – the documentarian. Those were the happiest times.

Mum and Dad would also have a Boxing Day party. When the pubs emptied, everyone would come down to ours and the house again would be filled with laughter and noise. Dad never drank shorts – the one and only time he'd done so he'd fallen down a hole on Salisbury Plain (he also felt that in a man it indicated getting above your station, being a bit pretentious). But for women it was different, and on big occasions such as these, Mum would drink gin. She was always sociable, but gin totally transformed her. At parties, my dad and his mates would gather in the backroom, the result being there'd be a fair bit of blokeish non-PC humour. My mum would walk right into the middle of that banter and invert it so that all the women were laughing at the men, all that schoolboy sniggering turned on its head. My dad's face would be one of embarrassment mixed with huge amounts of admiration. He could play the game, but because of my mum's incredibly strong feminine influence, decided he wouldn't. I watched this scene unfold, fascinated. I knew I liked it more than the boys' club. I was a big fan of my mum, and her ability to own a roomful of men was something to behold.

Dad beheld it too. Witnessing life through Mum was such an important part of my dad's relationship to her. He would delight, absolutely, in watching her pleasure. My brother, an upholsterer, once made her a chair. It was beautiful and she was a little overwhelmed. 'Oh, Alan, I don't know what to say.' Myself, being the watcher, wasn't looking at the chair; I was looking at my dad's face. He wasn't looking at the chair either; he was watching her, again vicariously living her happiness. He did that a lot. His first reaction when anything funny, positive or momentous happened was to look straight at her.

Dad had a fantastic laugh, which we called 'the guffaw', and we'd hear it ringing out at parties. He loved people and he was a great audience for a joke, but wasn't somebody who would stand up and entertain. He'd defer that role to my mum, or Alan, them both being the main source of humour in the house.

Dad's humour was more inadvertent and came from his bizarre way of doing things. For instance, he didn't like to ask people to do something for him, so would find a roundabout way of doing so. I'd be sat watching the TV with him – 'Are you going upstairs?'

'No, Dad.' He'd go back to the telly.

'Why?' I'd know where this was going.

'Doesn't matter.'

'Why?'

'It doesn't matter. You're not going up so it doesn't matter.'

'Why did you ask?'

'Well, if you were going up, I wouldn't mind you turning the immersion heater on.'

Why he wouldn't just ask, I don't know.

Other times, me, Alan and Keith would be watching something on TV when he'd walk in and turn it over.

'What's this?' he'd ask.

'I've no idea, Dad, we were watching the other side.'

Occasionally, he'd borrow a fiver off one of us. A couple of weeks later, it still wouldn't be back.

'Dad, can I have that fiver?'

'Fiver? What are you on about, fiver?'

'I lent you a fiver.'

'I don't remember.' We'd get it back in the end.

There was a genuine eccentricity in there, like him asking where his glasses were only for them to be on his head – all this very much pre-dementia. We all used to watch *Fawlty Towers* together and I felt then and know now that the four of us were laughing at Basil because we too had one in the house. He half knew that, I think. It fitted in with his ability to be self-parodic.

'France,' he'd say, 'they should build a concrete wall around it and fill it in with concrete.' He had another fate in store for the Gauls – 'All the French should be made to swim home and those that make it should be shot on the beach.' We knew he didn't believe it. It was just *Fawlty Towers* moved from Torquay to Salford.

There were certain things I loved watching with Dad because his reaction was so joyous. Me and him loved the Fred Quimby *Tom and Jerry* cartoons. Occasionally there'd be a sequence where Jerry would run through an open window only for it to come slamming down on the pursuing Tom's neck, at which point his mouth would open and his tongue shoot out three feet. That made my dad laugh more than anything. Laurel and Hardy we loved, too, not so much for the slapstick, more for the interplay, Oliver's looks to camera, his sheer unadulterated frustration. *Whatever Happened to the Likely Lads?*, the subtlety of the relationship between Bob and Terry, was similarly massive for my dad. We also used to watch *The Black and White Minstrel Show* because Dad loved the singing. Even if the overt racism was noted, it was certainly not mentioned. Of all entertainers, though, Eric Morecambe, without a shadow of a doubt, was the ultimate favourite. When Eric came on the telly, it was as though he was my dad's personal friend. If Eric was on, you knew Dad's mood would be good.

Dad found his pleasure in being with Elsie, reading his newspaper, or watching something good on TV. Unless it was a party, he rarely drank at home. If he did fancy a drink, he wasn't one for dragging me along, giving me a bag of crisps and sticking me in a corner. My mum wouldn't have that, and he wouldn't have been comfortable with it either. If I did happen to be with him when he went for a drink, generally I'd wait in the car, as happened when he had a pint in The Raven with my Granddad Pop and my Granddad Shaw. I spent that particular half-hour messing around with the lights, and when he came out they had to give him a jump start because I'd run his battery down.

Before the twins came along, Dad spent a lot more time in the pub. Granddad Pop demanded that all his sons be there in the Red Lion, in Irlam, known as 'The Cat', on a Friday night. But when Alan and Keith arrived it was full-on hard work for my mum. Endlessly, she'd be washing, feeding, cleaning. In the end, she put her foot down.

'I can't do this, Ronnie,' she told him. 'It's not just the work; we haven't got the money for you to go drinking.'

Dad listened. *I can either be in the pub with this lot,* he thought, *or I can be at home with my wife and twin sons.*

From that moment on, the other lads at the pub called him Cinderella because he was always missing the ball. Dad wasn't bothered. He could be a real man's man in the boozer, but Elsie allowed him a richer emotional life at home. He loved being a father to the babies. He knew also, from a tough upbringing, where hunger was a constant companion, that money was tight and was to be respected. Like many working-class people, Mum and Dad feared money and its power to dictate life in the starkest of ways. It's a hard habit to shake. To this day, waste of any sort upsets my mum. Worth remembering when we see elderly people rooting around in their purses at the supermarket that they really did come from a background where every penny counts. Mum and Dad, for instance, started out in a rented room with orange boxes for furniture in a house in Eccles Precinct. From there, they would set out every morning to the same bus stop to go to work at Colgate-Palmolive, the factory where they'd met. I asked them about that moment once when we were out in a restaurant in Manchester. Dad had dementia at that point, but he still had a keen memory of the encounter, although Mum gave it a rather more filmic quality.

She'd already heard about Dad when one day the lift opened and there he was on his stacker truck, typical Ronnie, with one pallet too many. 'He never took his eyes off me as the lift doors closed,' she told me. 'I thought, *He's tricky.*'

'If it had been any of the other blokes I'd have told him, "Eh, silly old, you've got too many pallets there," but I thought, *He won't take that very well.*' Instead, she told him, 'Oh, I'm not sure you're meant to bring two.' She was astute. She could see there was a fragility of confidence.

Elsie finished with a bloke to go out with my dad. Her spurned beau later became a professional footballer and wrote to her trying to get her back. She chose Ronnie. They had a church wedding. Dad had a very questionable haircut, Mum looked beautiful in a subtle, understated wedding dress, a locket round her neck. I am looking at the photo now – she looks gorgeous. You were punching above your weight, Dad. They couldn't afford a honeymoon. The nearest they got to a treat was when his brother Pete, his best man, stuck a fiver in his pocket at the end of the night. From Eccles Precinct, eventually Mum and Dad got hold of their first Salford council house in Stone Street, moving on to Blodwell Street, and Little Hulton, raising their three kids as they went.

Salford itself embodies Mum and Dad's determination to rise above adversity. In *The Condition of the Working Class in England*, penned in 1844, Friedrich Engels, who spent much of his life in the city, describes it as a 'very unhealthy, dirty and dilapidated district'. Little had changed when in 1931 a major survey concluded that while parts of Salford contained some of the worst slums in the country, infested by rats and lacking elementary amenities, inspectors were 'struck by the courage and perseverance with which the greater number of tenants kept their houses clean and respectable under the most adverse conditions'. People had nothing, but their homes glistened.

Salford actually became a pioneer. The Royal Museum and Public Library, opened in 1850, was the first unconditional free public library in the country, a link perhaps to the fact that so many notables who emerged from the area did so through a radical use of culture and words. Emmeline Pankhurst, founder of the suffragette movement, spent her early years in Pendleton, and her father owned a theatre in Salford for several years. Her ability to engage a crowd can be attributed to that very stage. Walter Greenwood, author of *Love on the Dole*, and the dramatist Shelagh Delaney, whose play *A Taste of Honey* questioned an array of social mores and prejudices, were both from Salford, as were Joy Division founders Bernard Sumner and Peter Hook, their non-conformist DIY outlook shared by fellow Salfordians the Happy Mondays and punk poet John Cooper Clarke.

Current Master of the Queen's Music and prominent gay rights campaigner Sir Peter Maxwell Davies also emanates from Salford, as does Alistair Cooke (whose *Letter from America* was broadcast for decades on Radio 4) and the actor Robert Powell. I'll reserve special mention for Albert Finney, the greatest of them all, although the footballer Paul Scholes runs him close. Indeed, one of the best moments of my life was when I met Scholes in Starbucks in Manchester, sat at a table with his wife and baby. In situations like this, I generally give people their space, but, on this occasion, I took the opportunity. I had to – I respected him as a footballer so much, watching him in the Manchester United reserves right through to his incredible performances in the first team. Equally, I loved the fact he could have earned loads more money by putting himself out there, doing adverts and the like, but wouldn't do it. He was the best player on the pitch but did the least press.

I sat myself down. 'All right, mate?' I said, with great originality.

'All right,' he replied.

His wife then interjected. 'Eh, you!' she said. 'You went on a date with my mate and she said that when she walked into the place you were reading a book. You were reading a book on a date! And you never rang her back.'

I saw a smirk on Scholesy's face, which only broadened when I started trying to dig myself out of the hole.

Thankfully, my all-time hero, possibly registering my discomfort, delivered a subject change. 'What was that thing you did about a schoolteacher?'

'*Hearts and Minds*,' I told him. 'It was on Channel 4.'

'It was good, that,' he noted. My favourite player had just given me a decent review.

My career meant that I got to meet, and very nearly play, several on that list of Salford greats. I took great delight in reciting John Cooper Clarke's poem 'Evidently Chickentown' in Danny Boyle's film *Strumpet*. We filmed that scene in a pub in Collyhurst. As Alex Ferguson once said, 'Collyhurst, where they take the paving stones in at night.' It was an audience of regulars and extras and the energy in the room as the poem went through the gears was incredible.

I was invited to ask a question of John Cooper Clarke for an article in *The Observer*. I knew straightaway what I wanted to quiz him about. I've always been obsessed with First World War poetry and had happened across a poem called 'Oh! Fucking Halkirk'.

He was obviously aware of 'Oh! Fucking Halkirk' when he wrote 'Chickentown' and had modernised the form to create another poem of incredible power.

The film director Michael Winterbottom, meanwhile, wanted me to play Peter Hook in *24 Hour Party People* but I couldn't because I was committed elsewhere. Ralf Little did a brilliant job, but I can't help feeling I'd have been great as Hooky, matching both the attitude and tonality of voice. I pleaded with Michael to shoehorn me in and he came up with Boethius, who was Tony Wilson's favourite philosopher. I had this extraordinary experience of sitting under Victoria Bridge – the same bridge where I used to get off the bus, the 38, the 31, or the 91, from Little Hulton to Manchester throughout my childhood and adolescence – relating Boethius's Wheel of Fortune.

It's my belief that history is a wheel. 'Inconstancy is my very essence,' says the wheel. Rise up on my spokes if you like but don't complain when you're cast back down into the depths. Good times pass away, but then so do the bad. Mutability is our tragedy, but it is also our hope. The worst of times, like the best, are always passing away.

All my ghosts were under that bridge, and all my experiences were in that speech, the bizarre nature of the situation heightened by the fact I was delivering those words to Steve Coogan pretending to be Tony Wilson, and then, out of the corner of my eye, I could see the real Tony Wilson who'd come down to witness that particular scene being filmed. The same Tony, an absolute cultural icon, who saw Shaun Ryder as W. B. Yeats – Shaun who was from my road, Coniston Avenue. And the same Tony who not long after would interview me on the set of *The Second Coming*, only for us to end up talking about Nobby Stiles (he was a mad Manchester United fan). The last time I ever saw Tony was outside Waterstones on Deansgate, appropriately enough for another lover of words, a man who allowed the disaffected a voice.

I saw Morrissey, actually a Mancunian, but whose photo with The Smiths outside Salford Lads Club is perhaps their best known, in exactly the same place. I had just voiced a documentary about the icon called *The Importance of Being Morrissey* and was talking to the producer outside a café, when I stopped mid-flow.

'You have no idea who's walking towards us.'

'Is it Morrissey?'

'Yeah.'

'Go and talk to him.'

'I can't.'

'Go and talk to him!'

He walked past me. I got on my bike and followed him. He'd just walked up to Waterstones.

'Excuse me, Morrissey.'

'Oh, hello.'

'My name's Chris Eccleston.'

'Yes, I know.'

'Oh, right . . . I just want to say thank you.' I stuck my hand out. He shook it.

'No, no,' he said. 'Thank you.' And walked off.

I'm fairly sure it was a more remarkable experience for me than it was for him, and the reverse anecdote doesn't appear in his own autobiography. But the significance of Morrissey knowing who I am will never be lost on me. I had been that classic callow youth sat in a bedsit listening to his plaintive tales of working-class existence. And there I was saying hello to him outside a bookshop that now (I rather blithely assume) has both our stories on its shelves. It's things like this that bring me up short sometimes.

Having little never means having nothing.

3

RED DEVIL

'Duncan Edwards, he was a player, eh?'
  'Uh. Uh.'
  'Legs like tree trunks, isn't that what they used to say?'
  'Uh. Uh.'
  'Those were the days.'
  He didn't say anything, but there was a glint in his eyes.

I never wanted to be an actor. I wanted to be a footballer – to play for Manchester United. I still do.

The first thing I committed to memory wasn't the lines of a play, it was the names of the Busby Babes. There was a drawer in my mum and dad's bedroom and whenever I got the chance I'd go rooting. I'd find sets of false teeth, ties, photos, watches, United programmes, leather lighters from the '70s, all sorts. It was fascinating. Boredom was our ally back then – we had nothing else to do so exploring the house was an inevitability.

I also found a *Manchester Evening News* special from the end of 1958, a commemoration of the desperate tragedy that unfolded on the tarmac at Munich Airport and the subsequent run to the FA Cup final with the team the club somehow cobbled together.

The Munich air crash was a huge event in our house. Mum and Dad both felt it deeply. Dad had been going to Old Trafford since the 1930s, while Mum actually worked at the ground during the Babes era, pushing a cart round the outside of the pitch, selling pies and beef tea, the money being passed down through the crowd before the refreshments went back the other way.

'We all fancied Roger Byrne,' she told me of the United captain and England international, one of eight players who perished in the accident, 'but you could tell he was moody.' Roger Byrne, as it happened, was the spit of my dad.

'Everybody fancied Big Dunc too,' she continued, referring of course to the prodigious talent that was Duncan Edwards.

My dad would talk about them as footballers. 'Roger Byrne never tackled anybody, Chris,' he'd tell me. 'He just used to jockey wingers into a position where they couldn't go anywhere and take the ball off them. He was that good.'

Duncan, meanwhile, was the best player he'd ever seen. 'Man at sixteen. Legs like tree trunks. Never seen anything like it.' His respect for Duncan went beyond his ability; it was wound up in him being masculine in a way Dad admired.

Dad didn't just watch football, he played it, centre forward. People would tell me all the time, 'God, your dad was a good footballer.' And he was. The army asked him to stay on beyond his two years' National Service purely to represent Southern Command. At that level, scouts from professional clubs came to watch, but my dad's attitude was rigid. 'I've done my National Service, now I've got to get back to Salford.' Because that's what young men did. They went back to what they knew, what they'd been conditioned to do. They were expected to go home and put money in the pot. My dad wouldn't have wanted to shirk that responsibility. He was always very firm about paying his way. One of his first life lessons to me was 'Always get your round in – stand your corner.' So wedded to this attitude was he that it was difficult actually to buy him a drink. 'I'll get this,' he'd say as soon as the glasses had been drained. I'd have to stop him. 'No, Dad – you already got yours. I'll do it.' That kind of social minutiae was very important to him because it said something about values and character. 'If a bloke doesn't get his round in, that tells you all you need to know.' And he was right. If you're in the trenches and you want someone you can trust by your side, it's not going to be the bastard who ducks his round, is it?

With that background, Dad never had the chance to say to his family, or to himself, 'I'm going to see where football takes me.' Instead, where it took him was the amateur leagues. By the time he stopped playing, he'd been heading heavy leather footballs for twenty-two years – in fact he was renowned as being great with his head. I'm convinced, as was proven with the West Brom striker Jeff Astle, such constant impact contributed to his eventual dementia. After an eighteen-year professional career, Jeff Astle's brain was shown to be more like that of a boxer. But it wasn't only professionals who headed the ball.

Dad grew up in different days. When I came along, the idea that working-class people could become something was far more accepted. Albert Finney was a case in point. Mum and Dad knew his dad, a bookie – Albert had been a bookie's runner before finding acting success.

Four years previously, he'd made his name in *Saturday Night and Sunday Morning*, part of the 'kitchen sink' movement that portrayed vividly a generation no longer willing to accept the preordained drudgery of working-class life. My dad was born in 1929 and was making his life decisions immediately after the Second World War.

I grew up believing I had choices. And my first choice was to be a footballer. But this wasn't a simple ambition; there was a psychological complexity behind it. More than anything, I wanted to be a footballer to please my dad, to strengthen the connection between me and him. I was always conscious that my older brothers hadn't bothered with the game, being more into catapults and generally messing about with the readymade pal who'd arrived in this world alongside them. I was eight years younger and football was something between me and Dad alone. He'd come and watch and, as I tried my utmost to impress, I'd be so, so aware of him stood on the side lines. Not that he was vociferous. He was very much the quieter type. He stood on his own away from the competitive dads, which taught me another valuable life lesson and made me love him even more.

Often, he didn't want to come. He'd been working all week, it was Sunday morning, and he just wanted to sit in his chair and read his papers. I'd badger him and badger him. I feel bad about it now, knowing how much he would have relished a rest, but the result of my nagging was he'd be there. It meant an unimaginably huge amount.

We'd play all over and sometimes I'd get a lift with another lad who was a much better footballer than me. After the match, we'd pile into his dad's car and listen as he lavished praise on his son. 'You were absolutely brilliant.' Me and my mate would be sniggering in the back as our pal, to his credit, became more and more embarrassed.

My dad never operated like that. He'd say nothing to me while always making a point of telling the other lads they'd played well. It didn't bother me. In fact, I admired him. I was proud of his democratic spirit, and I felt he was teaching me something. I know when the time comes, and my son Albert and his mates get in my car, I won't start telling him he's great – I'll be saying that to the other lads. Another tiny life lesson, but a very important one, and I can't help thinking that it, like so many others, comes from Salford, a city with an ethos running through it – 'Think of other people. Don't get too ahead of yourself.'

Of course, there might have been another reason he didn't praise me – I was probably the worst player on the pitch. At school, I was one of the best and captain of my team, but when I then progressed to Salford Boys I was struggling. Trouble was, while I inherited Dad's determination as a footballer, I lacked his gift. I was always in and out of the team. I was the fittest, very vocal (surprise, surprise), and worked really hard, but had very little actual ability. My first touch, pace and turning let me down – although at the time I couldn't see it. It was left to my dad to point out.

I had a Nana who ran a boarding house in Blackpool. I was sat on the floor in her living room and from her armchair she asked me the classic question, 'So what are you going to do when you grow up?'

There was only one answer. 'A footballer.'

'Yes,' my dad interjected, very gently and very obliquely, 'but if he doesn't improve a bit in the next year or so we might have to think about that.'

I felt disappointed, but at the same time relieved. My dad knew what it was to be a talented footballer. He had a good eye. More than that, though, he'd picked up that my ambition wasn't entirely for myself. He was letting me off the hook while

41

at the same time letting me know what he thought. He was, as they'd say now, managing expectations.

Trouble is, while football had been ruled out as a career option, very little else was being ruled in.

From the very start, I'd felt held back in the classroom. Bedtime with Mum and Dad meant that, by the time I began reading at primary school, I was already familiar with, among other books, *Black Beauty*, *The Adventures of Tom Sawyer* and, equally formatively, *The Boy Who Was Afraid*, by Armstrong Sperry, an incredibly emotionally layered story that tells of a young Polynesian boy conquering his fear of the sea and the loss of his mother. Books were ever present in our house. The library was only half a mile away and Mum and Dad were both in and out of there, she for her romantic novels, he for his thrillers, as was I and the twins. When I then entered the classroom, they gave me *Janet and John*. After the world of adventure I'd experienced, 'Here is a cat', 'Here is a dog' was of no interest to me. *Janet and John* is also extremely class-bound, with middle-class kids who had nothing to do with my experience or my view of the world. If they were trying to get me to be aspirational for that kind of life, it fell on deaf ears. Thankfully, the teacher introduced me to the Doctor Seuss books, which I consumed, loving their colour and clever use of language. There was also a book club at school where I read *Stig of the Dump*, *The Borrowers*, everything I could get my hands on. Back home, meanwhile, I was watching *Sesame Street*, education by stealth. I'd also read comics, obsessed with *The Numskulls*, now in *The Beano* but previously in *The Beezer* and *The Dandy*, about a group of little men who lived in somebody's head, one controlling the mouth department, another the brain, and so on.

The strip has many similarities to the Disney film *Inside Out*, which, coincidentally, my children are now obsessed with. I also read *Battle* comic, pretending to be Major Eazy, a character I now realise was based very much on Clint Eastwood's Man with No Name. Later I would get into all the usual suspects, such as *The Lord of the Rings*, while also going through a phase of reading ultra-violent sexual and skinhead stories and the Hell's Angels books by Richard Allen. Naturally, I hid those from my mum and dad.

Secondary school, especially, was a turn-off. I was never happy there, worn down by a culture, as I perceived it, whereby if you did your homework and worked hard, aspired academically, talked about university, or volunteered for sports teams, you were deemed a creep. Essentially, a communal fear of looking or sounding different, of being honest about ourselves, meant we were all colluding in holding each other back. I don't know what a sociologist would say about that, but we certainly weren't rebelling against the system; we were allowing it to define us in the exact way it wanted – 'Forget ambition, you lot are headed for the factory.'

Instead of following my instinct and doing what I thought was right for me, I got caught somewhere between the two positions. My education went to shot and yet at the same time I was made head boy. There was one reason for my elevation and one reason only – manners. Unlike my communication skills, they were impeccable. From day one, Mum and Dad drilled it into us about respect for other people. I am now engaged in that with my own children. They probably feel I'm a bit oppressive with the pleases and thank yous, but for my money they're the first step towards civilisation.

My dad put it slightly more bluntly – 'Always say please and thank you to someone because, if they don't say it to you, you know they're a bastard.'

Typical Dad. But he backed up those words with actions. If they went out, Mum and Dad were more polite to waiters and waitresses than they would be to the person in charge. Position and authority, per se, didn't warrant respect; there had to be more to it. Whenever we went to a guesthouse, my mum and dad's manners and respect for the people waiting on us was immense. There was none of that horrible inverted snobbery that remains so prevalent and was so hugely impactful on me as a child. I loved them so much because they could always put themselves in the position of somebody else. They treated people equally and I've always tried to do the same in a job that is full of levels of politicking and power-gaming.

At school, however, my considered manners backfired. All I wanted was to be one of the lads, but as head boy all the lads saw was a proxy teacher. The school, on the other hand, saw a child who was definitely not a rebel, was well turned out, had a bit of presence, and tended to be good at sports. I had a leg in both camps and a foot in neither.

Unfortunately, if the school hoped to gain any educational kudos from my position, they were to be very sadly disappointed. There was one area in which I excelled and that was English. At everything else, I was just dreadful. I felt it was a huge embarrassment to the school that the head boy was in the lowest set for maths, in fact the lowest set for pretty much everything. My head boy duties were suitably undemanding. Occasionally, I would have to speak in assembly, otherwise it was just giving out registers and the like. Even then I was lazy and let the deputy head boy do all the work. I should have been sacked and think the only reason the school didn't wield the axe was because of the embarrassment. Seemingly nothing could get me deposed, not even getting drunk on a school trip to Haworth to see the Bronte sisters' house. The headmaster went wild and carpeted me for it, but still I carried on in the position. How I held on to that job I'll never know. There'd be one or two other occasions where I'd think the same thing down the years.

I got seriously lost at secondary school. My reports weren't great but there was a subtlety in my mum and dad's reaction. They didn't come down too hard on me because their perception of themselves was that they too weren't intellectual, so for them to give me a hard time would, in their heads, be hypocritical. I never had the big 'If I'd had the education you'd had . . .' speech. They laid off me, a generosity that was misplaced. I could have done so much more but only wanted to do the things I was interested in: English, drama and sport. I loved drama, but we only did it until the second year and then it disappeared from the curriculum. I only reengaged with it when I went to Eccles Sixth Form College to re-sit my O-Levels, which again I failed. I was looning around the communal area one day when the drama teacher pulled me up – 'If you're doing that, you might as well do it in here.' At which point, I entered the drama department. It wasn't the huge moment of realisation it would be if I was in a US teen drama. I didn't suddenly 'find myself' and see a path laid out before me. But I did find myself in *Lock Up Your Daughters* and met Pooky Quesnel, one of my greatest friends, with whom I now co-star in *The A Word*. She would talk to me about

Stanislavsky and Brecht, at which point I'd become very self-conscious and we'd end up having a row.

I moved on to a two-year drama foundation course at Salford College of Technology. My early forays into the subject at Eccles had made me realise that with acting I could show off and use my physicality. The course was based at the Adelphi Building on Peru Street, a huge white stone structure, converted from a chemical factory, now knocked down. My mum told me on her first day of work, when she was fourteen, her initial task was to deliver a message to that same building. Every day when I walked up the steps I thought of my mum as a girl doing exactly the same.

Escaping from secondary school, first to Eccles College and then on to Salford Tech, meant entering a more reasoned environment where you didn't get battered for expressing yourself. I felt I could throw off the shackles and become more the person I wanted to be. The teachers only added to this newfound sense of discovery and freedom. They had no inhibitions and spoke openly, honestly and passionately about their fields of expertise. I still remember vividly an English A-Level teacher, Ms Sorah, saying to a classful of Salford students, 'I think there's something very moving about the sight of a ploughed field.' I know in isolation that sound pretentious, but I've never forgotten it – an observation about nature I would never have considered had I not gone to Salford Tech. Ms Sorah, so passionate, opened my eyes to poetry, its beauty and brutality, and its ability to educate and move. She was central in particular to my fascination with the war poets, which continues to this day. She so brilliantly revealed the depth of message, the disillusionment, the journey from valour to desperation.

War poetry was my way into art in every sense, in particular

Siegfried Sassoon's journey of conscience from a man deeply taken with the notion of spilling blood for king and country to an absolute abhorrence of the hideous slaughter he saw on the Front. There's a poem of Sassoon's that was deeply influential on me and what I thought theatre, poetry – the arts in general – could be. Sassoon came back from the Front and saw for himself the asinine approach to the war as represented in a weak and sickly West End review.

In his disgust and despair at this gross misrepresentation of war, Sassoon, in his poem 'Blighters', visualised tanks crushing the audience. He wanted to pull back the curtains on the reality, expose this contrivance as a sham, an insult to those lying dead in the mud.

Sassoon, Robert Graves too, opened my eyes to what theatre, poetry, could be. Rather than distant, the preserve of an elite, they could be used to fight a battle. Ms Sorah woke me up to that fact and I felt excited, emboldened, by it.

Twenty years later, I would find myself back on that self-same spot filming for *The Second Coming*. Right there, on the Croft outside the Adelphi Building, as Steven Baxter, the second coming of the drama's title, I would preach the New Testament. Strange doesn't quite describe the feeling I had that day. When I walked into Salford Tech, I never imagined I would become an actor. To be a lead in a landmark TV drama would, in my head, have required a miracle.

4

A VISION DENIED

I was a 52-year-old man lying on my old bed in my old bedroom in my old house, the semi-detached in Little Hulton where I grew up. I'd been there for weeks, just me, my mum, and massive doses of medication.

One day she pushed open the door — 'I'd like to go and see where we scattered your dad's ashes.'

She was trying to get me to do something, anything. I was obviously in a very bad way.

I wanted to say no.

'All right,' I said, 'I'll drive you.'

We were on a bridge above a river near Clitheroe. These acres had meant so much to Dad. During the Second World War, the nearby Whiteacre Boys' Camp was home to dozens of children evacuated from Salford. Dad was one of them. Overseen by the headmaster, Mr Targett, Whiteacre, opened in 1940 by Salford Education Committee, was run along the lines of a public school — dormitories, sport and a considered in-depth education — but, instead of a privileged elite, with working-class kids from the back streets of the north-west. It was part evacuee refuge, part social experiment.

Dad would come alive when he reminisced about Whiteacre. Suddenly, there he was, Ronnie Ecc, in the middle of the countryside, a raggy-arsed kid from Salford in beautiful rural Lancashire. He'd talk about walking mile after mile, drinking in the freshness of the air, plunging into rivers. He was captain of all the teams – rugby, football, the lot – and head of his dorm. In that environment, Ronnie was recognised as a bright and sporting child. He was given responsibility and respect. The teachers perceived him as a leader, the result being he got an improved sense of himself.

Previously, Dad had been struggling for visibility in a big family in Salford. Peter, his eldest brother, was the most handsome, and because he was the firstborn, he always had a special place. Then Jack came along. A 12lb baby, he was mutilated, disfigured and blinded at birth by the mauling and wrestling of the forceps. He had a perfect half division facial birthmark – the same, I would one day discover, as that of De Flores in the Jacobean drama *The Changeling*. Ironically, considering his size at birth, Jack would end up smaller than his siblings, and clearly, because of the consequences of his birth, he too had a special place. Then my dad came along – plain, unremarkable Ronald, nothing of note there – before my Uncle Roy appeared, very fair and short-sighted. Sheila was the only sister, and then twenty-five years later came Paul. Dad was very much lost in the morass of the middle. A baby raised in the Depression. Then, when the world emerged blinking from those depths, it was straight into war.

Throughout their long time together, Dad would tell Mum that Whiteacre was the happiest time of his life.

'Wasn't that hard to hear?' I once asked her.

'No, no,' she said, 'I understood it. He was loved, but there was a lot of them in his family, and Salford was rough.' She wasn't wrong. Money was thin on the ground, employment hard to find, food scarce, and homes bare. People's health suffered accordingly, and children often suffered from lice infestations and other hygiene-related diseases. The 1930s and '40s in Salford were akin to Victorian times.

For Ronnie, Whiteacre had an incredibly intense impact. The focus was on him – and he excelled. This ordinary child, once ignored, blossomed. He read prolifically. He wasn't bookish as such, he wasn't a Herbert, but he liked stories. Again, maybe it was the middle child thing. He was slightly overlooked so he found his stimulation elsewhere, including acting, featuring in school plays. Years later, the lines would still come rolling out. 'Cor, stone the crows,' he'd mimic a cockney accent, 'if it ain't Charlie. Move another inch and I'll blow your bleeding head orf.'

He boxed, he told me, earning the nickname Will-o'-the-wisp Eccleston. Forced into the ring with his best mate, he refused to take part – until his pal landed a blow. Dad punched him back, hard, and won the fight.

Not only was this working-class lad from Salford building a sense of self-worth, but he was actually listened to. At one point, he came home to Irlams o' th' Height, looked in a sports shop window, and spotted a billiard table. He went back to Whiteacre and told one of the teachers. In any other school, he'd have been laughed at or told bluntly to shut up, but at Whiteacre the teacher actually wanted to know more – 'Where was it?' He told them, and Whiteacre bought it. They put it in one of the dormitories. My dad always told that story, pre- and post-dementia – Whiteacre and Duncan Edwards were touchstones untrammelled by the illness – with such a sense of pride because it was his suggestion. He was listened to. He witnessed the manifestation of an idea he'd had. He loved that sense of comradeship, joint ownership, between him and the teachers.

I would listen to these tales at the knee, loving the vitality they brought out in him. Vocally, and in his eyes, he'd be transformed. Everything about him shone, sung, as if physically he was back there and he'd taken my mum and me too. I fell in love with his love for Whiteacre. To see that passion in him was quite remarkable. When I think of him talking about Whiteacre, I still feel the self-same deep emotion it brought out in me.

It was more than talk. When I was a kid, Dad would take me and Mum to Clitheroe.

'We used to stand on them stones there', he'd point out, 'and jump in the river. We swam in the water. Can you imagine that?'

Mum was already familiar with the spot – Dad had taken her numerous times during their courting days, having told her about the area and what it meant to him. He had a love affair not just with her, but with that place and time. My mum and that period of his life merged and Elsie became very important to Dad in the same way as Whiteacre.

That closeness was reciprocated. From very early on in the relationship, Mum knew my dad. Really knew him. Not surprising really – emotionally, Mum is very generous and giving, empathetic, and acutely observant. I expect at that point Dad would have been giving it a lot of the Salford swagger, but I imagine what a woman would really be interested in would be 'Does he go to work? Does he turn up on time? Has he got manners?' Only then would she look for the tenderness, and that's where Clitheroe came in. When Ronnie talked about

Whiteacre, Elsie would see the little boy in him, the man who, before he'd fallen in love with her, had fallen in love with nature.

For a lad from Salford, to be pitched from an intense urban experience to an intense rural one must have been like taking LSD. Dad wasn't walking past factories; he was walking past byres and barns. He wasn't staring into the dead murk of the Irwell; he was peering into crystal-clear streams. The air wasn't fouled by chimneys; it was a sweet confection delivered fresh from the trees. Trees – something else he loved for the rest of his life, to him the purist expression of life a person could ever see.

And it didn't stop there. Ronnie wasn't sleeping in a house any more; he was living in a dormitory. He wasn't held back by class; he was on an equal footing. He wasn't lost; he was found. Ronnie flew. It took a war to make it happen, but he flew.

He wasn't the only one. After the war, the *British Medical Journal* published research comparing the health and well-being of boys evacuated to Whiteacre to those who remained in Salford – the social experiment. The Whiteacre boys were found to be significantly ahead, not just academically, but in terms of weight, growth and nutrition. No doubt about it, the expectations of these children were raised far higher than had they stayed in Salford. I expect that the teachers were much more relaxed and stimulated in that environment as well. They too, after all, were living in nature, living in peace, far removed from the social injustice and deprivation of the city.

Dad always maintained a little piece of Whiteacre in his head through his enduring affection for reading and words. Working at the Colgate-Palmolive factory, he won a dictionary in a stacker truck competition. No surprises there – he used to say to me, 'Chris, I can make a stacker truck talk.' He'd jump on board and off he'd go, pushing this lever, pulling that. If Dad hadn't been best that day there's every chance I wouldn't be writing this book now. Another huge step towards becoming an actor came from him winning that dictionary, because through it my dad transferred his absolute astonishment and love of words to me.

'Association,' he'd announce. 'What do you think that means?' And then he'd read out the whole definition. 'All those meanings for one word – it's marvellous that, isn't it? Marvellous!' His childlike wonder made it a moment of intimacy. This was the man I wanted to be part of.

'Scholarly,' he'd ponder. 'A gentleman and a scholar.' It was one of his favourite phrases. 'What do you think that means?'

'I'll give you that one, pal,' he'd say if I got one of his questions right. 'Where did you get that from?'

He'd also have his pristine *Manchester Evening News*. My dad was a great man of papers. He'd get three on a Sunday – the *Express*, *Mirror* and *People* – while in the week he read the *Mirror*, until it became illiterate and, like many working-class people, he swapped to the *Daily Mail*, also taking the *Mail on Sunday*. He also had the *Pink* football paper on a Saturday evening. Always a paper. He never had them delivered, though – you had to pay more for that. He loved the whole business of 'I'm going for my paper now'. I'm the same; I love going for the papers, another bond that lives on, perpetuated also by memories of the crosswords we'd share, especially the giant ones at Christmas. Crosswords were our thing. They were how we expressed our love.

Dad read novels too – Jack Higgins, Desmond Bagguley, and then he alighted on the early Robert Ludlum thrillers. With Ludlum there was an existential element that took his enjoyment to another level. He loved John le Carré for the same reason and obsessed over Alec Guinness's TV portrayal of George Smiley. Books, dictionaries and newspapers surrounded his throne. This was Dad.

He and Mum also passed on their love of nature. Mum's family had a little hut on Pickmere Lake, near Knutsford, where, as a girl, she would occasionally be taken, so she shared Dad's nostalgia for adventure-filled childhood days. Their memories bonded them, and when it came to their own children they wanted to recreate that same deep attachment with the natural world. No way were they ever going to use their fortnight's holiday to go to Blackpool. They wanted to instil the values, not of the amusement arcade, but of open fields, big skies and unpolluted air. Blackpool wasn't unfamiliar to me. My auntie Sheila had The Alhambra guesthouse on Palatine Road and Nana had The Sunset on Hornby Road. But I was so influenced by my mum and dad that I was a little bit snobbish about the town. I sensed what they were thinking – *So this is what the working class aspire to, is it? Well, not this working class. We aspire to be in nature. They're not taking our money through those slot machines. We're not wasting money like that.* When my mum and dad took us on holiday, they were telling us that life should be led according to simple values – people, the natural world, not possessions.

We'd go to either Cornwall or Devon and stay on farms – I do the same now with my own children. More often than not I would get headaches on the first day because the air was so fresh. We weren't far from the seaside, but we didn't want to go to the beach; we wanted to stay on the farm and help the farmer. I'd get the cows in for milking or collect the eggs from the chickens. It wasn't just the fluffy stuff; I saw the reality. I went with the farmer once when he took a cow to the abattoir. It was hung upside down and a short metal bolt put through its head. It didn't seem odd or callous; it was simply part of the experience. Stay on a farm and you see it through the farmer's eyes. Another time we drove all over killing rabbits infected with myxomatosis. The farmer would shoot them and then it was our job to get out and finish them off. Some kids, tougher kids than me, couldn't do it, but I'd pick them up by the ears and chop the neck. I didn't enjoy it, but I had the mentality of not wanting to be embarrassed by looking soft, so I role-played it. In my head, it wasn't me doing the chopping, it was the farmer.

My dad was a man at his best on holiday. He would always make a big effort to get friendly with the farmer who generally wouldn't be hugely enamoured at his house being used as a B&B, but, like any working man, needed the money. The farmer would initially keep his distance, but my dad, very cleverly, would charm him. He could see there was tension, that this was a working man, and would approach him as such. Inevitably, they'd end up getting on, which also offered some welcome male time for my dad.

As the days passed, Dad would leave work behind and slowly relax. The only part of life at home he brought with him was his love of papers. In every picture of him on holiday, he's got a paper in his hand. More than anything he wanted to spend time with my mum. He really loved her, really enjoyed her company.

Years passed since Ron's divorce from Whiteacre until one night the relationship was unexpectedly resumed. I was sat in the front room and my dad was reading his *Manchester Evening News*, back to front, as he did every night, when he sprang to life.

'Elsie! There's a thing here saying, "Anybody who attended Whiteacre School, and is interested in attending a reunion, please ring this number."'

He was glowing. 'Ring it, Ronnie!' she urged.

Knowing what a big deal Whiteacre was to him, we stood next to him as he picked the phone up and dialled the number.

'Hello, is that Mr Targett?'

'Yes.'

'Hello, sir. This is Ronald Eccleston.'

We listened. Surely after all these years the headmaster wouldn't remember.

'Ah, Eccleston,' he cried, 'the footballer!'

It was incredible. Like the decades had been reduced to but a few months.

Dad loved those reunions, a reminder of such happy times, a life that had vanished as abruptly as it had begun when he returned to Salford, a city that, along with its own inherent deprivations, had now seen 2,000 homes destroyed or damaged beyond repair by the Luftwaffe while almost 30,000 more had suffered to a lesser degree.

At that point, Dad was plunged back into the reality of a school that recognised him only as a mark on a register and dismissed, often with a violent hand – him and hundreds of others as a mere nuisance to be herded on their way to the factory gates. Even when he had dementia, Dad used to talk about a teacher called 'Snuffy' Johnson who repeatedly singled him out as if he had a chemical reaction to his presence. This horrendous individual hit Dad again and again. He terrified him through violence, and, years on, Dad would clearly recall the Dickensian detail of his wooden thumb.

'Snuffy Johnson', my dad would say, 'was a bastard. If I could find where he's buried, I'd dig him up and kick him all round the cemetery.' Or 'cimitery' as he said it.

'Ronnie,' my mum would berate him. 'That's a terrible thing to say.'

'I would,' he'd continue. 'He was a bastard. He hated me.' It was said with a lot of force.

Before he knew it, Dad was on the working-class conveyor belt. He had a milk round and then worked on the railways – he always said the best eggs and bacon he ever had were cooked on a shovel put in the firebox. He would tell me how women alongside the line would lift up their skirts and show the drivers and shovellers their knickers, and how in return they'd throw them some coal. He told that as a joke, but when you think what's going on there it's not quite so funny – poor people being reduced to flashing at passing trains, to humiliating themselves, in return for a basic necessity. He also used to tell me how on a Saturday afternoon they used to stop the train on a line that ran along the top of Bolton Wanderers' Burnden Park ground and watch a bit of the game.

All this time he was basically a worker, a labourer, a number. He was a teenager, but his life had been mapped out to the grave.

I can never stop wondering about the attributes common to me and Dad, and where, in a less socially restrictive world, he might have found a place to shine. Like me, my dad was a pro-foundly non-practical person. He could make a stacker truck talk but wasn't quite so adept with his hands. He also enjoyed a stage, a spotlight, which in his case was forthcoming from sport. My first stage, too, was sport. That didn't work out but still I maintained a physical presence coupled with an intensity of drive and ambition. Basically, those are the qualities an actor needs. My dad had them, as well as the sharp features – the difference being that, for him, the doors to the creative world were welded shut. When I came along, social reformism meant they had been jemmied open a little.

It would have been incredible to see Dad act. Recently, I happened across a book written by an art teacher at Whiteacre. It revealed how in tune so many of the boys were with the idea of imaginative self-expression, how it allowed them to talk about their backgrounds, their sensitivities, and their view of the world around them. It offered an incredible window into the possibilities and potentiality of the young working-class mind. I can only imagine that for Dad the opportunity to act did exactly the same. What I saw in later life, through Dad's love of music, radio and television, particularly drama, was a man attuned to the intricacies of story, performance and character. He was a wonderful audience. If somebody could do something well, he admired them deeply. On a Friday night, they had a sing-song at the Morning Star in Wardley. Dad wouldn't sing but he absolutely adored watching those who could. The only time Dad had sung was, quite literally, for his supper. As a young man, he had a friend called Larry Morgan, an endless source of interest. They'd met during National Service at Salisbury in the Lancashire Fusiliers and on leave would go out drinking in Bath or Bristol to try to meet women. After a night on the town they'd go to the Salvation Army hostel and literally sing for a bowl of soup and a bed. Dad, as ever, never forgot generosity and always put money in the Sally Army tin.

Dad found Larry fascinating. Whereas he was completely fat-fingered and cack-handed, Larry was the opposite. He'd explain how he once watched him make a crystal radio from batteries and fuse wire – 'Incredible. Marvellous.' That enthusiasm for other people's abilities was a great quality. There was a quizzicality at its heart, which I experienced from him myself when I started getting somewhere.

'Marvellous, that,' he'd say. 'How did you do that?' He respected what I was doing more than the fact that I'd had success from doing it. 'You took off a good part' – that was always his phrase. My brothers would do it too – 'Wow, that was fantastic!' – and look at me like I was slightly alien. I was always uncomfortable with their admiration. I didn't want to be made separate. I didn't want my acting to be elevated to something special above what they did. They had their own talent. Aside from acting, I had none. I was given a chance to escape to a rare world. And, unlike Dad, I never had to go back.

5

RAGE

I went to the top of the path and faced the bottom of the road. I knew if I did, when Dad turned into our street, he would spot his little son playing, apparently unaware of his presence. In my head, he'd see me and think, There's my lad – isn't he vulnerable?

I heard the car getting nearer and nearer and still kept my back to him. He pulled up and opened the door. I turned round and smiled at him, looking surprised.

And he blanked me.

Dad would exhibit a great and frightening anger as he got older, and it's hard not to wonder whether the glimpse Whiteacre had given him of another life didn't act like a stick being jabbed in the back of his neck. 'What would have happened if . . . ?' He was denied any opportunity to find out, and the emotion that sparked in him had a direct impact on me.

Maybe Dad's anger came also from being what I've been labelled – an 'overthinker'. It's a term I dislike immensely. Why is a desire to analyse, to seek knowledge, presented as a negative?

'Overthinking' could just as easily be termed a keen inquisitiveness. Are working-class people not meant to enquire? Are they not meant to have an interest in the world in which they live? Dad was hungry for stimulation, as are my brothers and my mum. They are, like me, intensely curious people. We are far from alone in wishing to seek out information, to open our eyes to what the world has to offer. There are millions the same, sharing an attitude that comes very much from a sense of being denied education, or lack of expectation that a person who lives on a back street or an estate should have any. Overthinking would be considered a positive in any other strata of society.

Dad's frustration came from a restless intelligence, an intelligence not being met. You got the best out of him when he discovered something new, be it via a documentary or a book. Then you would see his sense of amazement. Occasionally, it would spill over into everyday life. He would stop me in the street and look up to the moon.

'Can you believe that man has stood on that?' he'd ponder. 'Can you believe it?'

I loved that. Again, the intimacy. There was a great deal of boyish wonder in my dad, and I'm the same. Knowledge is wonderful. I'm completely unabashed about going 'Isn't that amazing?' That was a value my dad passed on to me – a value not of money but of knowledge.

'Do you know how bees make honey?' he'd ask, and a thousand other questions like it. Life was an adventure. But that side of a person was never encouraged if they were working class. It was never going to be any use in a battle zone or heavy industry.

Dad wanted a life of the mind. Unlike me, it was never in his sway to find it. Instead he was left to recall a lost paradise of, as A. E. Housman put it, those blue remembered hills.

It could not come again. That was the absolute truth of Dad's life. And his frustration was only worsened at the factory. As time went on, there was a period when he stopped being a stacker truck driver and was made a foreman. The promotion wasn't undeserved. Dad was nothing if not bright, hard-working and punctual. His bosses rightly thought, *Reward this bloke, he can do it. He knows the place inside out, and he can handle himself.*

Fine, except suddenly, whereas before he'd been one of the lads in navy blue all-in-ones, now he was the boss of the lads, in with the suits, a lot of whom, having just come out of university, were younger than him. They were talking about new ideas, working models. My dad didn't know much about working models, but he did know a lot about twenty-five hairy-arsed Salford blokes who drove stacker trucks all day. He also knew the realities of the factory floor and how it worked, the tricks that were pulled, the blind eyes turned if something disappeared. He'd done it himself. It's how things were, how people thought – *This is a big industry; if we get a few tubes of toothpaste, fuck 'em.*

While the increased money and responsibility was welcome, being picked out of the pack created an enormous tension in Dad because he found himself in a no-man's land where he didn't fit with either side. Key in my dad's life at that point were some questions: 'Who do I belong to now? The lower middle classes or the working classes? Am I a suit-and-tie man or a boiler-suit man? Am I a stacker truck driver nicking a bit? Or am I one of the suits keeping an eye on others who might be doing the same thing?'

His answer was to try to occupy both camps. He was in the offices doing admin, but he was also on the factory floor, cajoling the men, talking to them. There'd be some blokes who'd say, 'That's it, my days on the truck are over,' but my dad wasn't like that. He always said he could make a stacker truck talk and he carried on doing so. There was a practical point – he could get things done – but it was also man management, showing the men that he could still do what they did. The unavoidable truth, however, was that he was trapped in a void. He was no longer the same as his mates and yet would have been highly uncomfortable sitting at the top table hearing managers describe people he used to work, eat and laugh with as 'lazy bastards' or using the phrase 'When I was at uni . . . '

Here was a very, very bright man who wasn't like this group of people on this side or that group of people on the other. No one spoke up and said, 'No, you're like us,' which is what happened to me. He was left to wander that no-man's land alone.

Dad's mental soup, like my own, would eventually reach boiling point. But the eruption was a long time coming. For years, he would come home in a very, very stressed state, filled with fury and frustration, which he would then distil around the house.

There was an anger in him, a tangible rage. And it could come. As a child, I felt the temperature in the house was dictated by whether he was there or not. If he was out, fine. If he was in and happy, fine. If he was in and not happy – 'What's going to happen now?' It was a question I was asking from a point of isolation. Everybody else in the house was older than me and so had more sophisticated ways of dealing with the tornado. Alan and Keith had each other. Mum, meanwhile, knew Dad in a way that carried the insight and understanding so lacking in a child. For me, though, while there was so much to admire, so much to love, about Dad, I feared him. And it got worse. There was a period when I was older, just short of my teenage years, when, so intense was his rage, my nervous system, my animal self, thought he might kill me. He wouldn't hit me, there was never a belt or anything like that. He rampaged around, and that was worse. His rage was so deep and so consistent, so fierce, it traumatised me. It definitely set me up for various issues going forward. He would be heartbroken to read those words, devastated – 'Me?' But I attach no blame to my dad. He was brought up one of six kids, the product of a Victorian father, the product of a system where men were brutalised, purposefully. He couldn't be expected to have a wider perspective. My dad, like me, came into this world thinking the glass was half empty, and in fact for him it was.

Dad's wrath, absolute wrath, could be about anything, but it would often manifest itself in a belief that everything had to be perfect. This was Salford in the late '70s. Perfection rarely visited.

'Bloody burnt offering!' he'd erupt. 'Bloody burnt offering of a tea! I'm sick of it!' Loud. Angry. Real anger. Ferocious. That's coming from someone you love; someone you want to make feel better.

I've thought about it a lot since I've become a dad. We have to be aware as parents what we are. If we're forty-five and 13 stone and have got a terrible temper and are imposing it time and time again over an extended period, which my dad did, then it is going to have an effect. All the time I look at my own children and ask myself how they are viewing the people around them. What I picked up from my dad, and my mum, at such an early age has made me hyper-sensitive to Albert and Esme's own emotional lives. I have been like that from day zero, because we have to be aware that our children take in our energy before they can speak. I arrived at consciousness thinking my mum was reliable, gentle, natural and unchanging. I came to consciousness thinking my dad was the opposite of all those things. He was not a bad man – he could be tender and we always knew he loved us – but amid that he was deeply flawed and emotionally very immature. He was infantile in the speed of his mood swings and tyrannical too, a mannerism forged in the tradition of many other working-class men. I'm sure my mum and brothers will see it differently, but I can only speak about my own sensibility. I can only speak about what my antennae were picking up. As a child, I had a definite proclivity to internalise what Mum and Dad were feeling, which makes sense when you think about the job I do, absorbing characters, filtering them, and playing with the results.

As in every working-class household, money mattered. Mum had started working Mondays, Tuesdays and Wednesdays cleaning at the baths. That meant Dad was coming home three days a week and having to make his own tea. Looking back, I think he felt emasculated by my mum having a job. At the same time, however, he knew we needed the money.

Thursday and Friday, everything was fine. Monday to Wednesday, the situation was different. I would be home first, then Keith would come in at five past five. Keith was always gentle with me – he knew what was coming. I knew what was coming too, but would have a slightly different take on it. Keith was nineteen, I was eleven. With Alan home too, we tried to do everything we could to have tea ready, but it was never enough. There would then be a short period of calm before the storm, which was when I'd regularly head outside and do my back to the top of the road trick, trying, hoping, really hoping, to summon up a bit of sunshine. The arrival of his green Ford Escort (UNB 172K – I can remember all my dad's number plates) generally signified the clouds closing in.

Not that I was aware of it at that point, but basically I was creating a piece of open-air theatre in an attempt to keep something out of my life, my house. But Dad wasn't thinking about my vulnerability. He was thinking, *Somebody else who wants something from me.* Whatever frame of mind he was in, he was basically saying to me, 'No, I'm taking this in the house.' He'd fly through that door in a rage.

I would look at him in his shirt and tie and think, *I don't remember this when he wore the blue.*

Even if everything was perfectly prepared, he'd always find a reason to be harassed or frustrated, banging cupboards, slamming drawers. He really didn't want to come back to a house without Elsie, not because she should have had his tea ready, or because he wanted to sit back and be lazy while she waited on him, but because his idea of family had been forcibly dissolved by financial imperative. He wasn't alone; we all missed that feminine presence. But for him it was much more pronounced. Elsie took the edge off things. He adored her, and his work was intensely male. He wanted his domestic life with her in it.

After he'd eaten, while we did the washing-up, Dad would disappear upstairs, have a bath, and get changed. Once again there would be calm in the house. He'd come back down with a shiny face from having scrubbed it so hard, to the extent I could almost see my reflection in it. I knew that ever since he'd left Colgates at five o'clock, all he'd been thinking about was sitting in his chair, clean, fed and reading his newspaper.

Ensconced in his *Manchester Evening News*, he'd have his shirt collar up, a mental reassurance, a reminder, that this was a time when he didn't have to wear a tie. I'd look at him and know his regret about his behaviour was starting – harder to watch than the behaviour itself. After a while he'd start making eye contact and conversation. There'd be a bit of payback from me, monosyllabic, uncommunicative, and I think he understood that inside I was angry about what had gone on.

Eventually, lack of communication would become a problem. When puberty came, I was more argumentative and less willing to accept the status quo of the house and how it operated, the way Dad dominated the place through petty mood swings and anger. As I edged into my teens, whenever I had a row with Dad I was definitely harbouring a feeling of 'I'm not going to end up like you,' which sounds nasty and aggressive but to me was just a matter of fact. This was a long, slow process of observation before the inevitable flashpoint. I was fourteen and he was doing his usual, bollocking me for something, when I felt consumed with rage, savagely angry about all the shit he'd pulled, the storming round the house, the instant and childish mood changes, the seemingly blithe dismissal of other people's feelings.

We squared up to each other. Me, back against the wall, staring him in the eye. Him tapping his finger on my lip. I did something with my eyes, which I now know to be an acting trick, to register my disgust.

'I wouldn't let a grown man look at me like that,' he said.

In my head, I was thinking, *Go on, you've always wanted to do this, so fucking do it.* But I was using the tool of 'Once you do it, mate, you'll never get me back. You can physically hurt me, but you'll be dead to me. Because you'll be a man who punches his own son.'

There was something in him that understood that, and he withdrew.

If he'd not imposed his mood on the house, shouted at Mum, I'd have perhaps been less critical of his attitude, but the basic dynamic was that I didn't respect his authority in a way I respected my mum's authority. By the time of the against-the-wall incident, I was properly 'Fuck you, pal.'

A decade later, I was sat, in my mid-twenties, with a therapist, the first of many. He listened intently, puffing on a cigar, Freud-esque, as I related the story of my doomed attempts to stem my dad's anger when he arrived home. It was the first time I'd ever expressed it.

'What do you think of that little boy in the road?' he asked.

I became quite emotional, but I wasn't pitying myself. I didn't feel as if I was talking about me. I felt distant, as if I was examining another human being. Here was this little boy, who happened to be me, and I quite admired him. He was brave and resourceful. I wasn't saying 'Wasn't I brilliant?' – that boy could have been any child – but I did admire his willingness and ability to summon up something, anything, to take the heat out of the situation. It was about more than standing in a road. On a deeper level, it was as though I was trying to excavate my dad's personality. I felt like I knew something about him. I internalised his frustration and his dissatisfaction with himself and felt it in a very primal way, as if I shared it genetically, as if I was seeing myself, although it could just have been proximity. Maybe I was one of those kids who, without realising it, takes in tiny nuances of other people's personalities and then uses them to draw a bigger picture.

Amid my overwhelming desire for recognition, I felt sorry for Dad. I had no idea what his life, seen through his eyes, was like. I knew there was a part of him that hated blanking me. I knew there was a part of him that wanted to give me that smile, give me that one-on-one recognition. But an infantility in him would overrule it – 'I'm going in this house and I will have it out.'

I also knew men were meant to be angry and brusque, in particular when they come home from work hungry. I wasn't a little poet with my head in the clouds. In those days, it was totally legitimate to be a patriarchal Victorian figure. I wasn't expecting Dad to walk through the door and be full of hugs. That wasn't the way. It was never going to be the way. I'd grown up surrounded by and embedded among the anger of the working classes, not just my father, but in general. Anger was not a rarity in lives like mine; it had a constant existence.

I understand now that his rage wasn't about me, it was about his relationship with himself. Here was a perfectionist, obsessive about punctuality and working hard. Each night he was carrying a metaphorical briefcase full of mental baggage – frustration, irritation, anger, despair – and coming home to a sensitive 11-year-old boy who thought the sun shone out of his behind. I hero-worshipped him, the way lads do. More than anything, when my dad came home, I wanted him to smile. What I got was the opposite – a shout, a snarl. I now comprehend that process in his head, that doubtless there were deeper-seated and longer-rooted issues at work here too. On his side, the twins had reached eight years of age when I came along. They had each other so he felt he still had Elsie to himself. With me, Elsie was experiencing maternity as most women do, one on one, potentially with a baby that was never planned in the first place. There is potential there for jealousy, a triangle rarely pleasant when it features two alpha males. On my side, when I got older, and denied a close sibling of my own, I was unarguably needy. My mum said Dad was wonderful with me when I was a toddler but when I got to the more demanding period, when I really wanted to do things with him, like go to football matches, it was more difficult. At that point, he was tired from the situation at work, wrestling with his own personality. My hope that he'd invest time in me turned to anger when he wouldn't. Even if we went to games, I could often tell he didn't really enjoy taking me. He just wanted to sit at home in his chair. He worked bloody hard and he was knackered.

Equally, though, while I can make these logical deductions, his rage scared me, and that hasn't always been easy to reconcile. It created a period of intense uncertainty about him in me. Yes, there was a background picture to his discontent, but essentially he was putting his own feelings before mine and everyone else's, and we all normalised that change in atmosphere when he came in because it was simply how things were. He was the man of the house. Whatever day or time, it was his right to dictate the mood. If you went in and he said, 'You all right, cock?', you'd think *Oh good, sorted.* If you went in and he said, 'Where've you been?', you knew you had to tread lightly. Ironically, that need to react quickly to unpredictability would help me enormously as an actor. At the Central School of Speech and Drama, where I ended up, there was a brilliant dialect teacher, Julia Wilson-Dickson, who said I was good with accents, which indicated that sound had been very important to me from early on in terms of taking the emotional temperature of a room. That certainly resonated with me, in terms of the temperature around my dad.

My mum has said to me throughout my life, 'You were a latchkey boy.' I wasn't. What she means is that, when she wasn't there, I ran full pelt into the brunt of my dad's anger and frustration. She feels complicit because she worked Monday, Tuesday, and Wednesday, when it was at its worst. She should never feel that because, if she hadn't worked, we couldn't have lived in that house. Dad's rage was itself seeded in the fact that he'd never had the chance to develop himself or go to university, instead put through a social experiment, Whiteacre, in a public school environment, which affirmed what was good about him and then stuck him back in a Victorian education in Salford complete with Snuffy Johnson and the rest. My mum also knew that only she was able to throw a fire blanket on the intensity of Dad's rage. Dad's anger would frighten me, but not my mum. Like many working-class women, she was tough and brave. Mum could quell the anger in Ronnie that a little boy couldn't.

When I was older, I showed Mum and Dad the film *Distant Voices, Still Lives*, in which Pete Postlethwaite plays the playwright and director Terence Davies' father in 1940s Liverpool. It's very arty and slightly abstract and for a while I could see they were a little dismissive. Then they couldn't take their eyes off it. As the best films do, it had made the jump from screen to real life, highly evocative of my mum and dad's period. Postlethwaite's character in the film is much more intense than my dad and yet that performance is the epitome of working-class inner turmoil, a quality my dad carried by the barrowful, heavy and all-encompassing, which is exactly how I experienced it at a formative age. The psychological and emotional impact on me of the passion of that anger was very, very considerable. My dad wasn't an abusive monster, but he was a very, very powerful presence. People tell me I've got presence when all I'm doing is standing in a room. When I was a kid, all my dad had to do was sit in a chair. I think presence, in those terms, is internal activity. There's something going on inside, like a pressure cooker. With Dad, that pressure would be released in short bursts around the house.

Mum told me once, 'I had to have a word with your dad. I had to tell him "You're frightening Chris."' At the time, I wondered if maybe as a kid I'd made his anger a bigger demon than it was. Now I've got children of my own, I see it differently. Until that happens, I don't think you're aware of your power as a parent. Children's inhibitors and filters are out so they experience us on a level that we as adults can't understand. As a child, you can't defend yourself physically, so your intuition is much more foregrounded, your psyche very impressionable. You remain highly sensitive to unpredictability, movement, noise. I wasn't scared of Alan, I wasn't scared of Keith, I wasn't scared of Mum, but I was scared of Dad. He never wanted to take it out on me – he loved me – he just never realised quite how powerful he was. I think of that so much now with my own children, and I want to make it a better experience for them than I had. As a parent, with children around you, no matter how bad your day is, that isn't their day – and you're taller and you're bigger.

Thankfully, as a counter to Dad, I had someone who was deeply, deeply fair. My mum was, and is, gentle, kind and emotionally intelligent. Alan and Keith were also gentle and loving. But they could all look after themselves. They were negotiating that house in a different way. They will also remind me that I'm the one who's the most similar to Dad. Conflict can often arise when two people have very similar personalities. Many great dramas are based in that very scenario.

Again, we are talking about the complexities that arise in families weighted down by non-communication. When Dad had me up against that wall, there was part of me thinking, *Prove you don't love me. Fill me in,* and another part telling him, 'I really need you – I don't want to always get the vulnerability and the tenderness from my mum. I don't want to always have to run to my mum, because I'm not female, I'm male, and I want to find it in you.' As a male, it's great to find that in your dad. It also helps women because then they don't become mothers to partners. But this was the 1970s.

I'm sure Dad knew, like me, there was a complexity to our big bust-up that went way beyond a simple confrontation. I'm sure he knew, like me, that life would be a lot easier if only we could just be honest with one another. And I'm sure he knew, like me, that none of that could ever be vocalised because we were working-class males and we didn't do that sort of thing. Why vocalise an issue when it can be left to fester and churn?

Dad's flame, the one with the power to scorch all around it, would eventually fade, rarely to flicker again. I've a feeling, however, that it may still shine in me. I'm not invisible to the words, justified or not, often applied to me – intense, angry, confrontational. More than that, I'm convinced the complexity and ferocity of my dad's personality and how I learned to coexist with it pushed me to want to be creative, to play characters who are at the same time good and bad. Thomas Hardy describes Gabriel Oak in *Far from the Madding Crowd* as a 'man of salt and pepper mixture'. On a good day he was a good man, and on a bad day he was a bad man. We were taught that book in sixth form and as a 17-year-old I was very attracted to what Hardy was doing there – presenting a man warts and all. That's exactly how I experienced my dad. I would like to have talked to him about that period when I was frightened of him. But I would have liked that to have come organically, not in an interrogative or forced manner. Maybe, had dementia not struck, that's what would have happened. He'd have seen me interacting with Albert or Esme and it would have sparked a discussion. It was certainly not beyond my dad, had he not gone down the dementia route, to have reached seventy and said, 'I'm sorry about that. I got that wrong.'

The anger and intensity I saw in my dad has, subconsciously or otherwise, dictated my career choices much more than any characteristics of my mum. Frustration, unhappiness, personal limitation – I've played them all. For certain, when I have to be angry as an actor, I don't have to go anywhere else but to my dad's rages.

Early in my career, I was in an episode of *Boon*, playing a bad lad, stealing cars – a terrible performance. The story sees me get caught by Michael Elphick (Boon) and locked in a room until the coppers arrive. I rattle the door, can't get out, and so smash the room up entirely. Fantastic. At that age, you're thinking, *Great, I'm going to do my De Niro here. Look how aggressive I can be.* Typical self-conscious young actor. We only had one take – Central TV budget – and I smashed the room up as requested. A few weeks later, I was up in Little Hulton staying with my mum and dad.

'I saw that episode of *Boon* you were in,' he said.

'What do you think?' I asked. 'Did you like it?'

'It was good, yeah.' He paused. 'Where did you get that temper from?'

'What do you mean?'

'When you smashed that room up. Where did you get that temper from?'

'Where do you think?' I replied.

'I'm not bloody like that!'

But he was, and as an actor, I have since concluded, I was thinking, *You scared the shit out of me and I'm going to use your anger right here, right now.*

The same happened in a film called *Heart* where I had to batter a door down with an axe. We did a take and afterwards I went up to the director Charles McDougall – 'Was that all right or was it a bit camp?'

'No, no – that was fine.' I think I gave it what he wanted.

Another occasion, this time as Willy Houlihan in *Accused*, I had to smash some bathrooms up on a building site. Again, not a problem.

It's a common theme. I've been cast as someone who carries anger a lot. The fact is I genuinely cannot fight my way out of a paper bag.

But I look like I can – and I knew a man who could.

6

FALL AND RISE

It's 2018, the third preview night of Macbeth *at the RSC in Stratford and I've just fallen off the stage. My crown has come off and I'm lying on my back looking straight into an audience member's eyes. He doesn't need to speak. Those eyes say it all — 'That wasn't meant to happen, was it?'*

Despite the desperation of my predicament, a thought occurs to me — how glad I am that this particular man is sat where he is. Here I am, in pretty much the worst spot a stage actor can be. I could be living this soul-destroying moment in front of someone whose natural reaction is to become uptight, panicky and embarrassed. Instead I have got a bloke looking at me as if to say, 'Mate, I'm really sorry that's happened.'

If ever we meet again, pal, *I think,* I'll shake your hand.

The crown is lying to one side. He glances at it. His eyes speak again — 'You need that crown, don't you?'

In this conversation with no words, my own eyes instantly respond. 'Yes, I do need that crown,' they inform him. 'But I'm making a decision.' Thing is a third party is now chipping in too. He's got a front-row seat in my head. 'Get on with it,' my dad's telling me, 'you're doing a show.'

I turn around and, as if getting out of a swimming pool, haul myself on to the stage. I run across the boards, grab my sword, and go straight into the fight. I make a slashing move — and as I do so it feels like my back has ripped open.

It would be easy to surmise that, denied his own opportunities, Dad lived his life through me. I've never thought that. The more accurate version of events is that I have lived my life through him.

In the aftermath of the plunge in *Macbeth*, there was, as you'd expect, something of an inquest. I'd stepped into nothing and, had I not been fit and agile and managed to turn as I was falling, shifting the bulk of the impact on to my shoulder, I could quite feasibly have broken my back. As it was, I had still suffered considerable damage, a physiotherapist confirming that my body had first been concertinaed by the fall and then brutally and violently opened up by the subsequent fight. Flicking from one state to the other had been a huge physical strain, tearing my intercostal muscles and rotator cuff. I was on painkillers for the next thirty performances.

The reason for the incident was clear. The production had been reblocked and I couldn't see where I was going in the dark. Blocking is the process whereby the director decides the position of the actor on stage. I was moving from one area to another in a blackout and the blocking had changed so many times I quite simply didn't know where I was going. The fall did nothing for my confidence. Even afterwards, though, as I considered what had happened, my dad's voice came into my head.

'Chris!' he was saying to me, his voice a mix of exasperation and amusement. 'You fell off the stage. I don't mind you getting bad reviews, but the least you can do is stay on the stage. Bloody hell, Chris . . . ' It was like him driving a stacker truck into a wall.

I wasn't lying. It was humiliating – and yet because I was seeing it through my dad's eyes, it was undeniably funny too.

It would seem that amusement at my expense is intergenerational. For the rest of the run, every time I told the kids, 'I'm playing Macbeth tonight,' they'd immediately reply, 'OK, Daddy. Don't fall off the stage.'

There was a lovely circuitous nature to Dad's voice appearing in my head. Almost four decades previously, *Macbeth* was the very first conversation I had with him about acting.

'What are you doing at the moment?' he asked one evening, ensconced on his throne.

'I'm doing *Macbeth*, Dad,' I told him.

I was seventeen and, through Salford Tech, in a production with a company called Theatre Beyond the Stage.

'What part are you playing?'

'Macduff.'

He roared – because 'duff' means hopeless in Salford. 'Lay on Macduff!' he laughed. 'Who's playing Macbeth?'

'A guy called Ayub Khan Din.'

'What, from Din's chippy? When me and your mum were courting, there was a chippy on Ordsall Lane, and the bloke who owned it was Pakistani. Me and your mum were always going in there.'

Next day, I went straight to Ayub. 'Did your mum and dad have a chippy in Salford?'

'Yeah.'

'My mum and dad used to go in there.'

Ayub Khan Din went on to write the comedy drama *East is East,* which won a BAFTA for Best British Film. When I look back at him and me at Salford Tech, I still think that's quite something.

Theatre Beyond the Stage toured *Macbeth* around the north,

rehearsals beginning the day the Falklands War broke out. When we took the show out on the road, I watched Ayub and listened to the whole play night after night. The character of Macbeth was incredible, tragic, but by no means a hero, and Ayub was brilliant in the part.

Ayub had natural ability on his side. The catalyst for my step into acting was one of the drama teachers, Steven Keating. After seeing me play Macduff and the Bloody Sergeant at the Royal Exchange in Manchester, he told me, 'I didn't realise until tonight that you can really do this.' Steven had been teaching me for two years at that point so he definitely wasn't one for throwing praise around wildly. He'd given me some good parts and encouraged me to believe I had some talent, but for him to actually say those words was massive. In two years, he hadn't seen any discernible sign that I really, truly had what it takes, and then, bang, that night it was there right in front of him. It didn't end there. I got a mention for being strong and powerful in a review by Natalie Anglesey in the *Manchester Evening News*. I couldn't believe I'd been picked out because the Bloody Sergeant and Macduff were such small parts. Getting a mention in the *Evening News* was a big deal, and that was the moment I began to think I could possibly achieve my dream.

Off stage, I was equally regularly adopting another persona – an amalgamation of George Best and Rod Stewart. In search of the rock star footballer look, I started putting blond streaks in my hair, wearing wild shoes, and inhabiting this personality mash-up I had in my head. On occasion, I would put shaving foam in my hair in an attempt to recreate the fringed bouffant of Ian McCulloch, lead singer of Echo & the Bunnymen (it was a bit Rod too – I was hedging my bets), a look topped off with my dad's long coat and scarf. He wasn't hugely impressed. 'You've got my coat on, my scarf on, and your hair like that?' he'd splutter. 'You look like a bloody coconut.' I actually think he quite liked that I was wearing his stuff, but for him to go with the hair was asking a little too much.

While in my head I was delivering a bespoke look the envy of the north-west, to the outside world I'd actually developed into a precursor to Paul Calf. Added into the mix was a touch of Arthur Seaton, Albert Finney's character in *Saturday Night and Sunday Morning*, and the man who me and my best mate Mark Sapple aspired to be. To round off the whole magnificent creation was the typical alpha male I'd become on the sports field.

The Rod Stewart obsession had been a thing for a while. Posters adorned the walls of Keith and Alan's old room, which I'd bagged when they moved out. While punk should have safety-pinned itself to my bosom, aligning perfectly with my childhood as it did, I didn't want to look scruffy. I didn't want to be Vyvyan from *The Young Ones*; I wanted to be a mod or a casual, to be a bit arty. The Rod I liked was not the parodic macho man he became; it was the more androgynous character he had inhabited while in *The Faces*, one who dressed and moved in a very feminine manner. David Bowie had a similar appeal. It wasn't just me. Androgyny spoke to many young men at that time, an androgyny that our fathers would never entertain, which was all part of the appeal.

Bowie had long been present in our house thanks to my brother Alan. He had a ticket on his mirror for weeks, green with black type, that stated 'Ziggy Stardust and the Spiders from Mars live at the Free Trade Hall'. This was 1973. I was nine years old and amazed he was going to actually see Bowie in the flesh. I asked him the next day what it was like. 'A bloke ran on stage and kissed him,' he said. Nowadays, a meaningless throwaway remark, but this was a time when a bloke kissing another bloke was very much frowned upon. I became increasingly fascinated by Bowie. I loved the way he had introduced a new way of looking at masculinity, partly because it put me in opposition to the status quo but also because he and those like him were sexy blokes. There was a message here – sexiness didn't have to mean machismo. Trad macho wasn't interesting, it was single faceted, and here were these people, including the glam-rock guys, doing something totally different – the hair, the make-up, the clothes. I didn't see that so much with punk. That was more straight-out trad-hetero aggression. Johnny Rotten, The Clash, were more a celebration of anger. It was great that punk happened, and I benefited from it as much as anybody in terms of that anybody-can-do-it attitude, but in terms of sheer masculinity it didn't interest me.

While I was captivated by Bowie, I didn't have the balls or the inclination to go the whole hog and mimic the way he dressed and looked. Rod, while having opened the lid on androgyny, offered a more comfortingly male yet interestingly bohemian position. As I tended to do with anyone I liked, I over-invested in him. I had pictures of him on my wall and saw him countless times in concert, including at Belle Vue and the Apollo in Ardwick, a fascination born from performance as much as it was voice. I knew all his albums back to front. I wanted to be him, to the extent at one time I even entertained the idea of being a Rod Stewart impersonator. I'd got the hooter after all and could do his voice having studied him in a way matched only by the depth I would later study the characters I'd play.

I knew everything about him. That he was born on Highgate Road on 5 January 1945, that he was once a gravedigger, everything. I pored over and absorbed it all. I now understand also that Rod was my way into black music, another cultural touchstone of the working class. I couldn't have my hair cut like Marvin Gaye, but I could have it cut like Rod, who was obsessed with Sam Cooke in a way I'm obsessed with Marvin and Curtis Mayfield. I still recall the hair-on-the-back-of-the-neck moment I first heard Marvin sing 'What's Going On?' and Curtis Mayfield's 'Pusherman', with my mum's backing vocal of 'That's about drugs that song! I don't know why you're listening to that!'

Dad had that cultural touchstone too. On a Sunday morning, he would listen to albums by Paul Robeson, the black American baritone equally renowned for his political activism in the US and Europe. Dad loved Sinatra (sometimes he'd have a bath and put the speakers in the bathroom), but he adored Robeson – 'Marvellous voice' – and thought he was a great man. Again, it set him out as different. None of my mate's dads listened to Robeson, and I found it very curious that he invested in this deeply challenging music. It's a big leap from Sinatra to Robeson, and, as a young boy, it only deepened the mystery of my dad for me. Looking back, though, there is a deep spirituality to Robeson, which I think explains it. My mum would always say it was depressive music, but to Dad it expressed something that ran much deeper. While the roguishness of Sinatra appealed, Dad loved Robeson for his moral strength, his fight for the underdog. Robeson would sing about slavery, most famously in 'Ol' Man River' – 'Tote that barge and lift dat bale' – and his work for the civil rights movement would have been featured on newsreels at the cinema. Dad respected Robeson the man as well as Robeson the singer.

Like me, music gave Dad a sense of self, whereas my brothers never felt it so deeply as a source of definition. The music they listened to, though, was equally startling. They started bringing in *Liquidator* by the Harry Jay All-Stars, The Upsetters' *Return of Django*. Again putting me out of sync with my peers, I liked the suedehead stuff they were into, which combined a punk ethic with a smarter, more formal, dress code. Keith even went through a bit of a dandy stage, velvet loons, or cowboy boots with his jeans tucked in. He was so macho in every other way, and yet he enjoyed the campery of that look and could pull it off. The twins demanded that we watch *Top of the Pops*, which delivered the spectacle of two identical people very unselfconsciously grooving to the music. My mum would be watching the lads, I'd be wondering if I could move like them, and my dad would be sat there going, 'You're bloody crackers, the pair of you. What are you doing? That's not music.'

The radiogram in the living room was the bigger portal to this whole new world beyond Salford. Reggae and ska entered my universe and I used to think the B-side of a single was absolutely extraordinary, because the only time you ever heard a band on the radio was when they played the A-side over and over again. Now I could hear them doing something entirely different. I'd put a B-side on with great excitement – and more often than not it'd be terrible. The B-side of 'A Whiter Shade of Pale' is 'A Salty Dog'.

I would buy singles while Mum and Dad had albums. They had *Whipped Cream and Other Delights* by Herb Alpert's Tijuana Brass. The cover stuck in my mind – a woman licking her finger, covered in a big mountain of cream that just stopped at her breasts. The music was pretty good too. Ray Conniff and His Orchestra's album covers were a little more staid.

The drinking came with the music, and by the time I got to college I was a regular in pubs in and around Little Hulton. I'd grown up knowing all about working-class pub culture. My dad might not have gone as often as he used to, but he still loved a drink, as did my mum, and I'd listen to them talk about the nights they'd enjoyed and the people they'd seen. I also had two older brothers who worked hard all week and then at the weekend pubbed and clubbed all round Manchester, coming home full of stories about the scrapes they'd got into. Inevitable, then, that as soon as I was old enough to get served, I was in the pub myself with my mates. We started out, aged fifteen, scallywags, in the New Inn on Walkden Road, and it wasn't long before we had a cluster of regular haunts – the White Horse, Stocks, Ellesmere, Bluebell, Albion, and Inn of Good Hope included. The whole idea of being a pub drinker appealed to me as a persona. I liked the acting of it as much as the drinking itself. Same when we'd drink bottles of cider under the railway bridge before discos. Again, I was looking around for a self, before going into an industry where I could be a multitude of them.

I have a black-and-white photo of my dad with his brothers and mates sat around a pub table heaving with glasses, everyone alive with laughter. He looks like he's in his thirties but in fact he's probably not that much older than me when I was doing the same thing. I love that picture. Dad's idea of a good time. And mine. Still is. I think back and know, while I might have been trying to be Rod Stewart, David Bowie, Ian McCulloch and Arthur Seaton, for sure the man I was most trying to be was him.

For now, I would have to wait. I would never truly find my dad until I stepped out at the RSC as Macbeth. I saw, and heard, him clearly then.

7

ADVENTURE

'Getting married? I don't fancy that. Settling down? No thanks.'

I was eighteen with a headful of mad dog-shit, women, boozing and acting. I have reams of teenage diary entries to prove as much, none of which will be appearing here.

There's very little room for refinement in that mix, but what I did know was that, as much as I loved them, Mum and Dad's life wasn't for me. My destiny in Salford was to get a job, get hitched, and have kids. Nothing wrong with that, but I'd had a keen view of my parents' marriage, and those of others, and decided to go a different way. I knew my mum loved my dad, and that he loved her, but I felt, rightly or wrongly, that there was something missing. My panic at the prospect of the 9–5, and being born, living and dying in the same area, which my family had done eternally, was manufactured from the same place. It didn't feel like there were any horizons. It felt as if decades of low expectations had become genetic. My grandparents had passed their institutionalised expectation of life on to my mum and dad, and now they – and I hold no blame in them for this, because it was based on reality – were passing it on to us. Keith had become an apprentice woodworker, Alan an upholsterer, and they would both go on to become highly skilled professionals, but there didn't seem much option beyond a traditional working-class trade.

More than anything, I was scared that if I didn't break out and do something different, it would make me like my dad. I would inherit his anger and bad-temperedness. I looked at him and thought, *I am not going to work nine to five in a factory because it will do to me what it did to you.* My dad had loads of happiness in his life. He loved my mum and he loved his kids, but there was something very unresolved in him. Unfulfilled potential had scarred him, and I was going to avoid the same fate at all costs. Otherwise I, too, risked turning into that man who came home and scared the living shit out of his own son.

The problem I had was that if I didn't want a trade, didn't want to stay in Salford, then what was I going to do? At that point, I was just a lad, a bit arsey, a bit different, who didn't fit, or rather didn't want to fit, into any preordained boxes. There was also, even at that age, an ego, formed, I believe, from having identical twin brothers. As I hatched a plan, how much of me was saying, 'I'll show you – I'll do enough for two'? It must have affected me. They were eight years older than me, handsome, and had each other. What had I done that I didn't get a twin? I was definitely competitive with them. I wanted to do things they either didn't or couldn't – hence the overwhelming desire to beat them on the squash court.

It was at that point I began to talk about acting, a choice so left-field that Mum and Dad went for it, because they, having seen what I was like, couldn't think of anything else I could do. They could see that somehow it fitted me, and I considered it the only chance I would ever have of adventure, an opportunity to go to London, see another side of life, one beyond the boundaries of a mapped-out existence. I'd seen my Uncle Paul already do so, forging a career in journalism that would later take him to Northern Ireland as head of news on the *Belfast Telegraph* and then Fleet Street as executive news editor on the *Daily Telegraph*. Paul, a truly lovely man, died in 2019 and is hugely missed.

Dad also recognised, as did I, that I was someone who would find it difficult to shut up and be constrained, and that could cause me problems in an office or factory environment. Overarching all that, he knew that to be an actor was to display what he had in abundance, a love of words.

Whiteacre was also in the mix. The fact he'd experienced that heaven meant that when I came home from tech one day and went, 'I want to be an actor,' in his generosity, and his understanding that there might be a way out, he went, 'Yes.' My acting was his Whiteacre. One could never have happened without the other.

'They've told me if I want to pursue it then I need to go to drama school in London,' I told him. This is where in the clichés of film and TV the working-class dad spits his fag out and chokes on his cup of tea. Not Dad.

'Well, how do you do that?'

'You send £8 in a letter and apply.'

'All right,' he said, 'we'll give you that.'

If Dad hadn't thought an acting career was a possibility, he certainly wouldn't have spent any money on it. The truth was it really captured his and Mum's imagination. Whereas before they'd been looking at me in mild bemusement, thinking, *I've no idea what this one's going to do*, when I dropped acting on them they had the capacity to think, *You know what? That might just work.*

Dad in particular was relentlessly positive, romancing about it in a way my mum most definitely wasn't. She wanted me to do it, but she was much more concerned about the more shadowy side, the uncertainty of the industry, what might await me in London. She had to rein in his enthusiasm a little. Dad wasn't interested in the ins and outs of the situation. For him, there was something more to it. The ambition I had always harboured was one day to play for Manchester United. Nothing more, nothing less. Thing is, when I said that to him I was always disappointed in his reaction. It didn't bring the sun out. The contrast when I said I was going to be an actor couldn't have been more pronounced. Not only did the sun come out, but it was scorching in its glow. The rock of my life at that age was my mother, but nobody was more emotionally touched and moved than my father. I had underestimated him hugely. He had an intuitive knowledge of my personality, that I wouldn't survive in an overtly macho world, not because I was sensitive, just because I'd get bored.

When I said to him I was going to be an actor, he believed it. His first thought was, *He could do that.* He was 100 per cent behind it, and yet there was no more evidence to back it up than there was to say I'd be that mythical footballer of my imagination. We didn't know any actors and there'd never been any family connection with the profession. What he did, I believe, was hold an inner thought – 'This might be your chance.' My dad – thank you, Dad – did that for me. Something that no one had ever done for him when football offered him a similar route through the exit door of a predictable working-class life.

The £8 was duly sent with an application to the Central School of Speech and Drama, and, on 5 January 1983, I travelled down for my audition, choosing a passage by Grandier, a priest accused of witchcraft, from John Whiting's *The Devils*, as my contemporary speech. Grandier has a melancholic tone that I felt I could embody, but I had no real understanding of the text. To say I was naïve would be an understatement. There was an underlying irony to the scene of which I was totally unaware. I just said the words.

I was also required to deliver a set Shakespeare speech, in my case Gratiano from *The Merchant of Venice* – 'Let me play the fool. With mirth and laughter let old wrinkles come.' Again, I had no idea what I was doing. No idea at all. I didn't work with anybody on either speech and had no self-belief whatsoever. I really didn't.

After delivering both pieces, I thought that would be it for the day. If I was wanted for a recall, I'd receive a letter. But I was sat chatting with some of the other hopefuls when a bloke came out to us. 'Right,' he said, 'we're recalling these four people.' He proceeded to read out the names. I was one of them.

'The recall', he added, 'is this afternoon.'

'What?' It was a shock to say the least. But there was nothing for it but to get on with it. Again, no idea. Hope over expectation.

Towards the end of the afternoon I was given the verdict. 'We'd like to offer you a place.' I'd be starting in September for three years.

I stumbled out into Swiss Cottage, found a phone box, and rang my mum and dad. Mum burst into tears. Dad was, to use one of his expressions, chuffed to little mintballs. By the time I got to Euston, all that was left was the milk train. It was the early hours when I got back to Manchester.

Stepping wearily off the train, I looked down the platform.

There was one person on it. In his hat, coat and scarf. My dad. He took me home, slept in his chair, and went straight to work.

Receiving the news that I'd got in at drama school was the first time it became real to the three of us. Again, Dad's passion for the idea was palpable. The day after I was accepted, without me knowing it, he rang the *Worsley Journal*. There was a knock on the door – a journalist and a photographer.

'What's this?'

'Your dad rang us.' Not my mum, my dad.

But we were all very naïve. Mum had expressed some reservations, but we didn't realise the odds were stacked so high against becoming a working actor, let alone a successful one. Ours was a very romantic notion. I had no idea about the levels of unemployment, which were a fact then, and a fact today. Only when I got to drama school was the reality drummed into me. Perhaps it was better to be naïve. Mum and Dad were, after all, required to make a considerable investment going way beyond that initial eight quid, taking out a covenant where they agreed to pay for my accommodation while Salford Council paid my fees, the lowest at the time because Central was grant-assisted by the Inner London Education Authority, which is now defunct.

It was odd in a way. Financial unpredictability wasn't something that Dad enjoyed. For working-class people, their lives are ruled by money. And yet, while the uncertainty of an acting income was never mentioned, he was very against the twins having their own businesses. The prospect scared the hell out of him. Maybe it was because they were going into a working environment where he understood the difficulties. He'd have been thinking about tax and national insurance and how much easier it would be to have a company deal with those things rather than doing it yourself. For him, it was much better to know the job was there, whereas for a small businessman there is always uncertainty. He couldn't have that kind of an opinion about me. He couldn't say, 'Listen, pal, you can't play Romeo,' because it wasn't his territory. It was so out there.

That weekend, my mum and dad bought me *The Complete Works of Shakespeare*.

'Oh, you're going to be reading a bit of Shakespeare, are you?' noted the woman behind the counter.

My dad didn't hesitate. 'No,' he said, 'it's for my son. He's an actor.'

'He's not an actor, Ron,' Mum interjected, 'he's just got in at drama school.'

To Dad, it was splitting hairs. His son had escaped the shackles of normal life and made it into a whole different world with all the possibilities that entailed. As he had leapt into that river all those years ago, now his son had jumped from the conveyor belt and refused to be boxed and labelled. His destination, unlike his own, was not going to be dictated. He was going to travel his own free path through literature, words and drama, given an education and ensconced in an industry and environment he would never have otherwise encountered.

He – I – was going to Whiteacre.

8

ANOREXIA

I gave Mum a kiss and then Dad came over. Silently, he hugged me, turned, and walked quickly behind the car. In that moment, I realised he was breaking down. He didn't want me to see him, and nor did I need to see his face contorted in emotion — I could read exactly what was happening from my mum's eyes. She'd known this moment of emotional collapse was coming for three days. I hadn't. I'd expected a big scene with my mum, but she knew she had to be strong. She knew if she fell apart I wouldn't be able to handle it. She got in the car, the engine revved, and Dad drove off. I was glad I'd not had to face Dad like that. Seeing a bloke cry? Be emotional? It would have been odd, embarrassing. Men don't show vulnerability — that's how he would have felt, and that's how I felt too. It was a window into myself — a window that now, thankfully, reveals a different view. I went upstairs to the flat and listened to Carole King's Tapestry. *That album will forever be connected with saying goodbye to my dad.*

Mum and Dad had driven me down to London and we'd had the weekend together. For them, this was an enormous moment — their youngest child was leaving home. Mum, Dad and me had suffered when the twins moved out. Keith went first and the four of us took it badly. Then, twelve months later, Alan went, and the three of us took it badly. We missed them both terribly. Four years later, I was gone too. Imagine what that was like for my mum. In a five-year spell, three lads leaving home. God knows how she handled that. I, of course, was so caught up in my own life that I was blind to their perspective.

For the first eight months, I shared with Mark Carroll, himself now a long-established and successful actor. Remarkably, we'd studied together at Salford Tech, both travelling down to the audition thinking the same thing, *This is going to fuck us up – they're not going to take two northerners, from the same college.* But they did. Living away from home wasn't an issue. I needed to get away, cut the apron strings, and toughen up. But I was very paranoid about drama school itself. I felt like I shouldn't be there. It was a massive culture shock for someone who had come from a very tight family and a very tight community to now be in the midst of the liberated, and also competitive, world of acting and drama. Thankfully, in those early days, I got close to an actor called Paul Higgins, a young lad from Glasgow, who would go on to star in *The Thick of It* among many other great roles, and an American actor, Dave Lansbury. In terms of the support that comes from friendship, those two were key, although there was a limit to my openness. The extreme self-doubt I was feeling wasn't a subject for debate in the pub. Neither was my body dysmorphia, a secret I'd already been hiding for more than ten years but now began to blossom in the most grotesque of ways.

'Chris,' my dad would say to me of his childhood, 'all I remember is being a hungry bastard.' Dad was very skinny. He had lived through the '30s, mass unemployment, and the deprivation that came with it. Respite was short – then came the rationing of the Second World War and beyond. Ronnie was one of six children. They were poor. Nana Ecc and Grandpa

Pop worked hard, but that was a lot of kids to feed. Food, as in most working-class households, was more than sustenance. Its availability, or lack of, made it a deeply emotional issue.

When Dad himself became a father, his attitude was simple – 'You eat what's on your plate.' And that, for me, was the first rebellion.

I was a healthy eater. I know because my mum told me. But something happened when I was between six and eight years old where I started to get faddy about food. It became a point of great conflict between me and my dad in particular. He was, after all, from a generation where, by necessity, you ate everything that was put in front of you. And there was me sat at the table refusing to eat.

I convinced myself that tomatoes made me heave, beef the same, and I wouldn't put them in my mouth. I'd get all the stuff about malnutrition and the situation in Biafra, but I wasn't going to be swayed. Neither were Mum and Dad. They'd make me eat and I'd retch at the table, which would make my dad really angry.

'You'll bloody eat it! You'll sit there until it's gone!' Or I'd be sent into the kitchen.

It was sheer defiance. A journey into how far I could push his temper. How much could I stand up to? Psychological strength used in the most negative manner. I wanted to defy him. Not my mum. Him. I was saying, 'Fuck you.' I was exerting my will against my dad.

More than that, I was trying to express some kind of fear and separation. Fear at the atmosphere around my dad, and separation at growing up in a house with two pairs. Food was the obvious place to start. It was such an enormous part of the mechanism of the family that the slightest interference with the cogs would mess it up. My mum, I think it's fair to say, is obsessed with food. She gets incredible pleasure out of talking about it, she's a very good cook, and her day is planned around mealtimes. She loves the ceremony of food, and the memories.

I was driving her through Hampstead once. 'Do you know where we are now?' she asked. In my pretension, I thought she was going to tell me something about the history of the area.

'That place there', she pointed at a building, 'was the first place I ever had chicken Kiev.'

Mum's obsession stemmed from the same roots as Dad's, rationing and scarcity. I feel like I got caught in the force of that. Rightly or wrongly – I feel more compelled to say wrongly – I felt oppressed by it. Not that I could have articulated it at the time, but it was like living the '30s in the '60s.

Mealtimes became all-consuming for me in a very negative way. I remember distinctly the way my dad ate. He had good manners, but I can recall the smacking of his mouth around food. It used to make me angry – irrationally angry.

He always got the most bread – and that was right, he was the biggest person in the house, the busiest, and the hungriest – but for some reason, from a very young age, again it irritated me. I wanted to challenge his dominance, as if I felt it wasn't deserved, or he'd done something to invalidate his right to be at the head of the family. I felt the power he had in his hands was being abused. He was using it in a way that shadowed the entire house. Too often in the darkness he cast, it seemed, was my mum. Dad was never a snap-the-fingers type, always said please and thank you, but I felt like she was put upon. I knew Dad was a hard worker, but so was she, and I somehow instinctively felt it was unfair that she should do all the cooking and cleaning. We're talking pre-feminism. As happens a lot, and especially in those days, the wife becomes a mother to the husband. Again, a mistake, but that was the social model, particularly for the working classes. This was the heyday of the patriarchy, when there was little or no expectation of equality in the home, but I twigged that our domestic set-up wasn't right.

Dad adored my mum but didn't always treat her as well as he could have done and, as a child, I was angry about it. I respected my mum completely, but I didn't respect my dad completely. I challenged him, and probably antagonised him. You could say that's what happens between the old line and the young, but my brothers didn't do that. Maybe I had sensed what they hadn't, that there was an injustice in the relationship between my mum and dad. And an injustice in the way he was with her compared to other people. My mum used to call Dad 'The Two Ronnies'. She was basically saying he was an absolute sod at home but then could be so totally charming with visitors. When no one was around, he could be moody, withdrawn and nowty. As soon as people were in the house, he was 'Hail fellow well met'. There was definitely a public and private side to his character.

I felt my mum had been worn down a little, that she loved my dad but had lost some respect for him along the way. I felt my mum could have lived without my dad but my dad could not have lived without my mum. She had a lot on her plate and there was a period when I'd do things she hadn't asked me to do, like tidy up, to help out. She would get headaches a lot, and I'd bring her a drink in a special glass that I'd won throwing darts at the fair. I was very 'mummy's boy' and I was angry with Dad a lot of the time on the simple basis of 'You can't not be nice to my mum'.

That feeling she was somehow being treated unfairly contributed massively to a highly unsettled equilibrium. Mixed up in that was my own heightened sensitivity, stubbornness, and inbuilt reaction to challenge what I feel is wrong. I was trying to provoke him, provoke something, as if I knew there were unspoken issues and thought, *I'll bring them to a head.* When it comes to confrontation, my career has been very much the same. If I encounter an authority figure who passes my X-ray, I can serve them happily. But if I find someone has been abusive with power, then it's a red rag to a bull. If someone wants to make it nasty, I can make it very nasty – and it began right there at that dinner table. 'If you want to cross me, if you want to abuse your power, I will challenge you.' I'm cleverer now, I avoid those situations, but, make no mistake, I can exist in profound discomfort.

I felt like I was an irritant to Dad, that he didn't have the time for me, and my behaviour was highlighting that as well. So much of my defiance at the table was about 'You don't like me'. It wasn't true. He loved me, but he was a hard-working man. The modern, laid-back dad wasn't around then. He'd done all the stuff with young kids running around the place with the twins, then, eight years later, I came along. I felt like I was a pain in the arse to him, which I probably was. I was flagging that up and did so by going for his Achilles heel – food. My not eating would, I knew, get to him. It wasn't conscious, it was instinctive. How could I wind him up? How could I get at him? It was attention. Negative attention, and frightening, but attention. I wasn't trying to get it from my mum, I was trying to get it from my dad.

Whether my mum and dad saw it as attention-seeking, I'm

unsure. I expect they thought, *This child is spoilt.* I don't blame them. I totally understand their point of view because all they saw was a kid who wouldn't eat, an image blurred by their own lifelong experiences with food. And yet, beyond that image, obviously, emotionally, something bigger was happening. I was becoming very aware of myself. I would look at myself in the mirror or in photos when I was six or seven and be highly critical of my aesthetic appearance. I thought I had a pot belly and knobbly knees. I looked at my body and disapproved of it. I almost found it horrifying. I contrasted it with my brothers who I thought were physically very beautiful. My mum used to tell me that when Alan and Keith were younger they were often mistaken for girls. I never was. I was lumbered with my big frame, my height, my broader shoulders. I idealised my brothers. I had a crush on them. My thought process was clear – 'There's two of them, and there's ugly me.' I had very self-critical, unrealistic expectations. It was the start of a serious condition. I am a lifelong body-hater.

My attitude to my body was only emphasised when I encountered acting. In my mind, actors were thin, aesthetes, sensitive, poetic. I thought I looked like a brickie or a farm labourer, and certainly thought of myself as lacking sensitivity. In effect, I saw myself the way I'd been told the working classes were by the 'great' institutions of society. People who physically looked like me and came from my background could not be actors. I really felt the only way I could progress was by physically looking a certain way. My answer to that was to make myself something completely different.

No surprise, then, that food and appearance became my personal commentary the minute I was accepted into drama school on 5 January 1983. Between that date and September when I started, I lost a stone and a half, and that was from a standing start as a perfectly normal lad.

I lost that weight while still eating quite healthily. The problem really started in earnest when I got to Central. I just did not know what I was doing. I genuinely had no idea how I'd got in. Outwardly I was going along with the teaching but inwardly I didn't feel I had any ability as an actor. At the same time, people had commented on my looks and my physical presence. That, to me, made me feel I was in quite a superficial industry, one not concerned with what's inside. I'm a unit, quite striking, and that's it. It was a view that was already formed in my head. Pre-London, my brothers had come to see me in a play at Salford Tech. Afterwards they told me, 'It's really weird, you look massive on stage.' That clicked with me – 'I'm here because of presence, I'm big, it's the way I look.'

I'd gone to drama school with a head full of negatives, and nobody at drama school was offering an alternative view. I had no one to turn to and found myself in an environment where the predominance of my fellow students were from London and surrounding areas; people who had, or at least appeared to have, confidence and expectation, having sailed through every test and exam put in front of them. I thought of myself as a dullard, academically inferior. I knew I had a lively curiosity but felt I was ugly, not just physically, but spiritually. If someone has a classical education, they have a frame of references, for example with Shakespeare, which I felt I was totally lacking. I wished I'd had a classical education, without ever actually understanding what it meant. I felt completely out of my depth.

I genuinely hadn't realised I was working class until I came to London. When you live a working-class life, working class is what you see. I had then entered a drama school in a middle-class area with middle-class people entering a middle-class profession. Aged nineteen, that was too big a realisation to process. With hindsight I can see my struggles. I had no sense of identity. The same can be said of being northern, not something I'd ever felt or considered before I went to drama school, other than an empathy with the life I saw in dramas such as *Boys from the Blackstuff*. When I was at drama school, though, being northern became very much a thing. The Smiths had broken through, as had a number of northern bands, and then the miners' strike highlighted the social and political difference between the two halves of the country. Unsurprising, then, that going to London politicised me in a none too subtle way. It was the first time I felt northern working-class. I acted up to that, subsequently adopting all the clichés of the angry young man, but inside was this lonely scared child, a state of flux no better illustrated than in the poetry of Morrissey, which I listened to in private.

Whereas appearing as the Bloody Sergeant in *Macbeth* with Salford Tech had made me feel I could achieve a life as an actor, as soon as I got into Central, that belief began to disappear. There was a Geordie, a Glaswegian, a Manc, and me, a lad from Salford. The rest were southerners who had a veneer of sophistication that was very, very intimidating. At least, that's how it felt to me at the time. Looking back now, I expect they were just as anxious as I was. All I felt was that I didn't belong at the drama school and didn't belong in my own skin. Maybe that's what a lot of late adolescents feel – there's just not a lot of late adolescents who then put themselves up for judgement. That churning inner turmoil meant food soon became one of the last areas over which I had the power to dictate.

When I looked at myself in the mirror, I was constantly seeing fat. Actually, I was skeletal, but all I'd see were exactly the same discrepancies I saw as that small child – the pot belly and the knock knees. Sometimes people would be shocked at my physical state – 'God, you look thin.' I'd be pleased. They were telling me I looked beautiful. I'd then try to kill the conversation. I was scared of anyone getting nearer to what was happening. At that point, I didn't know I was ill, but I was very aware of being unhappy. I hated my physical appearance because, no matter what I did, I was still fat and ugly. I was drowning in self-disgust. To drag my way back to the surface I would try to make myself look how I imagined Shelley or Keats looked.

At my worst, I'd have breakfast and then eat nothing else for the rest of the day. I had a period where I'd get up in the morning and go to a sandwich shop outside West Hampstead station called Mr Gingham – it's still there – and get two brown barm cakes with hummus, eat them, and that would be it for that day. I'd dream about food all night. All I'd think about was going to Mr Gingham in the morning and getting those sandwiches. I feel very embarrassed and very ashamed. I think how my mum and dad would feel reading this, and my brothers, and I worry, but it was a mental illness – and one that almost saw me choke to death. That particular day I had no breakfast but instead set out a meal for myself, Ryvita with cheese and tomatoes. 'You can eat when you get in,' I muttered as I pulled the door of my bedsit shut. I'd thought about nothing else all day, to the extent that when I finally got in, the door had barely closed when I took an enormous bite. The Ryvita was completely lodged in my throat. For five minutes, I thrashed around, desperately gasping for breath, before, somehow, I coughed it up. If I hadn't, no one would ever have known what was happening. I'd have lain there for days before anyone found me. I'd have died as a direct result of starving myself. A direct result of anorexia. Next day, I left that bedsit as I always did, wearing a mask. 'Look, everybody, I'm northern, I'm hard.' I wasn't going to go out shouting, 'Look, everyone, I've got low self-esteem and an eating disorder.'

I didn't help my condition by starting a relationship early on at college. The worst thing you can do when you enter a major new arena is find one person in that crowd and have a relationship. The newness, the fear, the nervousness generated by the move means you quickly become dependent on that other person. Effectively, you are finding yourself a mum or a brother or a sister. If that relationship then doesn't work, you are left fending for yourself.

In my case, that relationship was with a woman who was superficially far more sophisticated than me – and who also had some issues with food. While we should have gone into the drama school environment, found our feet, and understood how to handle what was a massive change in our lives, instead we became co-dependent. A major element of that was food, or rather the lack of it. Soon it became ridiculous, a sudden realisation of what extremes I could push it to.

In college, meanwhile, there was never any mention of mental health as part of the learning process. Life outside drama school wasn't monitored. Overnight, I'd gone from the family home to a bedsit in the middle of God knows where.

There were no halls of residence. You found yourself a room in the *Ham and High* magazine and that was the end of it. Even if there had been supervision, I doubt it would have made much difference. Men weren't being diagnosed as anorexic in the early '80s. The closest I had to a confidant was a woman in the college who was bulimic and anorexic. She wasn't alone. Eating disorders were rife among the women, but as far as I was aware, I was the only male in the group, who also happened to be the most alpha northern male. I watched girls go up and down in weight and I went up and down too.

It was my dirty secret that I was doing what those girls were doing. I felt emasculated to be suffering what I felt at the time to be a female condition. I didn't want to admit to wanting to be beautiful. The working-class male is a peacock, but we're not meant to talk about it. I come from people where you most definitely didn't talk about anything personal, and if you did it was very oblique. Down the years, my obsession with food and appearance has affected a lot of my romantic relationships because I thought of it as very unmanly. Again, that shame was something I was willing to tolerate rather than face up to. It was for the same reason, an embarrassment at the loss of masculinity, that, while I recognised that my relationship with food wasn't normal, if anybody else told me, such as family members, I would be very defensive. To be northern, working class and have an eating disorder, when you're not even supposed to look in the mirror, is a source of deep self-hatred.

At the same time, I was extremely hard on myself in performance. I equated giving a bad one to being a bad person. The mark of a great performance is truthfulness. As an actor, that is our raison d'être. We are supposed to tell the truth. Therefore, if I couldn't be truthful, in my mind I was a liar. It was as though a bad performance made me unworthy, like some kind of religious belief. I don't feel like that now. I've given dreadful, terrible performances in films and I look at them and think, *That is shite.* But it's not who I am, as an actor or a person. Back in the early days, though, it very much was. It was zealotry, not compromising, not settling for second best, perfectionism. That inner flagellation drove me, and it seemed quite normal, to the extent I could reconcile it as a perfectly reasonable tool in my armoury. But it is not healthy and it is not achievable. When Nadia Comăneci scored a perfect ten on the uneven bars at the Montreal Olympics, did that mean that some element of that performance, even in the most miniscule of ways, could never be improved on? Pursuit of perfection allied to self-punishment is extremely damaging. Even now I can detect it in young actors, that extreme self-consciousness and self-loathing. It hurts me to see it and I hope that they too can find solace in reasoned self-negotiation rather than an endless torture.

My predilection for self-punishment meant Central was never going to be a gilt-edged experience. Not that I had any real expectation as to what I wanted to get out of drama school anyway. I'm not sure it was particularly relevant training. The teachers who directed us were middle-aged people expressing interest in an art. With knowledge of the industry, I now look back on it as being unstructured and a little conservative. On the other hand, that might have been a good thing because, if I'd ended up at another institution, such as Drama Centre or East 15, both much more actively Method-based, I might not have made it to the end. Coupled with my own late adolescent intensity and internal mental spiral, it would have been too much of an overload. As it was, on top of what I was learning at Central, I began teaching myself, the start of my tendency to autodidact. If we were looking at Shakespeare, Ibsen, Chekhov, Tennessee Williams, I would naturally read around the subject. Angelo, from *Measure for Measure*, who I played at Central, was a case in point. Shakespeare found the inspiration for Angelo in St Augustine, in front of whom the devil appears in the shape of a nun to tempt him. Religious hypocrisy – brilliant. Because of that I ended up in Foyles on Charing Cross Road looking for books on religious iconography and St Augustine. Staring at the shelves, I looked round and there was a nun right next to me. I loved moments like that, and they came because I never saw a job as just acting; I saw it as an investment in the character and their situation. I read and read and soon felt I had a broader mindset than when I arrived. I also felt I had a stronger one. I fell to pieces under pressure when I played for Salford Boys in a way that I have never fallen apart under scrutiny on stage.

At drama school, the teachers cast the productions. It's a democratic process for the first two years. If the production is *Richard III*, five actors play Richard across five acts. When it comes to the third year, however, all that changes. The drama school is now advertising its wares. Some actors are in the window display, others find themselves at the back of the shop. At the time, Central and RADA were the best two drama schools, or so we were told, and so the agents and casting directors, like the big cats they appeared, would come for the raw meat. The idea was they would like what they saw and invite you to a meeting. Despite my own concerns about my aptitude, I was right there at the front of that shop window, with a big 'For Hire' sign around my neck. I got the best casting, a succession of fantastic roles, and yet, in my head I felt uncertain. Mentally, I thought there was a specific brand that was needed, and that brand was quite middle class. I was riven with the same conflict that had accompanied me throughout the previous three years – 'Am I a Hampstead taramasalata-swilling luvvie? Or am I a working-class socialist actor who wants to help effect change?' That muddlement left me in a no-man's land. I didn't know what or who I was. I'd been given a fantastic opportunity and yet all I could think was, *You're going to get found out.*

At the end of that process, I was the only one who ended up without an agent. No interest at all. It was confirmation of what I'd always thought – I was going to fail. Always coming back to the single same thought – *I'm not an actor, I'm not sensitive, I'm not poetic, I don't have an imagination.* My psychology meant there was a curious kind of satisfaction. 'See, I was right. I am shit. They gave me the best casting and I can't get an agent.' But there was still another part of me going, 'I don't want to give up on this.' It left me in a position that no amount of mental arbitration could resolve. I was determined to make it as an actor alongside the absolute conviction that I couldn't be one if my life depended on it. Those two standpoints absolutely coexisted in my mind.

A good deal of the determination to carry on came from me simply having nowhere else to go. I had no money, zero skills, Thatcher was ripping the heart out of industry, and I'd put all my eggs in the acting basket. It felt to me that I hadn't really learned anything at Central. I understood the superficial and rudimentary requirements it took to be an actor – the ability to do Shakespeare, accents, contemporary work. I knew how the system worked, and I was willing to work the system. But I had no self-belief that I could be an actor. I'd come out of there still at war with myself, the same glass-half-empty character, always expecting the worst. There's a segment in Johnny Marr's autobiography where he talks about standing on a street corner in Manchester, realising he's young, and being happy to be young. If that's true, brilliant. But that element of being young was wasted on me. I'd love to have had the wisdom of 'This is you at twenty-one – grasp it, enjoy it!', but I was just a mass of self-conscious confusion.

While never for a minute did I think I could succeed on ability and talent, I did maintain a feeling that physically I had something going for me. I was striking, and I was striking because I'd worked hard at turning myself into a razor blade. I was also very diligent about seeking work, buying the *Stage* newspaper and checking out every article and notice. I had a real work ethic and focus and maintain that to this day. There are far more talented actors than me, far more, but I am so focused and driven when I go after something. Same as when I played football. I wasn't the best, but I was the fittest.

For two years after Central, I lived in a bedsit in Belsize Park – 59 Glenmore Road. I wrote hundreds of letters to theatres, sometimes making up stories to tug on their heartstrings. I'd be a drug addict who was cleaning himself up and was desperate to get back into acting. Lurid, gothic stuff. I was trying to appeal to their generosity, but in reality anyone who read them would think one thing and one thing only, *I'm not having him anywhere near me.*

These were my *Withnail & I* years — without the glamour. My mum's not going to like this, but I did a fair amount of shoplifting. I would get up early and steal bread, left out the front of shops by the delivery man before they opened. I'd do the same with milk and newspapers. I didn't have a fridge so the milk would be kept out on the window ledge. The other thing I nicked were bottles of dry Merrydown cider and cans of Tenants Super. I'd mix them and get totally off my face. I would also go to the Swiss Cottage pub and drink really strong pilsner lager. The idea was always to get pissed as quick as I could. I had no chance of getting a girlfriend, stinking of failure and self-loathing, while trying in some ways to romanticise it, hanging around in libraries reading poems. I had the long student coat, Echo & the Bunnymen haircut, Levi 501s, docs, 501 sweatshirt turned inside out, donkey jacket — the works. If there was a 1980s student section of the Victoria and Albert Museum, I'd be in it.

There was definitely an inner feeling during those barren times that the whole idea of becoming an actor had been a pipe dream. 'What was I thinking that I could do this? Operate in this area?' I had failed. It was always going to happen. How could it have been any different? I was on the floor, self-esteem shattered, listening to The Smiths, in a bedsit, getting my dole cheque, and drinking it in two days. I was a very angsty young man and began to think I'd have been better off coming through in the '60s when there was a real emergence of working-class actors — Richard Burton, Albert Finney, Richard Harris, to name but a few. I soon realised, though, that actually, as ever, they were the exception. The rule was exactly the same. White, middle-class, received-pronunciation-speaking actors were the order of the day. Twenty years on, Gary Oldman, Tim Roth, Phil Daniels and Ray Winstone stood out in exactly the same way. I saw Phil in *Quadrophenia*, Gary in *The Firm*, Ray in *Scum*, and Phil, Gary and Tim together in the Mike Leigh film *Meantime*. Why was I so struck by them? Because there were so few others like them, that's why. Same when I saw David Thewlis in Mike Leigh's film *Naked*, I was stunned. He was one of my generation, my background, giving a performance that was as good as anything I'd ever seen. Why was I stunned? Because he was like me. People like me, I thought, reinforced by the evidence on film and TV, very, very rarely get to where they want to be.

My plight wasn't helped by the fact that an actor had to have an Equity card to work. To get an Equity card, however, you had to work. Catch 22. My mum flew into a rage when Derek Hatton got one by doing panto in Liverpool when I'd done three years at drama school and couldn't get my hands anywhere near one of the damned things.

I'd always managed to pick up bits and pieces of other work. While at Central I was an usher at the National Theatre on Saturdays and Wednesdays. I was selling tickets and ice creams and watching Anthony Hopkins on stage in *Pravda*. It was amazing to see so much real live theatre, to be able to drink in the bar – to see Anthony Hopkins eating beans on toast in the canteen. Out of Central, the job I found didn't quite offer the same access to the acting elite but at least the dress code was easier. I managed to boost my income a little by life-modelling at the Slade School of Fine Art. I would sit there eight hours a day with a fifteen-minute break every forty-five minutes. The sculptor Bruce Mclean was there, and I made a great friend in the artist Susanna Jacobs, despite the fact that the first time I ever met her I was stark bollock naked. I also life-modelled at the Hampstead Garden Suburb Institute. I was extremely body-conscious, and so what did I do? Went and took all my clothes off and had it spoken about as if it was a lump of meat. There's obviously some bottle in there. But there was also an element of me thinking it was a bit bohemian – 'I've studied Stanislavski and Brecht, I might as well be a nude model. Tell my dad about that!'

Perhaps it was life-modelling in the early days that persuaded me also, somehow, despite my own revulsion, to reveal myself on screen as often as I did. I have lost count of the nude scenes I've done down the years. Even now, when I think back to the shower scene in *Shallow Grave*, I can hear Danny Boyle saying, 'There it is, the Eccleston arse.'

I'd ring home once a week and every now and again Mum and Dad would send me a letter with a fiver in it. To them I was their son who was living in London as an unemployed actor. They were understanding. It was a hard game I'd gone into and now, after drama school, we were into the reality. I'd have odd jobs here and there – as well as the life-modelling, I worked on building sites, or leafletting, all cash in hand, which meant I could still get my giro – so Mum and Dad knew I wasn't sitting around doing nothing, although I did spend a significant amount of time in bed, in the pub, or lying around on the floors of bedsits.

In all that time, I got two auditions. One was for a part in Chelsea, for Attack Theatre, where the director Ian Brown sat me down and asked me how I was doing. I was honest and told him about my struggle to get work.

'I think you should keep going,' he told me, 'because I think you've got something.'

Sixteen years later, the same Ian Brown wrote to me. 'I now run the West Yorkshire Playhouse,' he explained. 'Would you like to come and play Hamlet?'

I remembered exactly who he was. I'd never forgotten his encouragement. And I did play Hamlet at the West Yorkshire Playhouse.

For now, that appeared unlikely in the extreme. But I was offered a job at the Royal Exchange Theatre in Manchester, a behind-the-scenes role on a touring version of *Don Juan* with Bernard Bresslaw and Jonathan Kent, directed by Ian McDiarmid. At the time, the Royal Exchange had a mobile theatre. They'd shove it in vans and tour round the region. At the interview, it was flagged up that I'd been to drama school.

'You do know you're not going to get an acting job out of this, don't you, Chris?' asked Ian. 'Because we don't want you giving any of the actors a hard time.'

Ian was very direct, and I knew what he meant, but actually I was glad not to have to think about acting. I was relieved to be doing something else. I wanted the pressure off. I didn't want the expectation on myself anymore. I'd never felt like an actor. I always thought I was too big and clumsy and stupid. It was like football all over again, another failure, and actually I just wanted a job and some money in my pocket. Working with the Royal Exchange gave me a sense of dignity because there were certain things in the show that only happened because of me. The gypsy lifestyle of taking shows on the road appealed to me also, and I became the court jester, the joker on the crew. When the tour finished, I then settled into a regular backstage job at the Royal Exchange. My mum and dad, and me, began to think that stage management was where I'd end up. The downside was I found myself living back at home. It caused a lot of tension between me and my dad and there were some bad arguments. I think in his head they'd got rid of me once and now I'd come back. Mum and Dad had formed a new relationship with just the two of them in the house and then suddenly there I was again, moody, belligerent, the lot. I was becoming a man and was doing so in my childhood home. It was horrible.

We were all saved when, out of nowhere, the phone rang one day. It was the casting director of the Bristol Old Vic.

'We're doing a production of *A Streetcar Named Desire*,' I was told. 'Phyllida Lloyd is directing it, and we'd like you to play Pablo Gonzales.' It was an odd moment. There was just me and my dad in the house. I told him, and I could see he was pleased, and not just because I'd be out of his house. Phyllida had seen me at drama school. Whether she had asked after me, found I wasn't working, and out of some act of kindness or generosity handed me that role, I don't know. What I do know is I've never stopped working since.

9

THE BONES OF ME

'Skinny is only one body type.'
Susie Orbach

Look at me as Derek Bentley. The bones I had then, or rather the way I displayed them, made me look as if I was fashioned from steel. Playing Derek in *Let Him Have It* was my break-through role. It came four years after I left Central. The control over food had continued way beyond drama school, the really worrying thing being that, as my career kick-started, it was working. I was climbing the ladder. My skeletal appearance was being rewarded. I was starving my system, which must have been affecting my cognitive processes, but at the same time I was still managing to turn up at rehearsals and deliver what they wanted. Yes, I was ill, but I was bold with it. I was Jekyll and Hyde — complete and utter self-loathing neurosis, and complete and utter unyielding determination. I knew the way I was behaving regards my body was unhealthy, but I also knew it was making me striking. I don't mean handsome; I mean physically different. After I played Derek, I didn't stop there. I lost a massive amount more weight. That was a straight reaction to, and I say this with due naivety,

'Here comes fame.' I had found a way into the industry and I wasn't going to lose it.

Acting has a lot in common with the modelling industry, and when I started out there was certainly a vogue for high cheekbones, that Daniel Day-Lewis cadaverous look. To achieve that, I needed to starve myself. I was quite practical. 'I haven't got the ability, but I've got a distinct physical appearance. Hone it, take it to its extremes, and I've got a chance.'

Taking it to its extremes was something at which I became very adept. There was an extended period when the anorexia had a grip on me that I was hardly eating and yet over-exercising to a ridiculous extent. For twenty-five years, I ran 10 miles, seven days a week, while still taking in tiny amounts, a couple of sandwiches or less. I was never bulimic but occasionally I'd get so hungry from the running that I'd gorge carbs – bread, cereal, crisps. Then I'd see a photo or a picture of myself – 'Oh my God' and feel sick with guilt that I'd given in to such 'greed'. The conversation about weight never ever stopped buzzing. The only thing I wouldn't stop was drinking. I didn't care how many calories, I loved getting drunk. Alcohol, sex and performing all offered a release from the torment of the rest of the day.

My view now is that I was deeply depressed. I didn't run for the usual health reasons – when I finished, I'd buy twenty cigarettes and walk back from the shop – I was running because I was self-medicating, giving myself a dose of endorphins. I also had clarity of thought while running. For a good few years, I had an internal dialogue with myself. I had enough about me to realise I was living in the West, I had my health, a successful career, friends and family who loved me, and yet I had this terrible negativity about life. I was repulsed by myself for having so much and not appreciating it. I can remember saying to myself on a run – and I can still picture exactly where I was – 'What you need is a near-death experience.' Maybe then I would find some perspective. Little did I know.

At that point, there was no voice shielding me from that self-hatred. No one telling me that such thoughts, such lowness of esteem and mood, were random across the population, and not based on 'success' or income. I needed to be diagnosed with depression to have that voice.

I always rooted my negativity in the anorexia. As time went on, I'd read enough about eating disorders to make the link. The most profound thing I heard about the illness came from the writer and psychotherapist Susie Orbach, who argued that because anorexics can't control the universe outside them-selves, they create a universe inside themselves that they can. And that's what I was doing with food. The manifestation of that was that it ruled my life. For many years, I would avoid social contact because it involved eating. I couldn't eat in front of people. It wasn't just about not wanting to eat. I felt by the act of eating in front of others they would see my problems, and so I spent more and more time on my own eating my strange neurotic little meals. My life was a 10-mile run, a tiny meal, and then two bottles of red wine. Wake up and repeat. I was completely imprisoned by anorexia. It isolated me. And yet somehow it offered me the control to which Orbach alludes. It allowed me to operate in a world that was totally counter to the dialogue of worthlessness in my head, one that anyone else would have run, not 10 or 12, but a million miles to avoid. Here was a very insecure young man from a working-class background, who'd grown up socially conditioned that he's not worth anything, and had deep-seated issues about physical appearance and ability, and yet had decided to step into the most public of all industries. Anybody with an ounce of common sense who's anorexic and dysmorphic would stay the hell away from being a television, film and theatre actor. It's set in concrete in this industry that you have to look a certain way. The ones who smash that concrete are the ones to admire, those who get work simply because they are brilliant actors. I never felt I had any ability as an actor so I did everything I could to make myself 'look like an actor'. I had an iron will to do that, allied to a serious mental health condition, which nothing could penetrate.

My enormous ego then exacerbated the situation. I wanted to be the lead, and you can't be the lead without the leading man looks, a fact borne out throughout time and the industry – James Dean, Laurence Olivier, Marlon Brando. I wanted to play Hamlet; I didn't want to play Laertes or Horatio. Michael Billington claimed that one of the great misunderstandings about Albert Finney, an incredibly striking figure, was that he was a leading man. Finney, he opined, was in fact a character actor with the looks of a leading man. I decided I wanted to be, or should at least look like, a leading man. That, to me, was the way to make a living. In reality, what I am is exactly the description Billington applied to Finney.

To some degree, the industry has agreed. Myself and Ralph Fiennes came through at the same time. There were four films we both auditioned for – *Oscar and Lucinda*, *Quiz Show*, *Wuthering Heights* and *A Dangerous Man: Lawrence After Arabia* – and he got them all. If you look at photographs of me and Ralph Fiennes in

1990, you can hardly tell us apart. The difference is he was more conventionally beautiful. Mixed in with my working-classness, I had looks that, in one light, could be seen as handsome, and in another not dissimilar to Plug from *The Beano*. I'd always been aware of my sticking-out ear and my big nose.

'You've always had that nose,' my mum would say. 'I took you back to the doctor's. "I've been looking at other babies," I told him, "and they don't have much of a nose. But he has. Is there something wrong with him?"'

'There's nothing wrong with him,' the doctor told her. 'He does have a rather prominent nose, but it means he'll find his way in the world.'

Ralph not only doesn't resemble a *Beano* character but is also a better actor. The only part I felt I should have got and he shouldn't was Heathcliff because of the class roots of the character.

At no point, no matter how successful I became, did that absolute need to look a certain way, the body dysmorphia, disappear. Rarely do I ever watch stuff I'm in. Not only don't I think it's practical – there's nothing I can do about the performance so I move on – but it can be a trigger. If I see an image of myself I don't like, the next step is to think *I'd better go on a diet*. I'm hypercritical of myself physically so I soon learned the best course of action was to do the job and end the association there. If I had to attend a screening, it could be excruciating.

Even now, I take a selfie every day to analyse myself. I have also weighed myself every day for decades as a matter of routine. I'm as near as anything 6ft, and big with it, and I never wanted to be above 11 stone 7. Ideally 11 stone 4. In *Our Friends in the North*, my weight goes up and down. I'm skeletal at the beginning but there comes a point where Nicky's middle-aged when he's carrying a little more weight, and it works for him. But it wasn't intentional on my part and I was horrified. Nine years on, the illness is still there raging within me as the Doctor. People love the way I look in that series, but I was actually very ill. The reward for that illness was the part. And therein lies the perpetuation of the whole sorry situation.

It never goes away, and it doesn't for thousands of actors today. It's absolutely normalised in our industry. I know for a fact that studios put women on diets, and that is undoubtedly happening to men now as well. I was making my way in the '80s and '90s when men operated to less blatant rules about appearance. The glare was on women, and the industry wasn't slow in telling them they had to look a certain way, hence the amount of anorexia and bulimia in my drama school.

There's a permanent hum in my head about food. It's rare that I eat and don't have some kind of internal dialogue. Billy Bob Thornton, who has also suffered with anorexia, called it a private radio.

Thankfully, I have improved. I still have a food and exercise obsession, but when I do eat, it's healthy, and when I exercise it's in a sensible way. If I have a day off from exercise now, I'm fine about it. Previously, I'd go into a depression of disappointment with myself. Of course, what had in fact happened was I'd not delivered my daily dose of endorphins.

My eating habits are eccentric but I've made a real conscious effort to tailor them so I can eat with other people. I cook for the children and, while I don't view them through the lens of my anorexia, I know I am going to be vigilant of any manifestation of what I went through.

I still have a negative relationship with mirrors. That's vanity and insecurity, all tied up with ongoing body dysmorphia. I will take a deep paranoia over my appearance to my grave. Even now, if someone says to me, in all innocence, 'In those days, you were all angles,' my immediate internal reaction is to think, *I need to lose weight.* That is an automatic click mechan ism. Hearing someone say that makes my stomach turn over. They are saying I'm fat.

I mentioned to my agent the weight I'd put on for *Macbeth* to make him soldier-like and she, again quite innocently, said, 'I think you should go back to running.' Straight away my brain was off – 'She thinks I'm too fat.' This is a 55-year-old man thinking this way, and the very fact I'm admitting it makes me feel like a spoiled child. But that's dysmorphia and anorexia in action. I'm fortunate in that I'm conscious of my mental process and have an angle on it. If I do put on weight now, I don't detest myself and I don't hide away quite as much. If a woman says, 'I like you as you are,' I believe it. Women deal with a constant noise about body image. If they say, 'You're fine as you are,' bearing in mind how oppressed they've been, I accept it.

Women have always had it worse, and still do by some dis tance, but for me there was a moment in the '80s that marked, for men of my generation, the beginning of a very slow equal isation in the genders about eating disorders. When Sting took his shirt off in the video for 'Don't Stand So Close to Me' and revealed that lean and muscular figure, combined with those incredibly defined cheekbones, it became a landmark image that would be repeated, in one body or other, on TV and bill boards across the decades. Travel on the Tube now, or through any city centre, or into a newsagent, and there are thousands of pictures of men with insane bone structures, eye-popping bodies. Young men are looking at those and thinking one thing and one thing only – *I don't look like that.* That's been going on for women for years.

There are many times I've been interviewed and many times I've wanted to reveal that I'm a lifelong anorexic and dysmorphic. I never have. I always thought of it as a filthy secret, because I'm northern, because I'm male, and because I'm working class. Similarly, I have never been diagnosed as anorexic. I never sought that diagnosis out. Why would I? I could easily self-diagnose. I could see it all around me. And, in the bizarre world I occupied, in my mind it was facilitating my success. I was a deliberate, practising anorexic. My challenge was to learn to manage the condition and have a high-level and visible career at the same time.

Over time I have come to understand what happened to me more and more with anorexia. I was shackled by fear, a fear that comes from who I am and where I'm from. It's facile to say we can shake off our past. We can't, and I haven't. What's more, I'm glad I haven't. I would never want to. I am shaped by my parents and my family. Their form within me is unmalleable.

I O

BREAKDOWN

I was running through the streets of London. Not unusual — I've pounded thousands of miles through the capital. Except this time, instead of shorts and a vest, I was fully clothed. Instead of early morning on Hampstead Heath, this was 1 a.m. on the Euston Road. In January. With a suitcase.

It was cold and wet. I tried to flag a taxi but nothing doing. I ran all the way to Paddington and banged on the door. They were expecting me. I'd rung earlier. 'I'm either going to die or kill myself,' I'd told them. 'I need help.'

They gave me lorazepam ,which allowed me to sleep for a while. Then they gave me some more.

Eventually, and inevitably, Dad erupted. He punched someone at work. His breakdown had finally broken through the mental and into the physical. The target for his long-pent-up rage was one of the university guys who'd been talking to him, or, more probably, patronising him, about how, from a sociological point of view, to deal with different characters on the factory floor. Of course, my dad was actually one of those men. The only difference was he now wore a suit. He found his colleague's approach disrespectful and knocked him out. Immediately, he was filled with remorse and, because he was very highly thought

I LOVE THE BONES OF YOU

of, the incident was papered over. Even so, he was home for about eight weeks sat in his chair. I asked my mum if he'd had a nervous breakdown. All she said was he was on tablets. It was all very Alan Bennett in its working-class unspokenness. There's a chance those words 'nervous breakdown' would never have been used by Dad's GP. I doubt very much that a man of his class in that era would have been diagnosed as having undergone such an event. He'd have been handed some pills, told to go home for a few weeks, and that would have been the end of it. There were no posters up in factory toilets about mental health back then.

As I lay on the mattress in my old bedroom in Little Hulton, the synergy of the contours on our life maps wasn't lost on me. When I thought of him, I was actually seeing myself. I had just experienced a nervous breakdown at exactly the same age. We were both fifty-two when we found ourselves dealing with a seismic psychological event.

My marriage had ended the previous Christmas. I'd landed up in the Marriott Hotel in Swiss Cottage. When the door of my room swung shut, it signalled yet another hammer blow to an already fragile mental condition.

That first night in the hotel room, I felt in a very heightened state. Eventually, I drifted off to sleep for a couple of hours before waking with a start to a terrible reality – the dream of my family had disappeared. I'd left Albert and Esme. To me it was the ultimate betrayal. They are my flesh and blood and the best thing that ever happened to me. I knew I'd left for the right reasons, but the missing of them, the fact that my head wasn't under the same roof as theirs anymore, made me very, very unwell. They were so young. And I'd learned to love in a very pure way, with all my attention, very hands-on. I'm no different to any parent – Albert and Esme are first, last and everything, and suddenly I had no outlet for all that love. I had failed, unable to give them a stable family with a mum and dad.

I was chain smoking, in a state of constant and fierce anxiety, spending my nights at the Marriott and days existing in a Costa. Insomnia, something I'd never suffered before, was my new companion. I'd always slept well, now I'd fall asleep for twenty minutes, wake, and be faced with the grim reality of my life. That cycle would revolve all night, turning, churning, again and again and again. Then I'd have to get up and go to work, when, inside, there was a growing fear. I didn't want to live any more. I thought I'd lost my children. I'd been a hands-on father and now it seemed, with solicitors involved, I might never see them again. Whatever happened, I'd never have what I had with them.

I alerted my brothers and my mum. They were talking about coming down to be with me, but I didn't want to spoil their Christmas. Anyway, I had to be back at work at the start of January, playing Maurice in the second series of *The A Word*, set in the Lake District, which only emphasised the physical and mental separation from Albert and Esme. Maurice is a comic character, one who couldn't have been further removed from my mental state at that time. The idea of adopting that persona seemed totally unrealistic. And yet on set I had this extraordinary realisation. I'd walk into my dressing room, see Maurice's 'uniform', and know I was at work. I'd climb into those cords, button up that check shirt, zip up his blue anorak, and be functional. At the end of the day came the reverse ritual. Taking off Maurice and putting my own clothes back on would bring the sheer hopelessness of my situation flooding back. It was the exact reversal of my dad's situation. For him, the shirt and tie signalled a descent into the world of middle management he so hated. He could only regain his true self when he took off his uniform.

I'd get back to the hotel and then the trouble would really start. I'd lie there in a state of abject mental agitation. Terror. Just living in terror. Then I'd wake up the next morning, put the costume on, and play the character. I had to. There were other people relying on me – actors, the writer, the director; I had to do my job.

In the middle of January, I returned to London to see Albert and Esme. I was missing them deeply. This time I ended up in a different hotel, the White House near Regent's Park. By now, because hotel rooms weren't my children's home, my place of safety, they had become phantasmagorical places, oppressive, pressing in on me. If the terror I had felt in Swiss Cottage and the Lake District was bad, now it was overwhelming. I was in a state of extreme anxiety, convinced I was either going to die or I was going to kill myself. I had absolute certainty. If I was to have killed myself, one of those hotel rooms is where I would have done it. In my despair, I reached for my phone and looked up a psychiatric hospital. I rang ahead, grabbed my bag, and ran. It must have made for a bizarre sight to anyone who might have recognised me. In my sheer terror, that was the last thing on my mind.

Behind the sophisticated frontage of the hospital, I sat in a consulting room. In front of me was a doctor. He was talking to me very seriously, asking me questions about suicide. I couldn't concentrate. Inside I was laughing, not at him, but at the situation. Even at this time of intense breakdown, I was doing something I'd done all my life – subconsciously stepping outside of myself, seeing myself from the point of view of an observer. It was ridiculous. I was ridiculous.

I was given lorazepam and shown to a room. Next day, I rang my agent.

'I'm in hospital,' I told her. 'I can't go back to work.'

'You've got to finish this job,' she told me.

It's all right for you, I thought.

But she was right. She was looking at the wider picture – that I would get well. She didn't want me to be known as someone who wouldn't finish the job. And, intuitively, she understood that when I was at work, I was OK.

I had two weeks to go on *The A Word* and managed to get back on the train north. I was full of lorazepam as I stepped aboard, and it worked. It stopped me feeling, which was an enormous relief.

I worked my way through the rest of the job, as before slipping in and out of Maurice, finding comfort in his shoes, stones in my own. If I did experience on-set anxiety, I now had the lorazepam. I was allowed up to four pills a day.

I didn't advertise my issues among the cast and crew but one particular day I was working with Pooky Quesnel, my old friend from Salford, now playing Maurice's love interest Louise. Pooky is one of those people who knows you better than you know yourself. She has inherent intuition. We talked and she understood completely. Not for the first time in the ensuing weeks, her willingness to listen was priceless. I also Skyped Anthony Venditti, an existential psychotherapist I'd been seeing in London. Twelve months later, I spoke to him about that session and he told me he knew I'd gone beyond his help. He could see I no longer had a sense of self. That's a very frightening thing to hear, but that's what happens with those with dementia and those who have nervous breakdowns. I also spoke to another old friend, Pete Bowker, the writer of *The A Word*, and the producer Marcus Wilson. But talk alone wasn't going to provide the remedy. Inside, my mental processes were in freefall.

We wrapped on location ahead of moving to Manchester to do some work in the studio. Everybody was saying goodbye, including me, but as I did so I was consumed by a thought.

This is amazing. We're all saying goodbye to each other, but they don't know that they'll never see me again – because I'm going to die. It wasn't an idle thought. It was an absolute matter of fact.

Everybody was saying, 'See you later. Cheers. Bye.' And in my head, I was going, *But I'm never going to see you all again.* This isn't me being dramatic. I'm talking about a mental state. I was immersed in it. That was my reality. My reality was that I was going to die.

When *The A Word* finally wrapped, I went straight back to the hospital in London and admitted myself officially. I was placed on antidepressants. Nobody diagnosed me.

One night I again became absolutely convinced I was going to die. My mortality was a constant conversation in my head – I was 100 per cent sure I was in the last few weeks of my life – but now it was shouting out loud, spiked and more pronounced. I found a pen and paper and started writing my will. I was putting it in black and white that everything I had would go to Albert and Esme. I was making an official document, and when an attendant appeared, an older guy who walked the wards, I asked him to witness it. Instead he disappeared and came back with a doctor. I was put on 24-hour watch. I was in bed and there was a man with a chair against my door keeping an eye on me all night.

As time went on, rather than just die I thought eventually I would kill myself. The doctors asked me if I had made any plans. I was always scrupulously honest with my doctors because I appreciated other people's attempts to do their job properly. As such, I would always say 'No', which was the truth. But it was sophistry really. There had been an occasion a month previously when my brother had dropped me at Piccadilly train station in Manchester. I was going down to see Albert and Esme but couldn't face the tumult of my marital situation. I walked away from my brother and on to the platform. A train was just pulling in.

If I jump in front of that now, I thought, *I won't have this feeling any more. I won't have to suffer this train journey feeling as bad as I do.* That moment passed. Serious intent or just an intrusive thought? I'll never know, but what I do understand is that on various occasions during that period, I got into a physical, physiological, emotional and psychological convinced state that, although I wasn't planning to kill myself, I was going to die.

Another part of me was telling me full square, shouting in my head, that I'd walked out on the best thing that would ever happen to me, my Albert and my Esme. Every arrow, internal and external, was aimed straight at me. Add in utter exhaustion and I hadn't the mental faculties to deal with what was happening to me. No wonder, like Macbeth, people in the grip of a breakdown start hallucinating – 'Is this a dagger I see before me?' I was no different. I was perceiving reality in an unrecognisable state. I hadn't killed myself – but I still thought death was inevitable. It was the only way out of the extreme horror of my existence. Moment to moment, second to second, it was unbearable. A permanent state of abject dread. However it might end, I was living out the last few days and weeks of my life. I was dying. I didn't want to live with all this pain in my head and my heart. It was impossible. I didn't have the energy, the courage, to face that existence.

Again, I was so grateful for Pooky. She came every day to the hospital to visit me. At a very distressing time, it allowed me to be with someone who knew how I functioned. But there was another element to Pooky: I didn't mind being unmanly in front of her. Mental health problems? In our family? In our class? I don't think so. We're stoic. We push our feelings down. To talk about depression is to talk about weakness, about effeminacy. 'He's got mental health issues? He can't be a real man – he must be a woman. He's weak. He's got no spine. He's not strong-willed. He can't stand up to things.'

I wondered whether Dad had suffered those exact internal and external feelings. He was off work for a significant period so it was inevitable, I think, that people would have been questioning if he was up to it any more. Did he wonder if people were talking about him? A man born from a much more overwhelmingly masculine world than the one even I grew up in can only have felt deeply emasculated and shamed. That was certainly how I perceived myself. Shame and self-hatred, disgust, a sense of disappointing people, all warped emotions that accompany mental health issues. That's why Pooky was so wonderful. There I was, need distilled, and she was calm, she was loving. I felt she understood.

In the background, another TV job, this time one in which

I was the lead, was looming. *Safe House 2*, again filmed in the Lake District, would, supposedly, see me repeat the role of an ex-cop persuaded to operate a remote hideaway for those forced to go on the run. Filming was due to start in mid-February and the big panic for the production company and ITV was whether I was going to make it. I felt an enormous pressure to fulfil my obligations. There were long-term ramifications of being known as someone who couldn't work due to mental health issues, what it could do to my future capacity to earn and, therefore, in my mind, provide for the children. *Safe House 2* was a massive show with me in every scene. There was a lot of money riding on it as well as my professional reputation. The last thing I needed was an industry talking as one – 'Chris? He's gone nuts.' My life, my career, were hanging by a thread.

My mum was also urging me to do it. She'd witnessed first-hand the state I was in when, a couple of weeks before I went to the hospital, I'd turned up at her house. She'd seen her son chugging through fags and unable to sleep. I was fully having a nervous breakdown and in front of me was this 83-year-old woman who was having to witness it.

A mother's instinct is to help, to put things right, but she was powerless. It was incredibly difficult for her to see me like that, and so hard for me also to see her distress at being unable to help me. The pain I saw in her eyes can only have mirrored what my dad saw during his own despair.

'I think you need to do this job, Chris,' she'd tell me in her plaintive voice. I knew her way of thinking – *He's always functioned well at work – work has always saved him.* Something which, after his breakdown, she was unable to say any longer about Dad. She was trying to give me a reason to go on. But, without being me, my mum could have no real perception of my state of mind.

A taxi picked me up for a read-through with the cast. *Safe House 2* was Chris Eccleston. Everybody was looking at me. All these people, right there, relying on me. Stephen Mackintosh was among them, a great actor, as were Ashley Walters, and Jim Cartwright, the same Jim Cartwright I wrote my first fan letter to, the first also, he reckons, he ever received, prompted by his play *Road*, exploring the lives of people in a deprived, working-class area during the Thatcher government. It remains the greatest I've ever seen.

'How are you doing, Chris?' he asked me. I couldn't tell him I'd come straight from a psychiatric hospital. I still haven't told him what happened to this day. I had played people who had encountered mental issues, such as Trevor Hicks, who had suffered profound grief and PTSD, and Derek Bentley, who had a learning disability, and now here I was, with my own problems, putting on an act as me.

I managed to negotiate the read-through. The question was whether I could get on set. The idea was I'd go back and spend more time at the hospital before filming started. But I was feeling troubled at the prospect. I didn't feel the staff had really engaged with me, to the extent I was going on the internet trying to find my own diagnosis. I felt like I was going under the radar, as if my renown was a barrier to them knowing what to do with me. I was also aware that people might talk about me because I was a celebrity. I didn't want to be the subject of gossip.

A great friend of mine, Davy Jones, came to the hospital and we travelled up to his home in Liverpool on the train. The idea was we'd spend the night at his house before we drove up to

Coniston for the next stage of preparation for *Safe House 2*. It caused an enormous crisis. During the course of that night, I changed from a human being to a mere embodiment of mental disintegration. I was reduced to an animal state. I felt very, very sorry for Davy. He was clearly scared, and understandably so. He was experiencing someone in the teeth of collapse, somebody he loved very much. We've known each other twenty years and are intimate friends and yet he barely recognised me. My self had disintegrated. He couldn't see me. I wasn't there. I wasn't Chris.

Davy is a very strong and resourceful person. Now all I could see in his eyes was fear, and that brought me back a little.

'Dave,' I said, 'I'm going to take two lorazepam to give you a break from me, and you're going to drive me and we're going to find a hospital in the north.'

While in London, I'd done some research about The Priory, in Altrincham. We drove along empty roads, knocked on the door, and somehow I got an interview. They couldn't take me in that night, so we went to a hotel nearby. I became very calm. 'You are yourself now,' Dave told me. He was right. I knew I'd found somewhere safe.

Next morning, I returned to The Priory and sat down with a consultant, Justin Haslam, and a questionnaire.

He looked at my answers. 'You're very ill, Chris.'

I almost laughed. 'What do you mean "ill"?'

'You're mentally ill. You have an illness.'

I pondered this. 'Well, I'm very sad and I have some problems . . . '

'You are mentally ill,' he reaffirmed. 'You have been in fight-or-flight mode for a long, long time. But your brain chemistry can no longer fight and it can no longer fly. Your brain thinks death is imminent.'

It was a moment of great realisation. I'd lived fight or flight for three years, some might say fifty the way I am. Chemically and neurologically, I had nothing left. All there is then is death. You don't know how it's going to happen, but your body and brain are saying, very resolutely, 'You won't go on.' The next part of that internal dialogue is to conclude, 'Well, I'll kill myself' or 'I'm just going to die.' And I lived in that shattered mental frame for months. Is that a suicidal state? I don't know. What I do know is I didn't want to live the way I felt any more, and I couldn't see a way of getting better. Every time I woke up, I thought I was going to die.

'Your brain chemistry is seriously disrupted,' Justin continued, 'and I can help that with medication.'

He asked me what I'd been taking. I showed him the drugs I'd been given at the clinic in London.

He was incredulous. 'This isn't enough for a mouse.'

He looked me in the eye. 'Did anybody diagnose you, Chris?'

'What do you mean?'

'Did anybody diagnose what you are suffering from?'

'No.'

'You are suffering from a severe clinical depression, one of the worst I've ever seen.' He paused. 'But I can make you better.'

BALM OF HURT MINDS

The consultant told me, 'Stop reading the Shakespeare sonnets, read something light.' I picked up Graeme Souness's autobiography in a charity shop. I'm not sure it was quite what he meant.

I was processed. There was no bed available on the private ward, but the feeling was I might get more privacy on the NHS ward anyway. Those on the NHS ward were severely ill. A guy who'd been the Doctor wouldn't mean anything to them.

A nurse took me to my room, and it was then, as I looked at the others on the ward, that one of the great shames of my life occurred.

I'm a celebrity, I thought. *I'm not as ill as these people. I shouldn't be here. I should be on the private ward.*

I'd been so used to being treated as different and now here I was on an NHS psychiatric ward. In my head, I was thinking, *I'm not being treated as special here.*

There was another thought, which makes me wince with self-disgust, and rightly so, to this day. *These people are being treated the same as I am? How can that be? Surely my illness is the most important. I'm an ex-Doctor — my illness must be more important.*

I actually thought, *Why am I in here with all these working-class people?* I can comfort myself a little that those thought patterns were a symptom of how ill I was.

I confessed my thoughts to the nurse, an admission of what I was thinking – 'I'm special.' He didn't sneer at me. 'Chris,' he said, 'you are very, very ill and this is where you have to be.'

The fact I'd come out with this snobbism, this sense of grandiosity, and he hadn't had a go at me, had heard me out, recognised I was mentally ill, calmed me.

The next day was my birthday. I was given a cake. I went round the restaurant and offered everyone a piece. In my head, they knew I was a celebrity and I wanted to show them I was normal. Whenever we ate, we all had to go over to the restaurant together. I'd gone from being a lead in an HBO series, a lead in *The A Word*, the Doctor, to being escorted with a load of other people for my dinner and back. It was as though I had been transported to *One Flew Over the Cuckoo's Nest*, to the extent I realised I was walking in a way I'd seen people in institutions on TV walk – a shuffle. 'Am I acting this?' Having played a lot of characters who are mentally challenged also warped the reality, like I was hovering above, watching myself.

The two words 'The Priory' conjure up certain images in people's minds, associated as they are with a pampered celebrity clientele being treated in semi-luxury. But the reality, certainly on the NHS ward, was very different. Here it was bare walls and lino floors, no attempt to cosy up what was going on. My room, in a corner, near to the nurses' station, had a bed and a shower and that was pretty much all. In the room next door was a lad who was paranoid schizophrenic. Like me, he operated in the controlled conditions of a psychological hospital environment. No sharps were allowed and anything electrical was checked – the back of a plug, for instance, can be taken off and drugs stored within. I've still got plugs with 'Approved' stickers on them.

Early on, another patient came and stood in my doorway. I didn't realise at that point, but patients aren't actually allowed to enter one another's rooms. He wanted an autograph. I have always been obliging on that front and I was again here. Soon after, Justin came to see me. 'You mustn't do that,' he told me. 'You're ill. You're not here as a celebrity, you're here as a patient.' I found that quite moving. He was looking after me. I felt like he was my dad.

There was a common room where we could watch TV. One evening, a new patient, a young woman, arrived and came and sat down. We were all men in there and I felt a bit concerned about her, but also pleased there was a feminine presence.

'What are you here for?' I wasn't exactly subtle.

She was equally blunt. 'I've got a personality disorder.'

It was the beginning of a friendship, based on that honesty. She was one of the few people I really connected with. There was another young man who'd been raped and tried to kill himself; we connected too. But apart from these glimpses into other people's lives, the immense and unimaginable burdens they had to bear, I tended to keep myself to myself in my room. The staff understood that and left me to my own devices.

I spent a lot of time researching clinical depression. I sought out the best book on the subject and found *The Curse of the Strong*, by Tim Cantopher, which posits the idea that depression can strike high achievers, for want of a less arsey phrase, because they are so used to coping. They cope and cope and achieve and achieve – and then wallop. Professional footballers have been in The Priory, doctors, all sorts of creative individuals. But you don't have to be well known, have letters after your name, to be a high achiever. Dad was a high achiever. He wasn't messing about on a stage or on a football pitch, he made a factory work, everything loaded up and out on time. He had pride in punctuality, another massive thing among the working classes. Dad, like me, found his ability in himself. His background meant he didn't have any other way of doing so.

Justin saw me with the book.

'Where did you get that?' he asked.

'I bought it on Amazon. I wanted to research what was happening to me.'

'That's a very good book,' he assured me. 'My friend wrote it.'

I believe he was encouraged by my resourcefulness.

When it came to visitors, I wasn't keen. I didn't like seeing them upset. I didn't like bothering them. But my mum and brothers would come. I'd not hidden my issues from them, but no one expected me to end up in a psychiatric hospital. One day Keith started crying. He saw that the Chris he knew had disappeared and he found that very distressing. On the next chair along, all my mum saw was a child in need. She was eighty-four. You don't expect to be sat in a psychiatric hospital with your supposedly successful 52-year-old son when you're eighty-four. What is it they say? You never stop being a parent. Their visits were too much for me. I'd be exhausted. Seeing them distressed, particularly my mum, was so hard.

Occasionally, a member of staff would come in and ask, 'How are you doing, Chris?' Often they'd find me crying. If not, I'd start talking about my predicament and then inevitably the tears would come. I felt very sorry for them that they had to listen to my misery. Looking back, I suppose that is part of their role – to walk in, say, 'How's it going?', and for you to have a cry. I didn't know that at the time, though, and it felt very self-indulgent, especially as a celebrity, which is why what Justin said to me about being a patient, nothing more, nothing less, was so important. He was impassioned about it, and put me in my place. In so doing, he gave me the ability to be that patient.

My respect and belief in Justin were total and immediate. A few weeks into my stay I had a conversation with him about suicide and wanting to die.

'Chris,' he said, 'think of the legacy you'll create for Albert and Esme.'

He was quite tough on me – 'You're a parent.' The legacy for Albert and Esme would be simple – 'Dad didn't love us enough to stay around.' Suicide would have accompanied them wherever they went. They'd have known me only through DVDs, and people idealising me the way they do when somebody's dead. You never hear people say, 'Oh, he was a bit of a twat.' It's always, 'He was a great actor, a lovely guy.' And they'd be thinking, 'Well, was he? He didn't hang around long enough for us ever to know.'

When Justin said that about Albert and Esme, it was my wake-up moment. I knew I had to get better for them. It was abrupt, but necessary.

Justin was like a god who I saw every Thursday. I could have left at any time, but he held the ultimate power because I so trusted his judgement. No way would I leave without his say-so.

One Thursday, I convinced myself I was going to get out.

'I think I'm ready to go home now,' I told him.

'Do you?'

I went from yes to no in a split second. I went back to my room and started crying. Always in my head, seen through a blur of medication, was Albert and Esme. The only reason I wanted to get better was because of them. I didn't want to go back to my marriage, wasn't interested in my career, I just wanted to see Albert and Esme again.

In came the ward doctor. She was amazing. I loved her. The day-to-day contact I had with her gave me so much, but in a very normal manner.

On this occasion, she was leaning against the wall with her arms folded, looking at me quite dispassionately.

'You'll be all right, Chris,' she said.

I almost laughed through my tears.

'I see people come in and out all the time,' she continued. 'There are things you see in people that tell you where it's going to go. You're going to be all right.

'Remember, Chris, you weren't sectioned. We didn't have to come and get you. You knocked on the door. That's an indicator of strength. You knew you were ill. You realised you needed help and you went and got it.'

That was a little step for me. Up to that point I'd thought of it as a weakness to knock on a hospital door and say, 'Let me in – I need help.' It confirmed to me also that I'd been so right to leave the hospital in London. It wasn't the right place for me. It wasn't going to help; it was going to hinder. Not only did the care feel like it was lacking coordination but, for me, there was something incredibly alienating about being in a city that had become a place of terror, of nightmares, an ogre.

A place that, whenever I approached it on the M1, made my shoulders hunch up.

I wanted to go home, be somewhere in the north, and part of that was quite definitely because of the accent. Psychiatric hospital is a rarefied experience, so if I could have it grounded in an accent that I recognised, then it had to help. The way people spoke, the ward doctor, a northerner, being a case in point, gave me some element of subconscious reassurance. Then there was Justin. It turned out his mother had taught me at secondary school and we'd been brought up a couple of miles apart. Justin was so very clear about my brain chemistry. 'You're ill, I can make you well.' And I believed him. My instincts about going north were good. I began to feel safe in the hospital. Maybe I was always going to be treated as a celebrity in London institutions, while up there they just saw the illness.

Every day, I had to tell people where I was going, what I was doing, until at 9 p.m. I had to go for my medication – 375mg of the antidepressant venlafaxine; 350mg of quetiapine, an anti-psychotic drug, which, at that level, is a sedative; 10mg of zolpidem, a habit-forming sleeping tablet; and 50mg of Phenergan, which is an anti-histamine, but, if you double the dose, becomes a sedative. I was allowed lorazepam during the day. Fair to say, I was very heavily medicated. The consultant said to me once, 'You have got the constitution of an ox. We are having to give you so much antidepressant even to touch this depression, and yet you're still not getting any of the side-effects that other people get.' I'm a unit, but he was talking about my psychological as well as physical make-up.

I didn't do much therapy in The Priory. They basically put me to sleep, and that for me was a huge, huge release. With my life crumbling around me, I hadn't been sleeping for months. I'd take my medication at nine and by half past I'd be asleep for the next eleven hours.

That sleep was the beginning of my recovery. I was starting to repair my brain chemistry and in so doing I reverted to type – I started reading. I'd read whatever books were around the hospital and then, occasionally, we'd be allowed to walk into Altrincham as a group. There was a Waterstones and a Costa. We were allowed to go off independently, but we'd always have to come back to Costa. School was the last time I'd heard someone say, 'Right, I want you all back here at one o'clock.' Then, it would have irked. Now I was glad of it, glad of the security it represented, albeit a little ashamed. This grown man should have been looking after his children, holding their hands, not having his own held while taken on a day out.

On one occasion, I bumped into Paul Abbott, the writer and producer who I'd worked with on *Clocking Off* and *Cracker*. I was with the group and so couldn't really explain what was happening; ironic really as Paul has been incredibly open with his own mental health experiences. On another occasion, I was sat outside a café and the director of the first series of *The A Word*, Peter Cattaneo, walked up.

'Hi, Chris, what are you doing here?'

'Oh, I'm just out having a coffee.' *Nothing to see here!*

There was a period in the last month at The Priory where I was allowed to go out on my own. I'd leave at ten in the morning and go back at six at night. The hospital approved it and were keeping an eye on me. During that time, I'd be trawling the charity shops in Altrincham, buying biographies, an escape from my own reality. But whatever the words in front of me,

I'd inevitably start thinking about Albert and Esme and how much I missed them. My heart would start to beat too hard, too fast, and I'd think, *I want to die.* Then I'd remember the lorazepam and, twenty minutes later, I'd be back reading the book. Sat in café after café, reading and reading.

It's interesting that in all that time I spent around Altrincham, I was never once stopped for an autograph. Perhaps that side of me shut down and I went unseen. As Justin had said, I was a patient, not a celebrity. It was something I came to physically embody. There were places I went where people might normally have gone, 'Are you that bloke from . . . ?' But they didn't. I was shut down, and my persona shut down with it.

In the unit itself, I happened across people whose lives had become invisible to themselves. On two consecutive days, I saw several teenage girls, skeletal, carrying drips down the stairs. Anorexia. My heart broke for them. I thought about the twentieth and twenty-first century and the bombardment of sexualised, idealised body imagery that had afflicted them, me, and, in all likelihood, will affect Albert and Esme.

Eventually, with spring in the air, I found myself functioning at a slightly higher level and was starting to think about coming home. By now, I was on the private wing, but whatever the ward, I had been in The Priory for approaching three months. Originally I'd only packed for an overnight at Davy's. I was wearing his T-shirts and undies for weeks. He never did ask for them back.

Justin concurred that it was OK for me to continue my recovery outside the environs of the hospital, and so I left. The Priory had done me a great service in allowing me to be in that environment and see people so much more ill than me. Not only that, but I'd felt part of a whole, not separated from normal people by being a C-list TV celeb. In my intense vulnerability, and I've never felt so vulnerable in all my life, I'd felt part of something larger. I'd had such fortune in my life and yet here were these people who'd had no luck and had then been landed with everything from anorexia to paranoid schizophrenia. Those days will stay with me for ever.

I went to live at my mum's house. But this wasn't the classic screen moment of the hospital doors shutting behind the man reborn as he stands there drinking in the beauty of the world around him. The credits don't role in real life. I'd spent seventy days in The Priory. They had passed in a fog, which was yet to clear.

The reality of those weeks post-Priory was that I would either lie on my bed all day in my old childhood bedroom or go to Waterstones in Manchester and just sit there in the café. Effectively, I was behaving at Mum's house just as I did in hospital, to the extent that at nine o'clock I'd even swallow the same cocktail of drugs. By half past nine, I'd be asleep, until half past eight in the morning when I'd come down and have some breakfast. I'd then go back up, lie on the bed, and read. All the time, I could smell the hospital on me. It took a long time for it to come out of my clothes and pores.

Mum didn't cajole me too much. She knew I was stubborn. But she's clever. She knew that asking me to drive her to where my dad's ashes were scattered was a tactic that would work. It would get me out of my bedroom and engaging with someone else's life, someone else's feelings. She knew she was asking me to do something for her, something that was about her emotional life, not mine.

We stood on that bridge and thought about Dad and what Whiteacre had meant to him. I am struck again now, especially in the knowledge of our respective breakdowns, how the years he enjoyed there contrasted so differently with what was to come. He left Whiteacre a care free young man, oblivious to the burdens he would accrue. A realisation would soon dawn that, for him, personal expectation was something only to be glimpsed at, that his own life would be dictated by the over-whelming need not to experience but to provide.

I think of his frustrations – how, as a very bright man, he spent a lifetime in a job that, although he was proud of his work, asked so little of him. That frustration, I truly believe, ate away at him, inched, and then plunged him into depression. The weight of unexpressed potential, conscious or otherwise, was simply too much to bear. When breakdown eventually came, whereas for me it offered a slow release from a tortured mind, for him, living in an era when psychological help was either not available or simply a matter for a higher social strata, it signified the start of the end. When Dad did return to work, he started to come home earlier and earlier. Some days he'd be back at half past three. It felt like he wasn't needed as much and in the end they let him go. My mum was cleaning at the baths when my dad turned up crying his eyes out. She thought something had happened to me, Alan or Keith. Eventually she managed to get it out of him that he'd been made redundant.

While from that day on the bridge, according to Mum, I began to improve, Dad never rediscovered his previous self. He was fifty-nine. Devastated. Never the same Ronnie again. He became much less active, less engaged, less interested, an isolation of the mind exacerbated by the fact he'd never really had any hobbies. While I slowly dipped back into my previous life with an audition for Mike Leigh's film *Peterloo*, and read the scripts for the third series of *The Leftovers*, practising my American accent at Mum's kitchen table, Dad's life descended into spending every day as he had his weekends away from work – sitting in his chair and doing nothing. Whereas before he'd been selective in what he watched on TV, now he'd watch anything. We kept urging him to go there, do that. One escape he had enjoyed in the past was golf, which would have been ideal for retirement, offering exercise, companionship, and the great mental boost that comes from a few hours outdoors, but he couldn't be persuaded. Occasionally, he'd go back to Salford and walk round the market trying to find old faces, and he loved the reunions for the Colgate factory and Whiteacre, but otherwise there was a refusal to break from the routine. My dad loved friendship and companionship but just wasn't very good at initiating it. He never wanted to start anything. I've detected all those things in myself but, perhaps with my dad in mind, I've pushed myself to be at least a little bit more proactive.

The latter stages of my recovery didn't come easy. The *Peterloo* audition was in London, the first time I'd been back since I'd been in the clinic, and the feelings of terror returned. I had a lot of lorazepam in my pocket as I sat on the train, but I didn't take it. I needed to negotiate the audition with something like a clear mind. As I left afterwards, I told Mike I'd spent some time in a psychiatric hospital.

'Keep smiling,' he said, a very droll, Salford kind of remark, which I appreciated.

The Leftovers, meanwhile, offered a larger step towards

getting better. At the end of May, I got on a plane and flew to Austin, Texas. It was vital I took that track. Had I stayed in my mum's house, it could have been dangerous. The isolation, the constant company of my own head, would not have been helpful. I knew I had to get back on the horse for practical as well as spiritual reasons. *The Leftovers* gave me exactly that, offering the comforting challenge of a role that had been a great success for me personally, alongside people I liked.

As soon as I got to Austin, I started reducing my medication. I joined a gym and began running every day. Exercise, again, became massive for me. I really stepped it up, including weight-training, which I'd never done before. Perhaps it was a response to feeling so spiritually vulnerable, but I began to build myself up. It was a discipline and I did it with trainers. The interaction and friendship I built with them was as important as what they taught me, while at the same time I revelled in wanting to learn again. As an actor, learning is key, be it accent, dance, or whatever. Through learning to weight-train, that desire came back. For my mental recovery, investing in my physical health was enormous. Austin allowed me space to breathe, to repair, so that I could get back to Albert and Esme and do my job – be their parent.

When I returned to the UK in August, finally I saw them again. I hadn't wanted them to see me in a psychiatric hospital, or in that state, full stop. Not only would it be awful for them, but I knew the emotional bruise left on myself could possibly derail what Justin was trying to do. I wanted to be recovered. Equally, I could barely imagine the impact on them of our separation. I'd been in their lives every day and then I wasn't there for six months.

The plan was I would collect Esme from nursery, picking up Albert from home first. I knocked on the door and, as it was opened, I could see through the hallway and down the stairs into the kitchen. A pair of legs were swinging on a chair. Albert was having his lunch. When he realised I was at the door, he jumped off his seat, ran through the kitchen, up the stairs and towards me as though he was going to launch himself into my arms. He then did an extraordinary thing. He stopped right in front of me and looked straight into my eyes, almost into the back of my head.

I knew what he was telling me – 'Do you know how important this is to me? Do you? You can't do this again. You can't disappear. Do you know how this has felt?'

I replied in kind. My answer too was in my eyes. 'Yes, I do know how it's felt, Albert, because it's felt like that for me too. I'm sorry, son. I'm not going to disappear again.'

He hugged me, and, as I held him, I felt a million emotions. Through them all, my respect for him was overwhelming. His complexity, and dignity, was amazing. We'd had a conversation and he'd driven it and taken control. I'll never ever forget what he did that day. I know it will be the last thing I ever think of. Through him, we had a conversation with our eyes. We knew that this, for both of us, was enormous – and then we got on with it. We got in the car and it felt normal.

I picked up Esme. She saw me – 'Daddy!' I went then – I burst into tears.

I wish I cried a lot more. I shed more tears than some of my generation, but they don't come easily. I hope they will. I want them to. Afterwards, I always feel fantastic. It's a rather more epic and excoriating scale, but I will be forever amazed at how much strength I accrued from my mental collapse. I would never have been disturbed had someone talked to me about their mental health, but I consider myself more of a man now because I am so willing to talk about my own. The flipside is how the industry views depression. Before *Safe House 2*, I'd never had a day off in thirty-two years. My breakdown meant meeting the commitment was impossible. As an actor, that's the biggest no-no there is. The upshot was the cast was disassembled and the programme abandoned, eventually to be remade with a different cast elsewhere. I'd let everyone down, left them floundering with no work. The result was that insurers demanded a much higher premium to cover my involvement in a drama. That production really has to want me if they are to make that investment. That's what acknowledging mental health issues can do for an actor. For some, there would be no way back, and for many, no doubt, it's an illness they prefer to keep hidden, with all the damage to themselves and others around them that brings. As it is, since not doing *Safe House 2*, I've never stopped. The more I work, the more the insurers relax, until my breakdown is seen as a blip, which is exactly how I see it – a blip that strengthened me hugely. My depression was triggered by close personal traumatic events and, from the education I received in the darkest of days, I know I now have the strength to deal with anything of that nature in the future. I wouldn't wish clinical depression on my worst enemy, but it launched me into a new, positive and different life. It deepened my humanity, deepened my tolerance, deepened my empathy and deepened my sense of brotherhood. It taught me life is a very delicate thing. I walk among the human race with a lot more sympathy, feeling and love. I've always had those elements but they're a lot more pronounced now.

I was in Melbourne in autumn 2016 filming *The Leftovers*, running along the river, when I saw a figure in front of me and people scattering, backing away left and right. He was right in my eyeline, to the extent he was shouting at me as I ran towards him. I stopped. He had the most beautiful green eyes, but was in a very heightened state.

'What's wrong, mate?' I asked him.

'What's wrong, mate? I'm going to kill myself, that's what's wrong.'

He was very distressed but quickly quietened into conversational mode.

'I hope you don't do that,' I told him. 'I felt like that once.'

'Why?'

'Because I thought I was going to lose my children.'

'Oh, I'm so sorry.' He put his hand on my shoulder.

Suddenly, in that exchange, he had started to think about me. It had changed his perspective, diverted him from himself. He wandered off. I don't know what happened to him, but my experience allowed me, perhaps unlike some other passersby, not to feel intimidated or threatened by his state of mind. Having lived through a very altered state myself, his condition didn't surprise me, and the fact I was calm in the face of his crisis meant he had a brief moment of contact.

There remains a stigma attached to the word 'breakdown', when actually it's a very legitimate response to life in the early twenty-first century. We are not designed for the non-stop world we live in, the pressures put upon us, and those we bring upon ourselves. For young people, especially, those pressures are becoming ever more intense. Social media, the battle for jobs, the speed with which we judge – it's a lot easier for kids now to be made to feel inadequate in so many different ways. I worry about what any child picks up in their subconscious just through their daily interaction with the world. Societal pressure has got worse for children, and I hope my own experiences will make me better able to help my children tread that difficult path.

I am on antidepressants to this day. I could be on them for the rest of my days. I do have an issue with that. I would like to attempt slowly to reduce the dose, to experience reality again, to see how I do. It's a matter of pride. It concerns me also that, artistically, the drugs may somehow deaden my creative side. And yet, interestingly, I have received some of the best reviews of my life since I started taking them. Perhaps it's because, while acting and my career was always the most important thing in my life, Albert and Esme came along and superseded that single-minded desire. I have come to realise that life – one with Albert and Esme in it – is much more important to me than work. Therefore, there's far less pressure on acting and I've found a relaxation in front of the camera. I do wonder if I have as much empathy and emotional depth as I had pre-breakdown, but, no doubt about it, medication has saved my life. I can't help thinking that if Dad could have had the treatment I've had, lived in my era, there's a very good chance he'd have avoided dementia. To have had access to counselling and medicines, to have seen, and learned, another way – simply to have been able to reflect and relax, to learn to shed the accumulated years of frustration and non-communication – would surely have acted as a pressure release on a cramped and complex mind.

As it was, Dad never had a chance of a reconciliation with his own past. The mental scars were too deeply ingrained. He'd lived a life dictated by others and to start again was asking too much. He was one of millions of (to those who know no better) faceless individuals who were never given access to psychiatric help the like of which I received. Part of that is about eras, but part of it is also about capitalism. If a worker breaks down at the end of their life, why fix them? You wouldn't spend that time and money if it was a machine. You'd just get another. The likes of my dad are expendable. Give him a few pills, send him home, get what we can out of him for a few years, and then that's the end of him. Remember Boxer? George Orwell didn't write *Animal Farm* for nothing. The working class are useful, then they're not. Binary. No grey areas. Politicians talk about the 'burden' of an ageing population. Presumably it was better when they died young from industrial diseases. Respect is what it boils down to. And the likes of my dad weren't shown any.

Two men, two breakdowns. One better for it. One who never recovered.

That's me and Dad all over. Same person, different eras. Time travellers.

12

DOCTOR DADDY 1

ALBERT: Daddy, your voice sounds different.

ESME: Is that your electric screwdriver?

ALBERT: Do you still have that jacket?

ESME: When was this?

ALBERT: It was made in twenty-thousand-and-five. It was before you and me were born. It was fourteen years ago. Look, Daddy's got no grey hair.

ME: Look, JFK – I was there at all the great historical events.

ESME: You mean you?

ME: Not me, my character, the Doctor.

ALBERT: But you are the Doctor.

ESME: What happened to him?

ALBERT: The plastic bin just ate him.

ESME: Is she your friend?

ME: Yes, she's called Rose.

ALBERT: Is that your telephone box?

BOTH: Christopher Eccleston!

ESME: Look! On the telly! It says Christopher Eccleston!

ALBERT: Is that Rose? Where's she going?

ESME: Who is this, Daddy?

ME: It's the scary guys – then I come and save the day.

ESME: Can you tell me when the scary guys have gone?

ME: I'm here – look, I'm saving her.

ALBERT: Did you take her outside?

ME: I saved her, yes.

ALBERT: I don't want to watch any more.

ESME: It's too scary for us.

ME: The Doctor's going to save the day. Do you find *Doctor Who* scary?

ESME: Yes, a dustbin ate up a man and replaced him with a plastic man. His girlfriend asked him to come in the house and then the plastic man's hand turned into a chopper.

ME: What do you think of me as the Doctor?

ALBERT: It's a bit weird because you're different and your voice is different. I thought you were American.

ESME: Daddy, I was worried you were going to be turned into a plastic man. It's good to see you as the Doctor but I don't want you to turn into plastic in it.

ME: The Doctor's a good guy; he doesn't get turned into plastic.

ALBERT: Where has the real boyfriend gone?

ME: He's gone, but the Doctor will help get him back because he's a scientist and a good guy.

ESME: But why is he called Doctor? Doctors just help people get well when they're sick.

ME: Doctor is also a name for a scientist.

ESME: What was that bottle thing, the lid, that you hit into the boyfriend?

ME: I opened the Champagne bottle and fired the cork

at the boyfriend and, because he's plastic, the cork was absorbed into his plastic and then he spat it out.

ALBERT: It fell into his mouth.

ESME: But what happened to it?

ALBERT: He chewed it for a minute.

ESME: Didn't he like it?

ME: No. He's a bad guy. He's been turned into the bad guy by the plastic bin, but if you watch the rest of the episode, the Doctor saves him and turns him back into a good guy – that's what the Doctor always does.

ALBERT: So the boyfriend was eaten by the plastic and it morphed him into a plastic thing.

ME: It morphed him into a plastic thing, yes.

ESME: So, like clay, and it squished his skin and then moved it all around.

ME: But then the Doctor, using his sonic screwdriver . . .

ALBERT: When you do it, he turns blue.

ME: He turns Mickey back into a good guy.

ESME: Wait, he's called Mickey?

ME: Rose's boyfriend is called Mickey.

ALBERT: How did you do it? Do you have amazing skills to avoid them?

ME: Yeah, the Doctor's really brave, and he's also really clever.

ESME: But, Dad, does Rose ask if she can be with you and go on your adventures? And then you teach her how to fight?

ME: That's right. She is braver and smarter than even the Doctor. So you, Esme, could be the Doctor's assistant or the Doctor. Now the Doctor is a girl.

ALBERT: Are you the main character?

ME: I'm the main character.

ESME: Because you're our daddy, we can call you Doctor Daddy.

ME: Rose is also the main character. The two main characters are a man and a woman, like Albert and Esme.

ESME: Doctor Rose and Doctor Who.

ALBERT: What are those on the DVD box? Are those the machines that make people plastic?

ME: Those are the Daleks.

ESME: The Garlicks?

ALBERT: Dad, I'm stuck – can you help me get down from here?

ESME: What do the Daleks do?

ME: The Daleks are the Doctor's worst enemy. The Daleks are the only thing that the Doctor is scared of.

ESME: Do they beat you?

ME: No, I win in the end.

ESME: What do they do?

ME: They're bad guys. The Daleks are bad guys.

ESME: What's their power?

ME: They're made of metal and they're really cruel. They can go sideways, forwards, up stairs.

ESME: What's that?

ME: That's the TARDIS.

ESME: What does it do?

ME: The TARDIS is Doctor Who's police box. It means Time and Relative Dimension in Space.

ALBERT: What's that spider? It's got a pink spider inside it?

ME: That's the console. That's the control centre of
the TARDIS.

ESME: Who's that?

ME: That's Captain Jack. He's a good guy as well. He
comes and helps. But Rose is my best friend.

ALBERT: What are you staring at?

ME: We're staring at the Daleks, that's why we all look a
bit serious.

ALBERT: You go serious because you are hiding your
fears inside you.

ESME: You feel scared but you don't show it.

ME: That's right. If the Doctor feels scared, that means
Rose will feel scared. But also the Doctor gets excited
by his adventures and stimulated rather than scared. He
wants to work out what the aliens are and where they
come from.

ALBERT: Even the plastics?

ME: Even the plastics.

ESME: But how does the living plastic do it?

ALBERT: This is too scary.

ESME: It's too scary.

ME: Would you like to watch some more of it?

BOTH: Noooo!

ME: Never again?

ESME: We can watch it when we're older – fifty-five,
like you.

13

LOTS OF PLANETS HAVE A NORTH

'The past is another country — 1987's just the Isle of Wight.'
Doctor Who

It was strange watching *Doctor Who* with the kids. Strange to see the younger me, no beard, no grey hairs. Strange to see me lean as a whippet. Strange to watch the work I did fifteen years ago. Strange to think how that character on the screen would so relentlessly follow me in real life.

More than anything, though, seeing my series through their eyes provided a much-needed answer to a growing phenomenon. Everywhere I go, Cornwall, Belfast, Glasgow, wherever, I now get people of a certain age, mid-twenties, coming up to me. 'You were my Doctor,' they tell me. Occasionally, and a little worryingly, they'll add, 'I had a little plastic model of you.' Yes, I was captured, looking mildly constipated, in plastic. I'll ask them how old they were, telling them, as their cogs whirr, 'I did it fifteen years ago.' I can see them doing the maths. 'I was nine!'

I'm even getting it via the children. Albert told me the other day that someone had told him, 'Your daddy is the best Doctor ever.'

'Does that mean you make people feel better?' he asked me. Which I thought was brilliant.

'Oh no, son,' I told him, 'I'm not a real doctor. I played a character on television called the Doctor, same as I played Macbeth.'

I'm loving the new joy I'm getting from *Doctor Who* fans, because I was never really able to take it in at the time. I spent my first day on set chasing a short Glaswegian dressed as a pig in a spacesuit around a studio and it never really got any more normal from there.

I can still remember the exact spot, the view across the field, where the Doctor first entered my consciousness as a character I could potentially inhabit. I've always been an actor who's actively looked for work, studied the newspapers and the trade press. Earlier that day, I'd read that Russell T. Davies was overseeing the much-vaunted return of *Doctor Who*. Now I was out running and I couldn't stop thinking about the show. When I was a kid, *Doctor Who* had never really meant anything to me. In my head I had a black-and-white image of Patrick Troughton. Then there were Jon Pertwee and Tom Baker, with whom, unlike, for instance, Patrick McGoohan in *The Prisoner* or *Danger Man* or Sean Connery as James Bond, I simply could never identify. *Doctor Who* seemed to me like your typical white middle-class authority figure. He was an upper-crust eccentric, very male, posh. The programme didn't grip me at all, to the extent I barely watched it, apart, that is, from the regeneration scenes when the Doctor would change from one body to another – I would always tune in for those. I wasn't fascinated by the phenomenon from a technical sense, the special effects, like some kids might be, but I was very taken with this notion that a character could remain the same in a different physical form. I would want to be there in front of the TV to see it happen.

Fast forward three decades and now here was Russell at the helm of *Doctor Who*'s rebirth. Aside from a film version in 1996, the show hadn't been seen for sixteen years. Neither had it ever gone away. Such is the passion for the series, its place in TV culture, that the clamour for a return had never disappeared.

Russell's involvement intrigued me. He was a writer and producer who'd never made TV by numbers; *Queer as Folk*, which followed the lives of three gay men in Manchester, being a case in point. Originally, *Queer as Folk*'s producers had wanted to see me for the role of uncompromising advertising executive Stuart. I've always regretted not pursuing that part but at the time I was very much in the grip of my anorexia. Playing Stuart would have involved nudity, something I'd never had an issue with before, but at that point my body dysmorphia was exerting an iron grip. I featured as a good twin/bad twin combination in an episode of the BBC One comedy drama *Linda Green* around that time and I was skeletal. Instead, I suggested Aidan Gillen for the role. I'm sure he was on the list anyway, but I've always been proud of that suggestion because he was brilliant. I have huge regret about my own non-involvement, but I don't think I'd have bettered Aidan.

Russell had followed up *Queer as Folk* with the equally origin al *The Second Coming*, which was where our paths first properly crossed. I took the part of Steven Baxter, a video shop worker who discovers he is actually the son of God, his mission being to avert the end of mankind. Originally, the drama was intended to be a landmark series on Channel 4. At the last moment, however, Channel 4 threw the production into doubt. I was never party as to why they nixed it – that's one of the frustrations of being an actor – but its makers, Red Productions, managed to pull it out of the fire by getting it to ITV, albeit in the form of a two-part drama, some way abbreviated from the original idea.

While the drama was still highly praised, and its content raised eyebrows with its central questioning of the worth of religion, one reviewer, Craig Brown, was fairly negative, calling it a 'shaggy dog story'. To a certain degree, my view chimed with his. I always felt like it was a missed opportunity. The expanded version Russell had originally concocted dealt with massive biblical issues. In my head I was thinking it would be up there with *Our Friends in the North* in terms of impact. Instead it ended up something of a novelty, but it always meant more to me, from having known the piece in its original form. For Russell, too, claiming a big spot on prime-time ITV for an ostensibly unusual, hugely original and very un-ITV piece of work was undoubtedly a big deal.

At the time of *The Second Coming*, Russell and I were at different points in our careers. Russell was climbing the greasy pole whereas I was flying high. I'd done *Our Friends in the North*, *Hillsborough*, *Cracker*, *Flesh and Blood*, and been in a couple of high-profile films. And yet we existed on the same plain because he and I looked at things in a similar way. Russell, for instance, was on set every day on *The Second Coming*, which impressed me. He also offered practical help. There's a scene where Steven Baxter is on the pitch at Maine Road, the old Manchester City ground, and starts to receive a message from God. I was a little perplexed at how to play such a concept.

I went over to Russell – 'How do I do this?'

'Well, you know,' he pondered, in his broad Welsh accent, 'it's like you are downloading it.'

Actors can work from abstract directions like that. Russell said it with so much enthusiasm and so much originality that it was a moment of absolute sense.

When Russell's name was then attached to *Doctor Who*, the fact that this man who I respected so much was so invested in the show meant a massive amount. If anything could make the return of *Doctor Who* work, it was his creative leap, and that was what I had in my head as I ran along. After lots of heavy drama for adults, I was also very interested in doing something for children. But I wanted it to be right. I knew how much I'd invested in TV as a child, how it had sparked my imagination, my sense of me. *Doctor Who* had to be the same. I felt Russell was exactly the man to do that. His previous work told me his approach to children was not going to be infantilised.

There was another element lurking in my mind. I wanted to surprise the industry. The idea of me playing the Doctor was very, very leftfield. So, so bizarre – and I liked that.

I considered, too, the nature of the Doctor himself. 'Time Lord,' I mulled. 'That means he's travelling through time. He's never at home. He's lonely.'

I had a thought – 'I can do lonely.'

The more I deliberated over the nature of the Doctor, the more I began to see the character as separate and apart.

When I got home from my run, straight away I emailed Russell and asked to be put on the list for the auditions.

His reply was instant – 'What!!!!!?''

But Russell took the idea to the BBC, and it appealed to

them. I can see now that attaching my name to the production, at that point a risky enterprise with no guarantee of success, gave them credibility. Along with a handful of other British actors, I was foremost among my generation for being associated with integrity. I didn't do advertisements, or even voiceovers for advertisements, and still don't to this day, but I had been in landmark dramas playing conflicted men. Therefore, I was regarded as a serious actor. If they were going to reinvent *Doctor Who*, a series that had ended in 1989 in a mire of disdain, my name delivered a much-needed dose of authority. The other names in the frame only added to that theory. I'm pretty sure Bill Nighy and Hugh Grant turned down the sonic screwdriver before it came to me. Maybe I should have asked myself why. What I now realise is that practically everybody else in the industry was thinking the return of *Doctor Who* was going to be a car crash. It had failed at the end of the '80s and there was no great reason to suggest it would do any better now. I, however, was seeing it differently. I felt it would be a success because of Russell T. Davies. Not for the first time, I believed in the writer.

And yet as the production date neared, I began to feel uneasy. Whereas in any series there will be discussions over personality and tone — a gradual portrait of the character being painted on a mental canvas — here there was nothing.

'The Doctor appears in a leather jacket,' stated the script for episode one. No more information than that. 'OK,' I thought, 'so he's modern.' But that was all that single scrap of information gave me.

I could have looked at any of the old series for a character. It was either a mistake or a virtue, but I didn't. Instead I decided

I'd play Russell. Right in front of me was a man who wore a leather jacket and whose brain was genius level, a tinder box of ideas. Russell had energy, he had humour. And there was no one who wanted to be the Doctor more than he did. I took the fizzing of thought in Russell's head and gave it to the Doctor. It wasn't a new tactic. In *Our Friends in the North*, I decided I would play the writer Peter Flannery. In any Jimmy McGovern drama, I feel like I'm playing Jimmy. With the Doctor, however, while Russell gave me a physical embodiment, the sketchiness of the character in the script still made me feel uneasy. How do I get a handle on this? And if I can't get a handle on it, how can I expect the audience to? It felt like I'd been given a platform I didn't understand. Perhaps I'm not alone in that search for the Doctor. It's an interesting fact about the show that a lot of actors, including myself, have been highly criticised for their performances, for being wacky, zany, or whatever other characteristics they injected into the role. It might be a fundamental flaw in the character that you can never quite get him right.

Russell's real brilliance was in the writing – I'm not sure he knew what he wanted from the Doctor. I don't think he had a very strong take on the character. There was never any discussion, for instance, about me being a 'northern' Doctor. But nobody told me not to and so I did it. As a working-class kid off a council estate, I certainly wasn't going to repeat what had gone before. I thought about people like Alan Turing, the scientist and codebreaker, born in Moss Side and credited by Winston Churchill for shortening the Second World War by two years, and Anthony Burgess, a brilliant and original literary figure, born in Harpurhey, both of whom would have spoken with my accent. I was aware also that, down through time, those with high intelligence, great scientific knowledge, a poetic gift, sensitivity, status, who made it on to radio or TV, had all spoken like the Queen. But brilliant people don't all sound like the narrator on a 1950s newsreel. I knew that for sure because I'd been brought up by two of them, Ronnie and Elsie Eccleston. I was always going to use my accent, and I think, in terms of tone and characterisation, it was one thing that definitely did work. It became a defining part of the Doctor. Just look at that beautiful line that Russell wrote – 'Lots of planets have a north.'

One area where I was definitely on wobbly ground was playing light comedy, an absolute requirement of the role, but one I wasn't used to. I loved comedy but I'd never done any. I'd positioned myself as this overly earnest actor. I wanted to be Hamlet. And to a large extent that was because I felt my mum and dad and so many others of my class hadn't been taken seriously. I wanted to navigate a path where someone of my background would be given that respect. Now, though, I was in a massive role, with massive responsibility, working in a style of light comedy I knew little about. Because hitherto I'd been so dour and serious, so tombstone solemn, when I started smiling on *Doctor Who*, it looked over the top. 'He's overdoing it. He's Timmy Mallett.' Watching it again now with Albert and Esme, I can see that actually, all I was doing, albeit a bit clumsily, was trying to create another character. I'd done it with Nicky Hutchinson in *Our Friends in the North*, and a dozen other TV characters, and now I was simply trying to create the Doctor.

Russell's great legacy would be the feminisation of the show. As a progressive man, he made Rose an equal, not a sidekick. It is she who, on several occasions, saves the Doctor, rather than the other way round. As can any parent with a daughter, I now look at Esme and think, *You could be the Doctor*. In 2005, as recently as that, such a thought would have been a pipe dream.

When it came to the Doctor's relationship with Rose, I was occupying the same territory as Russell, firm in my mind that she should never be one of those assistants we'd seen before – women basically there to be awestruck by the Doctor and tell him he's amazing. I knew even before I'd seen anything of the characterisation of Rose what Russell would want to do. I'd already seen it with his depiction of Lesley Sharp's character Judy in *The Second Coming*, a woman with an independent mind willing to confront received wisdom. In *Doctor Who*, where that was let down a little was in the kissing between the Doctor and Rose. I never wanted that. I was always against it. I felt it made the relationship too explicit. To me, the Doctor and Rose's love was pure and any physical expression weakened that precious commodity. Myself and Billie Piper had a chemistry that allowed the relationship between Rose and the Doctor to live in the mind of both them and the viewer. Better preserve that than make it too obvious. In my view, the Doctor loved this person – not this woman – and that was a trait of the Doctor I clung on to for all thirteen episodes.

Billie was magnificent as Rose. I knew she was good at the time but looking back now I can see her absolute brilliance. It reminds me how much we loved working together, which is palpably obvious on screen. Actors work at chemistry; it doesn't just come with a snap of the fingers, but we were fortunate enough to have something there from the start. We were also professionals and knew how to achieve on-screen banter. What truly amazes me is I know how nervous Billie was at the start. She thought I was some big serious performer and she didn't have the belief in herself as an actor. She proved herself, of course, to be way better than any of the rest of us. Her luminosity on screen comes from herself, not those around her, and instinctively she made Rose exactly the person she should be. When *Doctor Who* won a BAFTA for Best Drama, it was Billie for whom I was truly delighted. The reception she got when the show was screened made any lingering reservations on her part about her ability evaporate. It was admirable in her that she had zero arrogance that she could do it. The work she has done since has shown her to be worthy of every accolade that comes her way.

Watching our characters now reinforces what I concluded at the time: Russell enjoys writing more for women than he does for men. If so, I'm glad – there's been a lot of writing for men. Rose arrives on screen fully formed, one of the strongest female characters of any show of any year, painting a solid line leading directly to Jodie Whittaker. If you think about it, the relaunch in 2005 was actually the chance to create the first female Doctor. Why not do it then? Perhaps, really, we should be looking back on Billie Piper not as Rose but as the Doctor.

Billie made *Doctor Who* a delight but so also did Steven Moffat's scripts, which delivered my best work, bringing me closer to finally knowing exactly who the Doctor was than any other time during the shoot. Directors Joe Ahearne and Euros Lyn also allowed the character to blossom and thrive. I loved Joe. If he'd directed the show from day one, I'd probably still be playing the Doctor now. Joe, like Euros and Steven, had really done his homework. He spoke with the passion of a proper fan who had the knowledge that *Doctor Who*, along with

I LOVE THE BONES OF YOU

comic books and sci-fi, is drawing on the bigger-picture stories of Greek myth. There's a hugely intellectual and emotional content to that kind of output. If a director doesn't get that, they shouldn't be anywhere near the show.

Doctor Who has left its mark on me. People from both inside and outside the industry still say, 'I don't know why you did it in the first place. It just didn't seem to fit.' That reaction comes from my departure, which was enormously negative for me. Yes, I have felt bitter, and yes, I have felt betrayed, but I know also that *Doctor Who* was the best thing that, professionally, ever happened to me, not so much a learning curve as a plunge down a well and a long climb towards the sunshine I see now. These days, I feel nothing but positive about the show, to the extent I have even started doing conventions, something I'd been wary of because I always wanted to earn my money from acting. What I've actually found is some amazing people who want to talk to me not only about *Doctor Who* but *Our Friends in the North*, *28 Days Later*, *Second Coming*, *Shallow Grave*, *Cracker*, and so on. People bring memorabilia from across my whole career, which makes me feel good about my work and also about myself. It has healed something in me. Forget producers, forget politics – here are real people who have seen me do my stuff and want to shake my hand.

I sat here with my children again last night and watched myself. At first, some familiar nagging thoughts were apparent. *Wow,* I pondered, *you're young, and you have no idea what this is going to do to you.*

As the minutes passed, though, I felt more upbeat about what I was viewing. *I can see what you're trying to do here,* I thought, *even if you're overdoing it a bit.* At other times, I'd think, *That was all right — you're actually pulling this off.* I was watching it from a distance — and enjoying it. I liked what I was seeing.

So when anyone, including myself, tries to tell me *Doctor Who* wasn't a good fit, I tell them straight — 'But that's exactly why I did it.' I did something positive. The role — posh, received pronunciation — needed changing.

And I changed it.

14

DOCTOR DADDY 2

ALBERT: Daddy, what were you doing to that Dalek thingy?

ME: I was bullying him, trying to frighten him, getting my revenge on him because he's always scaring me.

ALBERT: Have you seen him many times?

ME: Yes, I've fought the Daleks many times.

ALBERT: Was he being kind or unkind?

ME: Who?

ALBERT: The Dalek.

ME: The Dalek was trapped and chained up. I would say that the Doctor was being cruel. He was shouting at and threatening the Dalek. What did *you* think?

ALBERT: I just thought the Dalek didn't mean any harm.

ME: So did you think the Doctor was being cruel?

ALBERT: No . . . I need to understand a lot of things.

ME: OK, I'll explain everything I can.

ALBERT: Who made the Daleks?

ME: Er, well, the Master made the Daleks.

ALBERT: The one with the moustache?

ME: No, the one with the moustache is an American bad guy who controls the internet.

ALBERT: But, Daddy, do you outsmart him?

ME: Yes, in the end I outsmart him and I outsmart the Daleks. That Dalek gets free and lots of Daleks come and I fight them all.

ALBERT: What about Rose and her friend?

ME: I save them both.

ALBERT: What was that white robot that you saw earlier on?

ME: The one in the case? That's called a Cyberman. That's the Doctor's second most frightening enemy.

ALBERT: What is a Cyberman?

ME: A Cyberman is a robot, an evil robot.

ALBERT: What does it do?

ME: It tries to take over the planet and destroy all human life on it.

ALBERT: What does Cyber mean?

ME: Cyber . . . er . . . it, er . . . what does it mean? I'm not quite sure. It's a technical . . .

ALBERT: We'll look it up on the internet.

ME: Yeah, OK.

ALBERT: You've no need to be ashamed.

ME: Thank you.

ALBERT: Who gave you the police box?

ME: I'm a Time Lord, and all the Time Lords . . .

ALBERT: Did you make it or did you not?

ME: Yes, the Doctor built the TARDIS.

ALBERT: But how could you move all those things?

ME: Well, he's a brilliant scientist.

ALBERT: When did you make it?

ME: I made it, er, millions of years ago.

ALBERT: When you were a teenager, or a little boy?

ME: Probably when he was a teenager.

ALBERT: Thirteen or fourteen?

ME: Probably, yeah. He had to make the TARDIS because his planet was destroyed by the Daleks.

ALBERT: That Dalek was making noises.

ME: Yes, he was screaming in pain because they were torturing him and keeping him in chains.

ALBERT: But who was going 'Aaggghhh!'?

ME: Well, that's a tiny green creature that lives inside the Dalek. There is a life force inside the Dalek.

ALBERT: But is that the one with the two things sticking out that goes 'Ex-ter-min-ate'?

ME: Yes, that's the Dalek.

ALBERT: Does he have lots of Daleks inside him?

ME: No, there's just one little green creature inside. The Dalek is armoured to protect this very terrified little green creature.

ALBERT: What is it, this little green creature?

ME: Well, it looks like something off the bottom of the ocean.

ALBERT: Green seaweed?

ME: Not seaweed. It's kind of like a mollusc or something.

ALBERT: If we could X-ray a Dalek, it might be useful.

ME: Would you like to see what's inside a Dalek?

ALBERT: Yes, that Dalek.

ME: What's it like seeing your dad be the Doctor?

ALBERT: Well, it's a bit amazing. I don't know how you could make that police box think, with all that amazing stuff.

ME: How I could make it think?

ALBERT: Yes.

ME: Well, it's a cloaking device. When *Doctor Who* started, those blue police boxes were all over London. It's a kind of camouflage.

ALBERT: But how do you keep it secret?

ME: Only the Doctor can open it and get in there.

ALBERT: Do you use your sonic screwdriver?

ME: He has a key for the TARDIS.

ALBERT: Oh.

ME: Do I look any different?

ALBERT: Yes, your hair looks Irish.

1 5

DOUBLE, DOUBLE, TOIL
AND TROUBLE

Early in my career, I was cast in a play by the director Sam Mendes. Then, all of a sudden, I was out of it. He sent me a letter – 'Let me explain to you . . . ' He told me all about the difficulty of casting a new play, the ins and outs, how these things work.

I wrote back: 'No, let me explain to you about paying the rent for my bedsit.'

Actors don't tend to be boat-rockers. They might want to impart a little motion, but they'd be worried they'd be thrown overboard somewhere down the road. There is a definite idea that you can say and do what you want to actors because they are desperate for work. I was very quick to say, 'I'm not that desperate.'

The attitude exists that, in the relationship between producer, director and actor, they are the adults and we are the children. I agree, actors can behave like children, they can be spoilt – but not this one, and not a lot of others I know. A working relationship can't operate on a basis of master and servant. If a director, or anyone else on set, comes in and has bad manners, then chances are they'll hear from me.

This idea that actors can be manipulated and pushed around

to suit the agendas of others irritates me. On *Shallow Grave*, prior to the shoot, myself, Ewan McGregor and Kerry Fox lived in a flat together for a week. We rehearsed, read scenes, and got to know each other. I considered it to be a budgetary and practical arrangement, but after the film came out Danny talked about it as being a social experiment, which I objected to because to me it was like the director playing God. If Danny wanted to conduct an experiment to gauge our reaction and interaction to one another, he should have told us. Had I known, I would doubtless have gained something from the situation. Danny, I expect, would argue otherwise, that the actors wouldn't get it. Well, I'm more intelligent than that. As it turned out, Danny's plan was counterproductive because all it did was give myself, Kerry and Ewan a week to realise we didn't like each other very much and didn't get on. We had entirely different backgrounds, approaches to acting, and sensibilities. All three of us were also very, very ambitious and insecure with it. Danny would probably argue that that tension then manifested itself on screen. I think that's bollocks. This idea of pitting one actor against another is dangerous, manipulative and patronising. The film would have been better without all that nonsense.

I'm not alone in feeling dismayed at misplaced directorial interference. Anthony Hopkins once arranged for the cast of *Frankenstein* to go for a Chinese meal during rehearsals. Anthony received a message from Francis Ford Coppola: 'Francis doesn't want you to go for a Chinese meal,' it read, 'because he feels it would break the atmosphere.'

Anthony Hopkins' reaction was simple – 'Bollocks, we're going for a Chinese meal.'

I'm not sure from where Anthony Hopkins got his instinct to challenge, but I know where mine came from. I remember a bloke approached me in the street in the early 2000s.

'You're Ronnie Ecc's lad, aren't you?'

'That's right.'

'I used to work with your dad. He was a great bloke to work for, but if he felt something was wrong he couldn't leave it alone.' I thought, *That sounds exactly like him.* And there are plenty who will say it sounds exactly like me.

Loyalty was all to my mum and dad. If they saw something wrong, they would speak up. Mum in particular had a great emotional intelligence but both my parents were very good readers of character. My mum always said about my dad that he could really suss someone out sharpish. If he thought you were worth bothering with, you were his for ever, and if he didn't, forget it. It was all they had in a sense. They didn't have material things, but they had an inner dignity – 'This is my view of the world and you're not going to change it.'

The same has happened to me working in this industry. From the start, you make a choice. You either lie down or you do it differently. I did it differently. Financially, I have regrets, and for the opportunities I missed I have regrets. But in terms of my children, and them seeing the choices I made, like I saw the choices my parents made, I have none.

It's black and white. Loyalty is massive; don't let people push you around. Stand up for those people you are working with. Community and togetherness, that is my mum and dad, and I always felt it. Never once did Ronnie and Elsie come on set, but so much were they part of everything I did, they should have got a credit when the titles came up.

When I'd tell them some of the things that happened in the industry that I didn't like, they'd tell me, 'Be careful – keep your head down.' And I'd say to them, 'What would you have done?'

There'd be a pause. 'Ah, well . . . '

Dad recognised that I was a member of the awkward squad. I certainly recognised that in him. Whenever an issue arose, I felt his presence at my side. Just before I started on *Doctor Who*, I'd sued Working Title, one of the biggest filmmakers in the country, behind *Four Weddings and a Funeral*, and *Bridget Jones's Diary*. I had appeared as the Duke of Norfolk in Working Title's film *Elizabeth*. A book was then produced containing despicable allegations that I had threatened to break the writer's head open for suggesting I play the duke as impotent. A straight lie, and a deeply damaging one, personally and professionally, presented wholesale as the truth. Interesting also that they should choose to reduce me to, in their eyes, the lowest common denominator, a thuggish working-class stereotype, which tells you a lot about class in this country. That's what they imagined in me, although perhaps not when I ran rings around them with words.

I got a lawyer and we wrote Working Title a letter. Their response was to say the reference was a joke. My response was simple – 'I didn't think it was funny. My mum didn't think it was funny. I'll see you in the High Court.'

I was advised not to go through with it – 'It's Working Title, basically the only film production company in Britain. They'll never give you work.'

That was never going to wash. I took Working Title to the High Court, as well as the publishers and the writer, and won a public apology and substantial damages. I didn't sue Working Title for the money; I did it for the principle. I gave the damages to Sport Relief.

Working Title's actions were but nothing compared to those of Mirror Group and News International, both guilty of accessing my voicemail messages during the period in and around when I was in *Doctor Who*. Again I took legal action and won damages against both. And, again, going for the two biggest newspaper groups in the country might not have been deemed a great idea by some. But to me the most important thing has always been 'Can I look myself in the mirror?'

Working Title, News International, Mirror Group – what they had back from me was Salford, my dad and my mum. Joe Orton once said, 'Everything I do is about revenge.' He was a working-class Midlands boy. For me, when it came to reacting to those who felt they could walk all over me, there was definitely revenge on behalf of a family who had been institutionally stamped down over the decades and centuries. My mum would say, 'But, Chris, I didn't want revenge.' My dad might feel a bit different.

As an actor, I was never going to be a company man – I was always going to be Ronnie Ecc. I can trace that desire for truth right back to my very first role of any real significance. On *Let Him Have It*, I felt Derek Bentley's challenges were being romanticised and idealised in order to make them easily digestible. My argument was, and is, that you don't have to make a narrative palatable, you have to make it real, particularly when relating a working-class story, as Derek's was, for a working-class audience. Don't forget I had grown up watching important drama with my mother and father. I knew about the complexities of their responses, how sophisticated they were in perceiving moral grey areas. With Derek, that grey area was that he was probably violent and definitely difficult. But I felt the writers and director were so desperate to portray him as a victim that the film we should have been making was getting lost. It was like we were making a film for *Guardian* readers. I didn't grow up as a *Guardian* reader and I didn't grow up with a *Guardian* lifestyle. But I knew someone like Derek, and so did most people.

I began raising concerns on the set as soon as I could see the direction the film was taking. It was a constant tension between me and the director, Peter Medak, whom I both liked and respected. Peter had worked with Peter Sellers, so had dealt with far more complicated people than me. I just felt if he had listened more to my instinct about revealing a darker side of Derek, *Let Him Have It* would have been a far more challenging end product.

In a way, *Let Him Have It* was an example of the British film industry bowing to American values. I hate *Forrest Gump*. I would like to burn every single copy of that film for the way it treats both mental health issues and women. A sexually free female character who ends up with AIDS? That tells you everything. I wanted to make an angrier, more polemical, more complicated film about a young man who deserved more than just to have the label 'simple' pinned to his lapel.

For me, the best film about capital punishment is Krzysztof Kieślowski's *A Short Film About Killing*. At its centre is a youth, not unlike Derek Bentley, who actually does senselessly murder somebody. He is a profoundly unsympathetic character and yet when they hang him, as a viewer, we feel it is wrong. We are taken on a much more complex journey. I felt I was betraying the working-class experience with my portrayal of Derek. One reviewer said I was a little bit too Smike-like, referencing the character, thought of as good-hearted but 'simple-minded', from *Nicholas Nickleby*. He was right. There was too much pathos up front, so the shock of Derek's murder by the state wasn't heightened; it was lessened. Derek wasn't Bambi, he was much more intricate, and I made my feelings known. Certain people around me, and I was having the same conversation in my head, were telling me, 'This is your big break – don't fuck it up.' But a big break at the expense of what? The truth? That sounds pompous, but it's how I was, and still am.

It wasn't an easy position to occupy. Derek's sister, Iris, quite understandably, didn't want any of her brother's shadow shown. To her, the story was straightforward – Derek's victimisation and betrayal by the state. She didn't want some unknown actor turning up and playing him 'unsympathetically'. But I felt we were letting Derek down, we were letting the audience down, and we were letting the argument about capital punishment down if we sentimentalised him. I have always been deeply understanding of the fact that, when you are dealing with real people, it matters so much.

This 'attitude' was coming from a 26-year-old bloke who'd been unemployed for three years, couldn't get arrested, let alone a part, but that was me, and I have to say I still think I was right. People don't remember *Let Him Have It*. The film has some kind of a legacy, but it is largely forgotten. *Dance with a Stranger*, about Ruth Ellis, the last woman to be executed in the United Kingdom, on the other hand, is not largely forgotten, and that's because of the intricacy of the way her story is told allied to Miranda Richardson's incredible performance. I have to put my hand up and say my performance in *Let Him Have It* is, at best, a C. If Gary Oldman or Daniel Day-Lewis had played the part, it would have been an A.

I criticised the film before it came out and writers Robert Wade and Neil Purvis were, justifiably, unhappy that I did so. From a business point of view, it didn't make great sense. Time has proven their outlook on films correct. Look where they are, look where I am. They now write the Bond movies. My own film work is a little more niche. But in terms of my sense of what is plain right, they are wrong. I had no ambition to be Robert Wade and Neil Purvis and knew it right from the start. They're millionaires and I'm not. I'd sooner have my career than theirs.

While I have no idea what Iris felt about my performance, I do know she was pleased with the film overall. Paul Reynolds, who played Christopher Craig, the 16-year-old who was holding the gun when Derek shouted those infamous words, said to me recently, 'You were just so earnest, Chris – you've always been earnest,' and I think that earnestness was a comfort to Iris. I don't think she thought my accent was perfect, I don't think she thought I looked like her brother, and I don't think she thought I was a particularly great actor, but I was genuine in my attempted portrayal of her brother. I wasn't trying to cause trouble; I felt a duty to her, the working classes, and to people with learning disabilities and epilepsy.

While it's easy to idealise and make heroic my motives, within that desire to do the job right was also a definite element of self-sabotage, a sense that I shouldn't be playing the role in the first place because I wasn't good enough, was unable to handle the job. I was a young man myself at the time. I was very insecure, battling my anorexia. I was ambitious and felt already that I was in a position that my talent didn't merit, which is often when you get bad behaviour from actors. I felt I didn't deserve what I'd got.

Yes, I was standing up for what I thought was right, but, looking back, a part of me was speaking up because I was trying to get sacked. If, on the second day of filming on *Let Him Have It*, they'd told me to sod off, my initial thought would have been one of relief. I'd had a torturous journey with the part. I had numerous auditions, got it, went through everyone in my phone book, told them, 'I'm going to be a film star,' and then the project fell through. I had to ring everybody back and tell them, 'Actually, I'm not going to be a film star.' Eventually, the casting director, Lucy Bolton, who really championed me, rang me up and said there was a new director on board – the original, Alex Cox, had pulled out – and he wanted to audition me. I had to audition for a part I'd already won. I'd been through the mincer with *Let Him Have It* before it even started, as had Paul Reynolds, except he was more experienced than me while I was nobody from nowhere. At that point, I'd had two tiny parts on television. Three years before, I'd been on a building site. I was that classic example of not feeling I was good enough, but then again that emotion was useful in Derek. My own naivety and self-doubt mirrored his. That may well be true about conflicts I've had elsewhere, where disillusionment and a lack of self-worth have coexisted. What intrigues me is that such low self-esteem could exist alongside such determination.

Whatever my motivation, I came out of *Let Him Have It*, my first major piece of work, labelled as a fully signed up member of the awkward squad. 'Difficult.' 'Hard work.' But I managed to keep working. There are plenty of people in this industry who will never work with me again. Equally, there are plenty who have worked with me multiple times. That argues against me being difficult. I am only difficult if I see something I feel to be an abuse of power or principle. The worst abuses I've seen on film and television sets have been by directors. They're the ones with the power and so they're the ones who are going to be watched most vigilantly by me. If a director is out of order, I go for them. If they're suggesting to me how to play a character and at the same time are treating a script editor or whoever like a piece of shit, I'm not going to listen to them. Call it a working-class hangover if you want, but for me, attitude, as served up by those whose views are laced, wittingly or otherwise, with a certain view of a certain type of people, comes clad in a gauntlet. When confronted with bad attitude, I am never going to see it as anything other than a challenge. I have been in situations of high conflict throughout my career on television and film sets. Why should actors be silent? And why should others want us to be? Actors should have an opinion on what they're doing. They should be inquisitive. They should want to know why before they do something.

I have undoubtedly seriously damaged myself with my adherence to a set of basic principles. Time and again I have driven a wrecking ball through my own ambition. But if I get in my head that I'm right, I won't let it go. I can't turn a blind eye, to the extent it's almost like I've been drawn to conflict, fascinated by how it feels, fascinated by saying things that 'people like me' never should. If I was cleverer, I'd turn away, I would get along with everybody. If I'd done that, I'd be a multi-millionaire, but I can't and I'm not. I am what I am. Before my career had even started, I always harboured an idea that if you stay true to your-self, that same ethos will bleed through to your work. That has sabotaged my career to some extent, but it's also in many ways made it, because in acting you are your work and if I become malleable to everybody, blind to my environment, in order to further myself, I will stop being me. When I go home and shut the door after a day's work, I have to live with myself. There have been some notable exceptions, but the vast majority of the work I've done has left me feeling personally comfortable. I have self-pride. Had I played a more professional game, my view of myself would definitely be a lot dingier.

Compromise, full stop, has only served to push my career backwards. The cynical career choices I've made have always rebounded. *Gone in 60 Seconds* (the ultimate metaphor for my chances in Hollywood) and *GI Joe* were both films taken for the wrong reason. Then there's *The Invisible Circus*, of which the *Observer* film critic Philip French, someone I read avidly, commented, 'This film contains an extraordinarily bad performance by Christopher Eccleston.' He's right. Again, compromise. I've given terrible performances in American films because they've been badly written, nakedly about making money, and have meant precisely nothing to me. At that point, a film becomes a hollow experience and consequently a hollow performance. I deserved every criticism that came my way for those films. I knew I was bad when I was making them. I was under no illusions that I was totally lost as a performer and a traitor to my true self. Sam Brookes in *Sight and Sound* said of my performance in *Gone in 60 Seconds*, 'Eccleston frozen with his own self-hatred.' He wasn't wrong. I hated myself so much I could barely look at my own reflection without wincing.

When I looked at the reception for those films, I had only one thought – *You've killed your film career. And you've done so by going against your gut instinct, which was not to go for the money.* I was influenced by agents but in the end it was my decision. I let myself be pushed. In so doing, I flattened my film opportunities under a stone. I pushed my career and my self-esteem down a hole. It hurt when I landed and it still does. Up until then my reputation as a film actor was relatively intact. *Jude* didn't make any money but was well regarded within serious film-making circles, as were *Let Him Have It*, *Shallow Grave* and *Elizabeth*, the latter despite it being nonsense historically and severely anti-Catholic, saved by a brilliant, luminous performance from Cate Blanchett. Those films gave me a cache, and then, idiotically, I took *Gone in 60 Seconds*. From that moment onwards, in Hollywood terms, I was just a low-rent villain. The only positive I can take from the whole experience is that I was allowed to portray Raymond Calitri as I saw him. The idea of a Salford accent in a Nicholas Cage film really appealed to me, and so that's what I gave him. I loved the fact that when I opened my mouth, what would come out would not be the stereotyped cockney gangster or an adopted American drawl, but me. Jerry Bruckheimer, the producer, never said anything about it, so why not? Often American producers or directors think I'm Australian or Irish. They are not well attuned to accent. They only wanted me in *Gone in 60 Seconds* because they thought I made for a good bad guy in *Elizabeth*, but in *Elizabeth* I spoke classic received pronunciation. The fact remains, though, that with Raymond Calitri I cocked up my film career. All it takes is one wrong move.

I would return to the States after *Doctor Who*. Initially, I had an unexpectedly enjoyable feeling of starting again. I arrived with no baggage and went to auditions, which I didn't always have to do in Britain, where I was often offered parts or my agent would be asked, 'Would he mind reading?' It always made me laugh. 'Would I mind reading?' Of course not, it's what actors do – we audition for stuff. In the US, I was in and out of auditions like I was back at the beginning. I even auditioned for the role of George Washington. A lad from Salford going all the way to America and ending up playing the first president of the USA? That would have been a coup.

But the cartoon baddie of Raymond Calitri was stalking me all the way. The first major role I was offered was Sylar, the serial killer in the top-rating NBC sci-fi show *Heroes*. I said no; I didn't forever want to be the British actor playing the villain. The role of Sylar became iconic and the actor who took the part, Zachary Quinto, went on to play Spock in the *Star Trek* reboot, but it was genuinely important to me to challenge the LA industry's perception of the British guy as the baddie. That policy paid dividends to some degree when another role came up in *Heroes* for Claude Rains, the Invisible Man. My dad was his usual subtle self. 'You went all the way to Hollywood,' he pondered, 'and all you got was the Invisible Man?'

I attended the costume fitting only to find the show's writers and execs waiting for me. They said they wanted me to wear a scarf. I knew exactly why – *Doctor Who*. I wasn't going to do that. I didn't appreciate the self-referencing element. How was that going to help me create a new character? My objection made them sit up a little – 'This guy has got a mind of his own.' And one of the worst things you can have as an actor is a mind of your own. If you really want to climb the ladder, leave your brain at the studio door.

'I'm not doing it,' I told them. But you can't win with these people. They inserted the line 'Fantastic!' into the script. I didn't realise until too late that it was a trope from *Doctor Who*.

I received decent reviews for *Heroes* but basically all I was doing was repeating the performance I'd given for twenty years in Britain, in America, with a beard. The show's producers were never going to let me carry an episode, which was what I wanted, and what I was used to. Similarly, I didn't love the writing of *Heroes*. I didn't feel like I was making the standard of television that I was back home. I knew also that eventually they would turn my character into a rogue. In the end, that combination of doubts meant I just didn't go back. They kept asking me to return and I kept saying no, which really puzzled them, but the message I was putting out was that I needed better material.

I was used to making drama with a meaning and, therefore, it suited me when I picked up a very low-budget film called *New Orleans, Mon Amour*, set a year after Hurricane Katrina. There I was, with a head full of issues about myself and my career, in a disaster zone, a place absolutely in the grip of trauma. But in New Orleans, even in its darkest time, I saw an honesty and dignity that was lacking in LA. The culture was far more integrated and diverse, music on every corner, a million miles from the politics of showbusiness and television. I found myself once again believing in a project and threw my heart and soul into it. But similar work was thin on the ground and, back in LA, I was cast in a terrible film called *The Seeker: The Dark Is Rising* (The Dark Is Risible, as I prefer to call it), where I was complicit in letting myself be that character I was so hellbent on avoiding – the villain. We shot the film in Bucharest and I gave a terrible performance. I look back it at now in disbelief, but it's only with hindsight that I can also see I was working with zero belief in my ability. In *The Dark Is Rising*, where I really had to come up with the goods, I couldn't do it. My confidence had gone. The type of work I was finding in America wasn't me.

Again, as with the great British film stars of the '50s and '60s, when it comes to American cinema there's a part of me that feels I was born in the wrong era. The American films I love were made in the '50s, '40s and '30s. I feel also that my sensibilities are very European. Even the American theatre plays I've done, such as *A Streetcar Named Desire*, and those of Arthur Miller, I've never honestly felt I can get inside them like I could with, say, Molière. What I did love about the American film and TV industry, though, was the utter classlessness of it. I could play anything. Ours is a cottage industry and its less expansive outlook reflects as much. Class rules here, but not out there.

I wanted to come home, and the opportunity came when I was offered a part in *A Doll's House* at the Donmar Warehouse in Covent Garden. A year later, thanks once again to the genius writing of Jimmy McGovern, I was back on the BBC in *Accused*, for which I won an International Emmy for Best Actor playing a flawed and self-destructive working-class character – territory I understood. I was delighted to be back at the BBC. So much of the work I've truly loved has been with them. All I ever wanted to do was the likes of those great shows I'd worked on before, and my wishes were soon answered. I found myself handed an embarrassment of incredible parts. In quick succession, I was in *Accused*, *Lennon Naked* and *The Shadow Line*.

Of those three, it was playing John Lennon that really made me think, *I'm back*. Being given the opportunity to play a character of such complexity and torment was massive for me. I was back in Britain, working for the BBC, in a lead role that would be judged and analysed to the nth degree. From a career point of view, *Lennon Naked* told people that, yes, I'd been the Doctor, but now I was going to continue the challenging work I'd done before. It told me something else – that I had overcome a situation that all artists experience, a crisis of confidence, the same that I would, a few years later, face once again with *Macbeth*.

I could have taken an easier, slightly quieter route than one of the most famous people on earth, but I have got a considerable ego and I like taking on big roles. Of course, there was another consideration with John Lennon – he's a founder member of the awkward squad. There's some great footage in *Don't Look Back*, the '60s documentary that covers Bob Dylan's tour of England, where the singer starts treating the press as his equals instead of the fourth estate. There's a sequence where a photographer asks him to suck his Ray-Bans, the classic tortured poet pose. Dylan gives him a long and contemptuous stare. 'You suck 'em,' he tells him. Slowly, over a period of time, he starts giving journalists a hard time, and they're offended. Back then they were authority figures. Lennon watched Dylan bring them down a peg or two, then did it himself.

From an early age, I recognised Lennon had an attitude where he wasn't going to be moulded to fit other people's view of the world he occupied. As I gained a bit of renown myself, I also respected his healthy disregard for the less palatable side of the press, accustomed as I was to people's view of me, in particular my perceived working-class abrasiveness, so often being informed by a small number of journalists. Google my name along with the words 'angry', 'prickly', 'confrontational', and there will be dozens of pages to justify those terms. But under whose definition? I personally do not believe myself to be any of those things – unless someone pushes those buttons. Those labels are tossed around because I work in a middle-class industry, defined by middle-class values. I'll freely admit I have been all those things with journalists, but generally it's because their interview has come from a very middle-class standpoint. The crucible for me was my family and those like them, people who weren't just not given the tools to advancement and self-expression, but wilfully denied them. I would sit there with a journalist and think, *Right, you've ignored everybody I've come from. You're not going to do that with me, nor are you going to patronise me, nor are you going to put me in a box.*

A working-class journalist might have a very different take on things, but how often do you see them? So often there's a narrative about someone like me having a chip on their shoulder. Really? Would the same term be applied to a middle-class actor highlighting a societal injustice of which they had direct experience and knowledge? Saying people like me have a chip on their shoulder is just another way of keeping them down. 'What's their beef? What's up with them?' Chip on his shoulder? No. What I have is an authority and, in my view, a requirement to explain that there are institutions in this country that serve to keep working people down. If even the supposed egalitarian, 'eyes wide open' and honest world of the arts shuts its doors on the working class, then ask yourself what the hell is everything else like? It's like the other one I get, 'professional northerner'. Amazing how the word 'professional' is one of respect and esteem when it's applied to someone of a higher social background. For a working-class person it's applied only to mock and put down. That anger, which I'm feeling right now, isn't me being a bolshie working-class bloke, it's me reflecting a longstanding and still apparent injustice that affects those I love. If only they'd had my opportunities, if only they'd known themselves a little better. I'm not angry because I'm a man – a working-class man therefore 'unable' to control his emotions. I'm not angry because my 'ingrained working-class masculinity' doesn't allow me to express myself in a 'finer way'. I'm angry simply because it is wrong.

It's for the same reason that I've never bowed to the 'establishment' in television. Bear in mind that TV is a very small industry. Many of those at the top go to the same dinner parties, speaking to similar individuals from other channels. That's where a conversation develops – 'He's difficult, he's an arsehole.' That north London dinner party circuit has always been something I've avowedly tried to avoid. I was aware from the start that if you went to the right places you could further your career, but that scene, with its Oxbridge and old school tie element, made me feel nauseous, to the extent that me and my old acting mate Paul Higgins had a pact that if we met a casting director in a social situation we would be openly hostile in order to make them understand we weren't trying to stick our noses up their arse. I'm very proud to have made my way in the industry without any of those connections.

Raymond still follows me round, though. I was having a drink in Stratford-on-Avon recently and a guy came up to me – 'Oh, man, I loved you as Raymond Calitri in *Gone in 60 Seconds*.'

'But I was terrible.'

'I know. That's the thing about you in that film. You're so bad, it's good.'

16

STRANGLED AT BIRTH

Mum and Dad had only one picture of me acting on their wall: Jude.

When I was seven, I woke up in the middle of the night. I was going to the toilet when I heard Keith, who at the time was struggling with his reading and therefore his confidence, crying. I froze.

He was heaving sobs. 'I'm thick,' he was saying, 'I'm thick.'

I could hear my mum whispering, 'Now you listen to me. You are not thick. Don't let anyone ever say you are.'

It pierced me to the core hearing someone I loved very deeply say he was thick. And it moved me to hear my mum's impassioned defence of her child. It was a little snapshot both into parenting and my big brother, the product of an age-old pattern of children being taught to think they had no worth. I feel angry about that even now. My brother wasn't thick, he is actually a highly talented individual, an amazing builder. He's very visual and one of the most amazing things for me is to watch him as he takes a building in, working out how it was constructed from the ground up. He is also a brilliant artist. He once created a picture of George Best with his hair made of snakes and the rest formed of images of the footballer cut from popular magazines. Keith should have gone to art school, but it would never have occurred to him. Alan, meanwhile, could well have been an actor, but, eight years earlier than me, a significant timeframe in terms of self-expectation, it would never have occurred to him either. Art school? Drama school? It just wasn't what people did. But never was anyone in our house considered unworthy or thick. They were respected for what they could do, not dismissed for what they couldn't, or rather had never been given the chance. If only they'd had my opportunities, if only they'd known themselves a little better, but they weren't shown how to exploit their talent. A state-sponsored veil was drawn over it.

Mum in particular loved Jude. She identified quite fiercely with him. And so did I.

The part had come my way when I was in *Cracker*. Michael Winterbottom, who was directing an episode, was trying to get *Jude* off the ground. He mentioned the role to my agent and I went through the audition process. Rufus Sewell and Linus Roache were also in the frame. My view is I got the role because just looking at me I evoke someone who comes from peasant stock. By the same token, I'd heard enough stories of poverty and hopelessness even if I'd never lived it. I had lived a very comfortable life compared to my mum and dad and those who came before them.

I read with Kate Beckinsale and Kate Winslet, the latter securing the role of Sue. I was already a big Thomas Hardy fan from studying *Far from the Madding Crowd* in sixth form, but I didn't know *Jude the Obscure*. Obviously, once I realised it was a story of working-class exclusion, I understood exactly why Michael wanted me. For him, too, there was a personal connection. Michael was a normal lad from Blackburn who, against the odds, managed to get into Oxford University. The idea of a young man, an outsider, considered by many incapable and unworthy of attending such an institution, meant for him the film had an autobiographical feel.

Unlike Michael, Jude's own dreams of making something of his life amid the spires of Christminster (Hardy's Oxford) are left forever unfulfilled. The self-educated scholar he makes himself is dashed against the rocks of ingrained prejudice protecting the educational corridors from a tide of lowly inter-lopers. Instead, as a stonemason, Jude is kept physically and metaphorically on the outside of those grand buildings, leading to a key scene, which stands undoubtedly as one of the greatest moments of my career, when he graffities 'I have understanding as well as you' on the gates of a university college. I remember vividly the night we shot that sequence and how emotional I felt. When I wrote those words, I was doing so not just for Jude Fawley, but for my mum, dad, and the many, many others like them denied access, learning and expression across the gen-erations. To perform that scene was very, very profound, the words a monument to those fed through a system that not only strangled their dreams but knowingly made them feel foolish to have harboured any in the first place. Challenging the institu-tionally sanctioned smothering of working-class hope has been the driving force of my life. It is very clear to me that my mum and dad were handed a rudimentary education on purpose, kept in their place because they were intended for the factory and/or the cannon. And so, by extension, were me and my brothers.

Everywhere in *Jude* are scenes that link effortlessly, a mental hyperleap, to memories, situations; so poignant. When Jude is reading, learning, taking pleasure in words, that to me is my dad.

Ronnie read voraciously, as, interestingly, does my son Albert. The only time he's quiet is when he's got a book, at which point he becomes completely transformed and absorbed. I used to love reading to him – memories again of my dad and Huckleberry Finn – but now he wants to read for himself. It gives me great comfort to see him reading so avidly. I hope that he and Esme will be part of a society that respects knowledge and individuality and doesn't make people feel stigmatised for having any. That hope for the next generation, however, can never quell my deep-rooted anger about what happened to my mum and dad and how they were viewed by the middle and upper classes and society in general. They had a perceived notion of those two people. I know them in detail and they are extraordinary.

Bearing in mind where I was coming from, it would have been easy for me to overplay the raging young man figure that Jude presented, and no one was more aware of that than Michael. Early on in the process he jumped on me for my anger levels.

'I know what you can do,' he told me, 'I know what you can feel. But I don't want too much of it. There are times when that side of Jude will come out, but essentially he's a gentle soul. There is more subtlety to him.'

It was a good lesson for me. Michael wanted me to explore Jude's more sensitive side rather than it be one note. The Jude presented on screen, as we all are, is a complex emotional bundle, the culmination of me working not only with Michael, but Peter Flannery and Jimmy McGovern – *Hearts and Minds* with Jimmy; *Our Friends in the North* with Peter. Jude is a 10,000-piece jigsaw of Peter, Jimmy, Ronnie, Elsie, me, friends, relatives, characters – any working-class person.

Playing Jude was also a reminder of my own great fortune. I was one of the lucky ones, a working-class lad who had got to a position where I could play that character. I had benefitted from the Labour governments of the mid-'60s and early '70s, which meant that by the early '80s it was still possible for a kid like me to rise up the ladder. With university fees and constant austerity, those doors, sadly, have now closed again. The social revolution of the '60s is a long time ago.

For that reason, Jude's experience is closer to my dad's than to mine. *I* got the chance. My sense of injustice was on behalf of my parents. I was having experiences like filming *Jude* and my dad was stacking boxes. And yet he had the same level of intelligence, sensitivity and curiosity as me. The difference was timing.

Whether Dad had that sense of injustice himself is less clear. 'I'm in a warehouse stacking boxes and I'll do it the best that I can, and I'll do it with some relish and some dignity, but is this it?' Maybe. After all, get him at home and he'd be poring through that dictionary – 'Onomatopoeia – what does that mean?' But it's possible also that, thanks to decades of social conditioning, my parents had accepted their position and never questioned it. Why would they? That was their lot. That was how it was. They were frustrated, but the root causes were not analysed because they were buried beneath layers of social reality. I came along and questioned that lack of equality and subsequently was angry on their behalf. And I'm still angry on their behalf. When I made *Jude*, or any other socially challenging drama, I didn't want them to love me more, because I already knew they loved me, but I wanted to make them proud. When it came to my career choices, I always wanted to say, 'It's because of you. It's the way you brought me up.'

Unsurprising, then, that *Jude* felt like a very, very powerful thing to do. No acting required, it was all there on the page, all there on the wall. I was totally caught up in the importance of the film as a social, political and religious statement. It consumed me in a way with which I was unfamiliar. I've never worked with someone who stays in character, but on set some have actually told me that's what I do. I can kind of see it. I know that I chat to crew members as Chris between takes. I know that I go back to my trailer, check my phone, read the news or about United. But what I also know is that if you spend a day, as in *Jude*, exploring what it's like to discover your child has hanged himself and killed his half-brother and sister, you're going to carry that around. It does things to you rather than you doing it to yourself. I'd felt the same happening with Derek Bentley. While I was filming, Keith told me, 'You've changed your face, you're frowning,' which if you look at pictures of Derek he did all the time. I'm not a Method actor in any way, but it was my first sense that what a person does can take over the person who's doing it. Prior to filming, I'd made a conscious decision to personally involve myself in Derek. Aged nineteen, he had a mental age of eleven. My way into him was an emotional immaturity comparable with his. My secret, my emotional imbalance and my anorexia, both deeply shameful to me, is in that performance, my first instance of using something deeply personal to inform a role. But, invariably, whatever the job, I'd carry something of the day away with me, as would my dad, as does surely anybody whatever they do. Thankfully, I didn't have the same visceral life pressures to deal with as Dad, the stress of an inescapable working landscape coupled with the need to put food on the table. But I found them in *Jude*.

With *Jude*'s themes still, sadly, relevant to a modern audience, Michael also wanted it not to be a film trapped in its era. Liam Cunningham, as the teacher Phillotson, Kate Winslet and I were rehearsing one scene when Michael really got a grip on us.

'Why are you acting like you are in a period film?' His face was palpably shaking with frustration. He was absolutely right. He wanted to shoot a period film as Ken Loach would, hence the graphic childbirth scene, the intimacy of the sexual content.

I felt Michael's approach, a period film addressing the classic imbalance in this country, would make *Jude* a great critical success. I was also very, very ambitious at that time. I had plotted my way through the business to reach the point of being a lead in a film and I thought this was my take-off point. I'd seen Gary Oldman and Daniel Day-Lewis become major movie stars because of performances in small British films and, in my arrogance, I believed the exact same fate was awaiting me. The sound of that bubble bursting echoed from Christminster to Salford and back. I overheard somebody mention a review of *Jude* in *Variety*. They hadn't wanted me to see it as it was hard on me and hard on the film. My heart sank. But the more I thought about it, the more I'd had it coming. My performance in *Jude* is deeply flawed. As an actor, I was frozen in my own issues. I was anorexic. I wasn't good at intimacy. I was a depressive. I was unhappy. I was tight, an emotional mess. I didn't know how to enjoy my life. And I let all that invade Jude. As with *Let Him Have It*, I'd had an opportunity to deliver something extraordinary, and I didn't. I delivered something that was solid. I thought *Let Him Have It* was going to be my version of *Sid and Nancy* or *My Beautiful Launderette*. But I did not deliver in the way Gary Oldman and Daniel Day-Lewis can, and that's because, with the best will in the world, I'm not in their class, not as good an actor, or don't work as hard as them. I'm a decent actor, a good, solid actor, but I'm not touched with what they are. To use a football analogy, George Best was created in heaven, but Kevin Keegan made himself. I'm Kevin Keegan, and, like Keegan, I had a focus and a determination, but sometimes it wasn't quite enough.

Some observers also questioned mine and Kate's chemistry. We were friends, we liked each other, and got on really well, but I'm not sure I was ever really Kate's idea of Jude nor she my idea of Sue. Kate is a very beautiful woman, while Sue isn't described that way in the book. To me, what Jude is attracted to is her defiance, her intelligence, and fire, while the film puts great stock also in her beauty. I felt it weakened Jude that it looked initially like he'd gone for a pretty blonde when actually Sue is a proto-feminist, braver than him, more willing to challenge.

I also felt there was a double standard at work on *Jude* that sidelined its more radical agenda on sexual parity. There's a love scene in which Kate and I are fully nude. Michael came up to me afterwards – 'We have to go again because we saw your penis.' It frustrated me. They were, after all, showing everything of Kate. *Jude the Obscure* was a ground-breaking novel, the last Thomas Hardy ever wrote. He was so destroyed by the self-righteous conservative reaction that he never wrote another. *Jude the Obscure* was provocative. I wanted to push those boundaries. How could it be that we were showing Jude's children die, but then couldn't show his penis?

We went to Cannes with *Jude*. While we were shooting, Kate Winslet had been nominated for an Oscar for *Sense and Sensibility*. At the same time, Ewan McGregor was there on a junket for *Trainspotting*, very much the film of the festival. And there was me with a film about a bloke who's in love with his cousin, can't get into Oxford, and whose kid has hanged himself.

I had actually been offered the role of Begbie in *Trainspotting* and said no. Instead I sent Danny Boyle a letter outlining why I should be Renton. I don't have a problem with turning down Begbie because I've always really liked Robert Carlyle and I've always thought he's a better actor than me. I'd also worked with him on *Cracker* and felt he was one of us.

Myself and Kate went to do a press call. The paparazzi trained all their cameras on her. I was blinded as all the flashes went off. I couldn't see them and they didn't want to see me. As a young man, in comparison to Ewan, who was clearly going to be enormous, and alongside Kate, already established as an incredible Academy Award-nominated actress, I was invisible. I wasn't jealous. But I was acutely aware that it wasn't going to happen that way for me.

I'd had a similar experience with *Shallow Grave*. If I had been more business-savvy, I would have taken that performance, got myself a publicist, and flogged the arse off the good reviews I received. As it was, I slightly missed the boat. Danny was very, very angry with the American distributors. *Shallow Grave* was a massive hit in the UK and could have been a massive hit in the States but was handled badly. To some extent, I'm glad that boat sailed because, if I'd experienced what happened to Kate and Ewan, I don't know what would have happened to me.

George Foreman said the best thing that ever happened to him was getting beaten by Muhammad Ali because he was out of control with his arrogance. Take the anorexia and combine it with the fame that Ewan and Kate experienced, and I wouldn't have been able to handle it. Also, I'd already fallen in love with the scripts for *Our Friends in the North*. I'm sure in this day and age, my agent would say, 'Don't do the telly, darling, go after the film,' but my agent then, and my agent today, would know, with one or two notable errors of judgement, I will only ever do what matters to me. Some actors run their career with their head, others with their heart. Ewan McGregor has done some fantastic work and has had a great career. I have done some fantastic work and have had a great career. The difference is I haven't the kind of money he does or the cache to get the roles he does. Maybe a bit more head would have been useful at times.

Perhaps if *Jude* had come eighteen months later, it would have been seen in a different light. One senior exec at the American arm of Polygram, which co-produced the film, said to me, 'Chris, if *Jude* had come out after *Titanic* and *Elizabeth*, you and Kate would have probably got Oscar nominations. It's just how the business works.' I've had an amazing career but so many times I've watched that ship sail over the horizon. In all honesty, I'm not sure I've ever understood when I was in positions of influence, or 'on the rise', sidelined mentally as I was with my anorexia and other problems. The good part of that is that I've had to keep making interesting choices. Instead of trying to promote *Jude* all over the world, I did *Hillsborough* because I felt a moral imperative.

Kate is a great example of how, even with great success, you

Let Him Have It (1991). Derek's scaffold was the platform for my career — it was a huge responsibility. © Alamy

Cracker (1993–94). Bilborough's death scene in this show gave me a television career. © ITV/Shutterstock.com

Playing David Stephens in Danny Boyle's
Shallow Grave (1994). © Alamy

Hearts and Minds (1995). The best performance of my career so far.

Hillsborough (1996). The most important drama I have been, or will ever be, involved in.

Our Friends in the North (1996). Considered a landmark drama in British TV history and rightly so – the breadth of writer Peter Flannery's vision was extraordinary. © Alamy

Jude (1996). The only picture of me acting on Mum and Dad's wall was from *Jude*. © Alamy

Gone in 60 Seconds (2000). A terrible performance. I was informed recently that I was so bad in it, I'm good. I'm happy with that. © Alamy

Doctor Who (2005). I loved playing this character almost as much as I loathed the politics of making the show. © Alamy

The A Word (2016–present). I've never loved a character
and a show more. © Alamy

Macbeth (2018). To play Macbeth at the RSC was my
ultimate ambition. A deeply flawed performance
and production. © RSC

can maintain integrity. Just look at the choices of films she's made. She's played some incredible roles, especially considering the limitations of parts for females in the industry.

Jude might not have taken me where I thought it would from a career point of view, it might not have been viewed by others as I viewed it, but there is one review I hold dear. Mum and Dad went to see the film in Bolton, a midweek matinee with only two other people in the cinema. As they were walking out, my dad turned to the other couple.

'Did you enjoy that?'

'Yes,' they replied.

'That's my lad,' he told them.

I'm not sure they believed him.

17

THE TRUTH

'Not both of them. They're all I've got.'

He handed me a faded Polaroid. On it was a picture of two girls. Their eyes were shut. The firmness of how they were closed told me they were dead. 'That's what it's about,' he told me.

Sarah Hicks and her sister Vicki died in pen three of the Leppings Lane end of Sheffield Wednesday's Hillsborough ground on 15 April 1989. Liverpool fans, the sisters, aged nineteen and fifteen, had, with great excitement, gone to watch their team's FA Cup semi-final with Nottingham Forest. Shortly after 3 p.m., they held each other as the life was crushed out of them. The picture Trevor Hicks was showing me was of his daughters in the morgue. I knew what he was telling me: 'You're going to act this, but it really happened to me.' He wasn't just telling me that for Sarah and Vicki; he was telling me for all ninety-six victims of that unimaginably dreadful event.

Seven years earlier, I'd been playing Pablo Gonzalez in *A Streetcar Named Desire*, my first professional job, at the Bristol Old Vic. We had a Saturday matinee starting at 2.30 p.m. and during the show, as we entered and exited the stage, we could see a terrible tragedy unfolding on the TV in the dressing room. I couldn't believe what I was watching. Bodies were being carried across the pitch on advertising hoardings by fans. I was absolutely stunned. Like everyone else, I was asking over and over again, 'How has this happened?'

The Sun then took over with its foul and despicable lies of 'the fans were pickpocketing the dead, pissing on the police – they'd forced the gate'. In the Thatcherite language of the day, Liverpool was a place of feckless, lazy layabouts. A bunch of thieves, spongers and cheats. The Sun took that narrative and blithely smeared the name of a city lost in grief in the most sickeningly awful of ways.

I was reading The Guardian at that time so was aware of an alternative voice. I was already imbued with a profound distrust of The Sun and a hatred of its toxic disdain for the working class, masked, as ever, in a tub-thumping right-wing rhetoric. But the damage was done, and only with time did it start to emerge that the Hillsborough families were victims of an industrial-scale institutional injustice dripped down from the very highest level. Margaret Thatcher was only too happy to ally herself with the self-same South Yorkshire police force that, just a few years previously, had broken the miners for her. Thankfully, there will always be those dedicated to scratching beneath the surface. The investigative work of academic and author Phil Scraton was key to uncovering what really happened that day. Scraton's book Hillsborough: The Truth is widely accepted as the definitive account of the disaster and its aftermath, focusing on the inadequacies of the police investigations, official inquiries and inquests, and revealing the extent of the systemic review and alteration of the statements of South Yorkshire police officers. It also detailed the treatment of the bereaved in the immediate aftermath of the disaster and the inhumanity of the body-identification process.

Like most people, I'd struggled to comprehend the scale of the emotional pain of those involved in Hillsborough; not just the families, but those who witnessed those terrible events, and the tens of thousands more deeply affected across Liverpool. While Hillsborough had shocked and revulsed me, I, like the rest of the country, had got on with my life. And then, seven years on, I was contacted by a producer. The Hillsborough Family Support Group had approached Jimmy McGovern, himself a Liverpudlian, and asked, 'Will you tell our story?' Jimmy didn't need asking twice. And when I was asked to take the role of Trevor, neither did I. But it was important to me that Trevor should give me his blessing. Morally and ethically, there was no way I could do it otherwise. I wanted to square it with him, at the simplest level to ask, 'Is it all right?' That's not something that drama school had taught me; it was the way Mum and Dad had brought me up. If I was going to start digging over someone's uncommon grief, there was no way I could possibly broach doing so without speaking to that person first. I'd felt exactly the same three years before with Iris Bentley.

It was when I went to see Trevor that he showed me the picture of Vicki and Sarah. He had a room in his home that contained all the information and documentation surrounding the tragedy. I was already aware of the responsibility of playing someone who had experienced a profound personal loss. Now, though, in Trevor's home, surrounded by the tangible memories, presence, of his girls, I felt that responsibility acutely. It was entirely right that I should do so. I was thirty-two, and a young thirty-two – childless too. What did I know of Trevor's experience? He was reinforcing in me the reality of it.

As I got to know Trevor better, I gained emotional knowledge as well as what was required from a purely acting point of view – mannerism, expression and accent. But I felt it was equally important to have a panoramic view of his life. Trevor differed geographically from a lot of the other relatives in that he was a businessman who lived in Middlesex. He was an establishment man who believed in the establishment – the police, Conservative Party, and judicial system. That same establishment had killed his daughters and then told him they had killed each other and themselves. Despite that, Trevor maintained dignity at all times. He kept his composure and pursued a plan of using the establishment way against the establishment. He felt that if the families ranted, raved and ultimately disintegrated, then those with something to hide had got them exactly where they wanted. If an external body, i.e. the judiciary, does not perform its role, people turn on one another and are weakened. Those in the establishment hope for that. It cements their power and position. That's what injustice does: it creates more and more injustice, belief that is fractured and broken. But the Hillsborough Family Support Group still gathers today. They've had their ups and downs, but they are still unified. Within that group, as they sought justice, were all kinds of different standpoints, all coming from people who were emotionally fraught, grieving deeply. Trevor himself could, quite justifiably, have been consumed with a rage so blinding that fighting for justice would have been impossible. That day in Sheffield, stood in the half-empty paddock next to the murderously packed one in which Sarah and Vicki perished, he attempted to draw a policeman's attention to the plight of his daughters and those suffering with them. He was told to 'Shut your fucking prattle'. He then witnessed death all around him. He had post-traumatic stress disorder even before he had to deal with the death of Sarah and Vicki.

And yet together the families did it. And it was that endeavour, that pursuit of the truth, that myself and Annabelle Apsion, who played Jenni Hicks, Trevor's then wife, came to understand as we met not only Trevor and Jenni but others who had lost children, including Eddie Spearritt, who went through the abject despair of seeing his 14-year-old son Adam die in his arms. I found it hard then to imagine how he dealt with his loss. Now, as a father, I find it impossible. The same can be said for Trevor and Jenni. That they could carry on at all is a source of wonder to some. They have, after all, lived through every parent's greatest terror, the thing that ends all human beings: the death of a child. I have said it myself – 'If my child died, that would be it.' But the last thing a child would want is for their mum or dad to die too. When it comes to Trevor and Jenni, and so many others, such as the parents of Tim Parry, killed aged just twelve by the IRA in Warrington in 1993, their strength is incredible, as is that of the mothers whose strained voices we sadly hear so often now, when, on the same night their child has been stabbed to death, find it in themselves to say, 'I forgive.' Astonishing.

Trevor and I were, on the face of it, worlds apart. But, as time went on, we found some odd common ground, such as always ordering the same thing off the menu, and occasionally adopting a bluff northern persona – Trevor is originally from North Yorkshire. Eventually, when he remarried – and I still find this remarkable – I would be best man at his wedding. But my surprise at being asked was born out of honour. I knew we had made a deeper emotional connection than that of simply actor/ subject. Movingly, I had my one and only spiritual experience with Trevor. I was struck that in the field next to his house were two racehorses. Maybe I was being pretentiously poetic, but in my head I thought, *Vicki, Sarah.* Trevor, being an engineer and very practical, had built a stable for them. I was visiting one time when we went out about 10 p.m. to get them in. They came straight over to Trevor. I'd never been that close to a racehorse. It was enormous, with a huge, long face. It made me think of a dinosaur. Trevor was stroking it, talking to me in his bluff way, when I noticed that his eyes were wet. At that moment, I became aware of something in Trevor, an unimaginably deep wound that, for the rest of us, unless we've been through it, is just beyond comprehension. It seemed to me that the horse was communing with Trevor, drawing the emotion from him, to the extent the animal was actually vibrating. Then the horse seemed to create a circle between me, Trevor, and it. There were a thousand questions in my head – 'Is this happening? What am I feeling here? What is going on? Does Trevor know what this horse is doing? Does the horse know?' It was as though the animal was running the entire thing. And then the circle broke and that was it. It remains the only supernatural thing that has ever happened to me. Only years later did I hear about equine therapy and its benefits to disturbed adults and children.

Maybe Trevor did that often, went out and found something soothing in this vast horse. I just happened to be there to witness it that one time. I felt what that experience gave me was an affirmation that what had happened between me and Trevor was positive. That was important to me. I had found it hard to reconcile that our friendship had arisen out of the death of his two daughters, just the same as Derek Bentley's scaffold had been the launchpad for my career. I'm being a little melodramatic there, but it's only natural to make that connection. It had taken other people's deep distress to place me on film representing them or their family.

When it came to the demand for truth, the drama only made a small contribution, but it was, nevertheless, a contribution. After it was broadcast, there were questions asked in the House of Commons. If nothing else, the anger of the families felt expressed, reinforced further by the disgust of millions that they, and therefore the memories of their loved ones, should have been cast aside by those in authority in such a hideously insulting and grotesquely insensitive way. As so often, names had been besmirched, lives dismissed, to protect those in power. The truth is now out. As tends to be the case with high-level scandals, it has taken thirty years to do so. In that time, evidence is lost, memories become hazy, key figures die, and mass outcry is distilled. The self-protectionism of the powerbrokers is clinical in its cynicism. The emergence of the truth has appeased the pain a little, but it still exists in stark measure. Thousands of ordinary people live the torture of Hillsborough every day, and that emotional tautness continues to cascade down through the generations.

I have a photograph on my fridge of me trying to turn myself into Trevor Hicks. I took it on the way to meet him that first time. But I could never turn myself into Trevor Hicks. Only he knows what it is to be him, just as only the other relatives know what it is to be themselves. All we can do is pay them the respect of remembering, and of seeking to understand.

Hillsborough is the performance that gives me most personal fulfilment. I wanted to be in dramas that prompted questions to be asked in high places, that caused embarrassment for the country's all-powerful elites, the same as had happened in the wake of *Cathy Come Home*, *Boys from the Blackstuff* and *The Spongers*, my favourite drama of all time, a classic *Play For Today*, written by Jim Allen and directed by Roland Joffé, set against the backdrop of the Queen's Silver Jubilee, which follows a young mother's spiral as she and her children are battered into an early grave by welfare cuts. Right from the start I wanted to be in dramas like that – dramas that matter. That's what I wanted to do then and that's still what I want to do now.

Roles such as Trevor Hicks have given a drive to my career. I have never felt that acting is a proper job. My mum, dad and my brothers grafted manually and so I went into acting with the attitude that it was a little bit indulgent. There was a sense of guilt that I had got to do things they hadn't. I felt a certain amount of embarrassment, shame and unmanliness about becoming an actor, and the antidote to that, for me, was to do work that I thought was valuable. I was determined that my output should in some way matter. So, of course, I felt a duty to do things like *Hearts and Minds*, which highlighted the abandonment of the working class in the education system, and feel filthy when I did things like *Gone in 60 Seconds*, which highlighted the abandonment of my principles. On a selfish basis, *Hillsborough*, and other similar projects, made me feel better about doing what I thought, in what I now know to be my ignorance and innocence, wasn't a real man's job.

At the same time, right from when I can remember, I was massively impacted upon by television as viewed by my mum

and dad. When it came to TV, they were nothing if not consistent. The set was only on if there was something worth watching
and that meant good drama, sport, news and documentaries.
Television in our house was there to entertain, inform and
challenge. It wasn't there to be moving wallpaper. Definitely
no soaps. My mum and dad were violently opposed to watching
soaps. *Coronation Street* in particular was loathed. We were from
Salford and so we had two constant problems with those who
made *Coronation Street*. One: were they laughing at us? And
two: if they thought *Coronation Street* was representative of our
lives, they didn't know what they were talking about. People
still have an idea that soap operas – *Emmerdale*, *EastEnders*, all
that bollocks – give working-class people a voice. They don't.
They're just fantasy horseshit. Pointless. Irrelevant. Mum and
Dad embraced the Dennis Potter view, that television is a way
the working classes can better themselves. Potter described it
as 'their window on the world'. Reflecting its sausage-machine
output, he also called it the 'idiot lantern'. Mum and Dad never
watched it as the latter. They were both autodidacts, always
wanting to use every part of their mind, and that influenced
me hugely. I knew in particular the power of TV for people
who didn't have season tickets for the laughably titled National
Theatre or enough money to go to the pictures. Potter knew
it too. He believed in television as an absolute instrument for
education and enlightenment. That's how it had come into
our home and how I had observed my mum and dad watching
it. *The Spongers*, for instance, had destroyed my mum, just
as the increasing numbers of dramas featuring homosexual-
ity had challenged my dad. For Dad – as perhaps it was for
homosexuals when finally they saw themselves represented

realistically on TV after years of being little more than sitcom stereotypes – television, done properly, delivered a metaphor for real life. For a man who I never heard use the phrase 'working class', television was definitely an expression of his sense that he was born into an unequal society, expressed obliquely in ways such as siding with the native Americans in a western. Dad was a man who enjoyed seeing an abuse of power turned around. Every week, for example, we'd watch *Branded*, a black-and-white American series about an army officer wrongly court-martialled for cowardice, and his fight for justice. It was basic good versus bad, right versus wrong. I learned so much about him from those precious times in front of the TV and developed a similar love of drama with a socially relevant edge.

As well as *The Spongers*, which I watched when I was thirteen, the drama that really pierced me as a kid was *Kes*, Ken Loach's telling of Barry Hines's amazing story of a young boy with a wonderful gift, an intuitive relationship with a kestrel, a relationship doomed, as is his own life, to the dustbin. It's Loach's greatest film, where his politics and poetry mix perfectly. I saw it first at the pictures, Unit 4 in Walkden, when I was about eight. I saw it again not long after on BBC Two, back when it used to show great films. It struck me how the light in the film was just the same as on my estate. I came later to understand that was because they were shooting with available light, like a documentary. But to me it was revelatory. That light, same as above those council houses in Little Hulton, was something I never countenanced seeing at the cinema. Same with the everyday dynamics of a working-class upbringing, the mocking, the casual violence, the cruelty in the showers after a game of football – I'd never seen any of it captured on screen. *Kes* changed my entire idea of what film was, as did *Blackstuff* and *The Spongers* with television. Drama, made for a mass audience, could actually have a realist element. It was then I saw what acting could be. And it was precisely those experiences that led me, on my first major acting job, to draw a line on *Let Him Have It*, to stand up and say, 'No, Derek's not like that.'

Television and film have power. Given the opportunity, it would be remiss not to use it. *Hillsborough* represented a miscarriage of justice and so did *Let Him Have It*. Both those dramas were in effect part of the process of righting a vast and deep-seated wrong. It took another twenty years for an inquest jury to find those ninety-six Liverpool fans were unlawfully killed. Everything that was said in Jimmy McGovern's drama was proven to be true. In 1998, five years after *Let Him Have It*, and forty-five years after his trial, the Court of Appeal quashed Derek Bentley's conviction for murder. Sadly, his sister Iris never lived to see the day. She died of cancer the year before.

So it feels entirely natural for me to pursue political and societal topics in television. I will always seek them out. It's impossible for me to do otherwise. I appreciate drama when it speaks truth, so of course I'm going to be a pain-in-the-arse social campaigner. Of course I am.

To this day, I think the job of film, theatre and TV is to give a voice to those who have none.

Hopefully that voice is present in at least some of the work I have done.

18

MY FRIENDS IN THE NORTH

My mum looked at me. 'You know you keep getting all these funny parts? It's not because of us, is it?'

I was experiencing a rush of instinct. Lying in my bedsit, I was perusing the script, laid out on blue paper, for *Cracker*. Three pages into episode one was a line – 'I rehearsed the death of my father for years.'

I had one thought: *I'm in.*

Cracker marked the beginning of my relationship with Jimmy McGovern, the writer I've worked with more than any other. The line wasn't particularly significant in the big scheme of the drama, but something told me it came right from Jimmy's life. And it came right from mine. I'd done the same right from being a little boy, preparing myself for my mum and dad's death. My mum told me I was always asking her, 'When will you die?' My kids do the same now, a natural curiosity. The difference is I asked a bit too much. I said to her straight once, 'What was I like as a child? Was I troubled?'

'No,' she said, 'you were a happy child, but you did ask me when I was going to die and what would happen a lot.'

'Did the twins do that?'

'No.'

I would still be doing it nearly twenty years on from *Cracker* when I had my breakdown. Sat on Mum's stairs, I started babbling to her that all my life I'd been scared of her dying.

'I know, Chris,' she said. 'You've always been like that.'

Anxiety. Not curiosity. So when I saw Jimmy's line, I thought straight away, *I've got to work with this writer.*

That was a decision made on pure emotion. In all honesty, the role itself, DCI Bilborough, I never really rated. I knew, however, that this was a series that was going to say something. *Play for Today* and its ilk had long gone by the mid-'90s. TV had changed, and social reality was deemed dull, dry and unstarry. The only way Jimmy, and others like him, could write about deep social issues and get them on TV was by creating a Trojan Horse. In Jimmy's case, he gave ITV what they wanted, a cop show, and slipped in the social issues around it. Jimmy was forever one step ahead of the game. There would have been no drama about Hillsborough without *Cracker*. With Robert Carlyle's traumatised antiauthoritarian killer, Jimmy broached the subject first right there.

Cracker was a classic of its form. As much as I knew the show would be dominated by Robbie Coltrane as Fitz, an incredible part, and as much as I didn't wish to play second fiddle (I wanted the part of Fitz and I told Jimmy as much), I wanted to be part of something that had a voice shouting far, far louder than another formulaic detective drama. *Cracker?* That's not like any police procedural I've ever seen, and Jimmy had no intention of it ever being that way. The first thing he ever said to me was, 'I really liked that thing you did about the skinhead.' He was referring to a twenty-minute short called *Business with Friends* in which I played a Nazi skinhead. He was sending me a message. I was playing a TV cop, but he wanted me to know this wasn't *Midsomer Murders* – 'Whatever you were doing there, Chris, I want that.' The fact he'd seen this very obscure piece of work of mine was very important. It told him a lot about me, and it told me that he was a man who wanted very much more than bland surface character.

Despite my respect for Jimmy's cunning, his absolute adherence to a reformative ethos, I left *Cracker* on purpose after one series. We had actors coming in like Robert Carlyle, Andrew Tiernan and Susan Lynch playing fantastically complex antagonists, Robbie Coltrane with the part of a lifetime, and what was I? A TV cop? I wanted to play leads in Jimmy's dramas, not plot characters. I wanted to be at the epicentre of shows highlighting institutional and political rancidity and social injustice. When I said I was going, no one on the show could believe it. But I wasn't stupid. For one thing, I knew I'd get a good ending, the associated attention acting as a springboard for my ambition. For another, I knew it would appeal to Jimmy's sense of the perverse, because back then killing off a main character so early into the life of a series just wasn't the done thing. More recently I did it with *Fortitude*, the psychological thriller set in the Arctic. But by then, killing off major actors early on was vogue. We'd seen it with Sean Bean in *Game of Thrones* and Jed Mercurio had made it a feature of *Line of Duty*. I didn't just let them do that to me in *Fortitude*, I positively enjoyed it. I liked the audacity of it and got to spend an afternoon with Michael Gambon. It appeals to me to surprise an audience, and with *Cracker* I knew I'd get a lot more attention than if I stayed. That was the ruthless side to me. I knew almost instinctively how to manipulate the system. I knew how to look after myself, which came from my dad. I could have sat in *Cracker* for five series, but why would I? Money, yes. But I was ambitious for me, not my bank account. I wanted Robbie's part, but that position was intractable, and so I left.

My instinct was entirely right. I'll never forget the thrill of the night Bilborough died. Jimmy created the incredible ending I knew he would, and 13 million viewers watched my character perish in the street after being knifed by Robert Carlyle's vengeful killer. It was exactly the shock I knew it would be. I can imagine many actors watching would have been saying, 'I bet he didn't want to leave that series.' Wrong. That moment gave me my television career. I walked straight out of that show and my awkwardness, allied with how passionate I was about Jimmy's writing, put me straight in line for the lead in his next project, *Hearts and Minds*, exactly the kind of socially relevant and intensely multi-layered drama I so desired to be in. My character, Drew Mackenzie, was a young man who goes from working in a factory to being a teacher. It was autobiographical for Jimmy because that, essentially, is what happened to him. Unlike Jude, Drew does manage to scale the educational edifice, only to have his dream beaten out of him by the institutional self-preservation and paralysis he finds inside. He is, like me, my dad, and Jimmy, another fully paid-up member of the awkward squad. I've played a lot of working-class men who come up against compromise and deal with it the only way they know how – head on. They headbutt it. And Drew was no different. He was also, like my dad, a man angered by work who takes it out on his family. But the true brilliance of Jimmy is to bring not only ingrained prejudice against Drew into the piece, but to draw Drew into a race row of his own making. Jimmy gives the audience an incredible problem, because they thought Drew was the hero. No other writer would have done that.

Jimmy was such a find for me because until that point I didn't really have a direction. I wasn't going to do Chekhov or Shakespeare. I wasn't going to be auditioned for it and it wasn't a world I knew about. Then along came Jimmy who had all my influences – Dennis Potter, *Play for Today*, *Play of the Month*. He saw something in me, and that was my emotional attachment to words and language. He has the same and goes out of his way to find actors who share it. Jimmy's genius is that he writes in the rhythms of working-class speech and how we use language. Perhaps it's because we're told we don't really own language or verbal skills that we are able to articulate through our inarticulacy. We use language sparingly. Often speech is to be used quickly and briefly and like a weapon. You get in there before the next person. Language mirrors emotion, something else used sparingly. Someone once said to me, 'There's a lot of love in your family but not a lot of closeness.' It wasn't a criticism, it was an observation, and it was correct.

I built my reputation on Jimmy. I felt I'd found in him the perfect ally. He was a man who would always put the honesty of his work before anything else. He left *Brookside* because they wouldn't let him include a mention of the sinking of the *Belgrano*. He knew himself he was just trying to jemmy it in. What that told him was he needed to be off. He'd gone as far as he could. Honesty with Jimmy, always honesty, with those he works with as well as his writing. He's as critical of me, hard on me, as anybody. He hasn't always wanted me on board. He didn't want me as Trevor Hicks in *Hillsborough* because I was too young. He was right. He thought I didn't have the emotional depth. He was right. Jimmy wanted Tom Georgeson to play Trevor and I still think he was right. But the producer and director really wanted me and so I did it. On the other hand, when I was in *Sunday*, Jimmy's film about the Bloody Sunday killings, in which I played General Sir Robert Ford, Commander Land Forces Northern Ireland, he wanted me, but quite openly told me it was only because 'We need a star.' 'Forget your acting ability, I need a name.' Thanks. He redeemed himself slightly with probably the nicest thing that's ever happened to me as an actor. He rang my house one day to talk to me but instead got my dad.

'Your lad's a wonderful actor,' Jimmy told him.

My dad wasn't one to compliment, but he told me what Jimmy had said. The fact it had come from somebody within the industry, who spoke his language, was massive for him and, therefore, for me. Forget BAFTAs, Jimmy McGovern says you're OK to your dad – now that's big.

I felt exactly the same rush of instinct as with *Cracker* when I first read the scripts for *Our Friends in the North*. Danny Boyle had alerted me to the project. I was on the set of *Shallow Grave*, stood with him at a monitor, when suddenly he looked at me – 'I've seen some scripts you'll like.' I went straight into the office and rang my agent – '*Our Friends in the North* – can you get me in?' The chasing of something you want – exactly what my dad would have done. So thanks, Danny, for sounding the starting gun. When I saw the writer Peter Flannery's words, my gut instinct was confirmed. I had an immediate rush of recognition for what this was – social drama of the most ambitious and very highest order. The scene that really convinced me I wanted to be on board wasn't one I was involved in. It was an elderly Felix having a pit bull set on him after politely trying to negotiate with a thug in a block of flats. I was intrigued by what Peter

Flannery was highlighting – the working-classes turning on one another, the brutalisation of a man and his ideals, the ultimate failing of a system riven with corruption and hypocrisy. It didn't matter that I wasn't on screen. The point is that the scene made me think, *Something is being said here and I want to be part of it. This writer feels this very deeply, and so do I.*

This flurry of socially informed dramas meant, at that point in the '90s, I felt I was part of a movement akin to the actors of the '60s and the deeply politicised performers of the '70s and '80s – Roland Joffe, Jim Allen and Ken Loach to name but three – all deeply of the left, social campaigners as well as commentators. That feeling was further accentuated by the unarguable fact that what writers like Peter Flannery and Jimmy McGovern were doing was wholly out of kilter with the cultural movement of the day.

The rancid posturing of magazines like *Loaded*, I hated. It was nothing more than a cynical, exploitative packaging of the working class, combining supposed ignorance with consumerism. It may sound pompous, but to me that movement was a sell-out, a betrayal of the working classes, and I wanted no part of it. My dad was a man, not a lad. He liked a pint and he liked his football, but he also liked his dictionary.

I can see how it happened. A generation was saying, 'Throughout the '80s, you told us we were thick – so here we are.' I get it and I can deconstruct it. But my generation was going, 'I got a chance – I got a better chance than my mum and dad.' As the comedian Stewart Lee points out: in the '90s, being politically correct became uncool, while in the '80s it was a matter of pride. My adherence to those values means that *Trainspotting*, which became the visual expression of Cool

Britannia, was not the film I would have made about heroin, but my film would not have made money. The path of political astuteness I was treading in the '90s was out of style, but so be it. Again, it shows how brave it was to make a drama like *Our Friends in the North*. And I'd sooner be in *Our Friends in the North* than *Trainspotting*.

Look at the scene where all four of the original characters are together at the end. No mawkishness, no big speeches, we all just look at each other. Nothing said and yet everything said. The fact that I love that set-up speaks again of my European sensibilities because it's hard to find that subtlety of emotion in American drama. Peter Flannery's attitude to an audience is that wherever you are in life, it's not Disney. Life is compromise, life is a grey area, life is living with disappointment, and relishing what you've got. That's why Nicky was such an incredible character to inhabit. In his hopeless search for what he hasn't, he wrecks what he has. The scene in episode eight where he knowingly destroys his long-yearned-for relationship with Mary by having sex with a young student is just devastating.

On a personal level, I felt playing Nicky in his later years was a cautionary tale of what might have been and what possibly could be. At that point, I wasn't a middle-aged man. I felt like my life was mapped out for me if I wasn't careful. The regrets Nicky Hutchinson has in late middle age, I didn't want those. Indeed, I have been careful and so have missed those preordained trig points.

The parallels with me and my dad were also apparent – the arguments, the gulfs in attitude and opinion. The desire of the son to have his voice heard. The constant search for personal and emotional recognition. The difference between Nicky and Felix and me and Dad is that the fictional father-and-son relationship was much more damaged. Nicky wants his dad's attention, support, respect and love. He wants to finish the work his dad started politically. His dad's response to that is utterly dismissive. Nicky is the soul of the left's journey, and all his father can say is, 'You're wasting your life, son. Don't be like me.' Thankfully, while Dad and me never had a deep and searching discussion about our relationship and each other's part in it, via a somewhat circuitous and occasionally torturous route we reached a point of understanding in the end. With my dad, my idealism, my path, was completely supported. There wasn't an iota of disapproval and jealousy. Me and my dad always loved each other. We had our ups and downs, but I knew he loved me and he knew I loved him. Felix and Nicky's situation, however, is left unresolved. The minute Nicky tries to talk about his search for his dad's soul, in comes Felix with, 'You've always been a waste of time.' Brilliant, dramatic, poetic.

Then, with great tragi-poetry, just as Nicky is finally ready to confront his dad, to tell him that he should have encouraged his son to make his own mistakes rather than offer the constant and destructive message of, 'You're throwing away your life,' Felix goes vacant, lost to dementia – 'Who are you?' The conversation, at the very heart of their damaged relationship, can never be had. There we have drama that is so incredible, so cunning, in its creation.

Of course, at the time I was playing Nicky, my dad was, unbeknownst to us, in the foothills of his own dementia. Eventually, myself, Freda Dowie, who played Nicky's mum Florrie, and Peter Vaughan as Felix, would film the scene where he is put in care. Taking him, leaving him, going. There was part of me even then that could see that self-same scenario unfolding with my dad. I wasn't wrong. Within five years, I was reading the seven stages of dementia. A decade later, there he was in that home. There are times when life mimics art and art mimics life so much that you begin to forget where one ends and the other begins.

I consider my portrayal of Nicky as far too one note. I got nominated for a BAFTA and I've no idea why. I made a mistake apparent in a lot of my performances – solemn, pronouncement. If you look at what I did in *Our Friends in the North*, it's juvenilia.

Peter Flannery once said to me, 'You were very, very hard on Nicky. You always majored on his unsympathetic side.' Which is interesting, because I'm similarly unforgiving about myself. There are a lot of American actors whose on-screen persona is all, 'Love me, love me. Mother me, mother me.' In my desire not to be them, I went too far the other way – 'Hate me, hate me.' But again, that's about my attitude to audience. Their threshold for sympathy is much higher than many directors understand. After my issues with the filmmakers' view of Derek Bentley in *Let Him Have It*, I wasn't going to let that happen again. Nicky was going to be shown in his true complexity, a man who takes part in his own self-destruction. It comes as much from within as without. It's why I saw him as by far the most interesting character of the three male leads. Initially, they wanted me to audition for Geordie. But I felt Geordie was very much a victim of circumstance, of the system, something I'd already explored with Derek. I wanted to play someone who self-sabotages. Nicky messes himself up, much closer to me than Derek and, later, Jude was. I wouldn't have been crushed by the system – I'd have done it myself. That's why I wanted to play Nicky rather than the working-class guy lost in Trafalgar Square.

It's Nicky's idealism that leads him down the wrong path. That's why I see my performance as one note – there was a lot of righteous working-class anger. What was it Joni Mitchell said? 'All romantics meet the same fate someday. Cynical and drunk and boring someone in some dark café.'

There is another reason I couldn't have played Geordie. For that role, you need somebody with rock star sexual charisma. Daniel Craig has that, I don't. No way could I have done what he did.

The performances I really loved were those of Gina McKee and Mark Strong. Myself and Gina, I feel, were quite similar – we just turned up and did the job. Gina is a very private person, much more so than me, and oddly, considering the depth of our relationship on screen, I never really got to know her. I got to know Mary, her character, instead. We didn't socialise. On any job, I like to turn up, get the make-up on, and do it, and Gina was the same. Myself and Gina also shared a deep love of what Peter had written. I was very happy to be part of something I felt was part of my experience. Gina, too, had her roots in the story. She was from the north-east, the crucible of the drama, and her father was a miner – bear in mind the story covers the miners' strike, which was only twelve years previous. It felt to her, as with me, that the script resonated on a very personal level. That resonance is acutely delivered.

Myself and Mark Strong, meanwhile, didn't speak. We disliked and distrusted each other to the extent we didn't acknowledge one another's existence. We hated each other, but then our characters hated each other too. The only time we spoke was when we had lines. Whenever we had a scene together, we both understood the job. He and Gina gave the best performances in the series, in my opinion. I thought Mark was brilliant. I was deeply admiring of what he did with Tosker, a very unsympathetic character who, with great skill and talent, Mark allowed the audience to maintain some compassion for. But, personally, we had no time for each other. We were very young and immature. What the production had accrued was three very ambitious young men. I felt Mark was being competitive with me. I didn't get that from Dan. I think Mark thought I returned that competitiveness. I didn't – I was too busy competing with myself.

Mark and Dan were very close, so inevitably that affected my relationship with Dan. I didn't dislike Dan and I'd talk to him, but I don't think he particularly liked me. That's fine. It's unrealistic for every actor to get on during a production. Does everyone get on in the office or on the building site? There will be similar situations in changing rooms at all levels of football where people don't get on, or see rivalry where there isn't any. The point is you deliver on the pitch or on screen.

What united everyone on *Our Friends in the North* was the absolute knowledge that we were making something very important and of extreme quality. How could it be any other way? There were so many very bright people involved with it. Nicola Shindler, who now runs Red Productions, was script editor and co-producer, enormous in her close relationship with Peter Flannery and what it brought to the screen. Charlie Pattinson, the producer, would go on to produce other landmark TV shows such as *Shameless* and Jimmy McGovern's *The Lakes*. Gina McKee won the Best Actress BAFTA for Mary; Daniel Craig is James Bond; Mark Strong, too, is a major film star, and they are just the most visible faces of an incredible cast and behind the camera team.

I've always trusted my instinct about British television – I've not made many mistakes, recognise good writing, and know what I can do with it – so I wasn't in any way surprised with the reception *Our Friends in the North* received. The affection for the series is incredible. Only yesterday I was in a café and someone came up to me – 'I'll never forget *Our Friends in the North*.' I get that all the time, and I totally understand how and why people love it. I was part of it, and I love it too. It was nine months of my life when I could have been cashing in on my profile from *Shallow Grave*. Nowadays, that would be the option taken by 99 per cent of people. They want to be famous because celebrity and fame has been positioned right at the centre of our culture. When I came through, however, celebrity culture was in its infancy. Yes, I wanted to be famous, but I wanted to be famous for being a great actor. There is an option where you just go for fame, but I always wanted to be a tradesman, and slowly I'm getting there. Whether I'll actually get there, I'm unsure. Peter Vaughan was seventy-four on *Our Friends in the North* and he was still working away at it, and competitive with it. We both got nominated for the Best Actor BAFTA. I walked into the venue and there he was. 'Hello, Peter.' He gave me a little smile, one that just said enough. I would have loved a BAFTA, obviously, but I knew the flaws in my performance and in all honestly would have been embarrassed to win ahead of Peter. As it turned out, the debate was irrelevant. The late

Nigel Hawthorne won for his role in the medical drama *The Fragile Heart*, which made us both smile. Peter never got any of those major acting awards, and he too has gone now. I know, though, that there's a lot of Peter, not just the nose, that lives on in me. He's the actor I've worked with who I've learned the most from, not just in terms of acting but in standards. I was sat on the set once – we'd done our rehearsal, the camera was up, and the director of photography was in place – and Peter wanted to talk to me about a scene. It required him to walk in front of the camera to get to me. 'Crossing camera,' he said as he came across. 'Thank you, Peter,' said a voice. I watched as he did this. *Manners,* I thought. *Manners on set.* Not only did I love Peter's manners, but I knew also that, if he messed up a take, those same people he'd shown such respect to weren't going to be muttering about him under their breath. When I'm on set now, I do exactly the same as Peter. Some young actors take the attitude of being a little nonchalant on set. But it's always worth remembering that people are working when you're not. Peter applied to acting what I had already acquired from Mum and Dad, an enormous work ethic, manners, punctuality and bettering myself. I would always turn up on time on set and I would always have my lines learned. My rebellion came in questioning authority – but you always had to be there on time to do it otherwise you didn't have a leg to stand on.

Hang on, I've turned into Norman Tebbit. Nicky, I'm sorry.

I've never come close to anything as epic in its timeline as *Our Friends in the North*. The drama covered so much ground, four decades, from 1964 to 1995, and required so many shifts in character, appearance and costume that I felt like I was being paid to go back to drama school. When I talk about the wigs and the make-up, that's me getting in the criticism before anybody else does, although they did seem to convince. I once left the set when Nicky was at his oldest, fully padded up in character and in a grey wig and glasses, and went to an Italian restaurant next to the Crown Posada, a famous pub in Newcastle. The waitress was entirely different with me than if I'd gone as myself. Everyone else went on their own journey of transformation. There was the boldness of Dan, taken from sharp Soho suits to alcoholic destitution, and, finally, trailing hair and big glasses. Mark, meanwhile, travelled from one of the finest heads of hair ever seen on TV to an overfamiliar flirtation with male pattern baldness. For me, as ever, I looked to the writer for the physical inspiration for my character. Right from the start, I said to the make-up people, 'Let's get as close to Peter Flannery as we can.' Considering where we ended up, I'm not sure how flattered Peter will be with that revelation. I'm fifty-five now and realise the 50-year-old Nicky I portrayed aged thirty-one was bordering on decrepitude.

To have found one writer who would act as both ally and influence is amazing. I am fortunate enough to have found several. I first encountered Peter Bowker on *The King and Us*, a very low-budget drama for BBC Choice based loosely around the Manchester derby of 1974 that saw ex-red Denis Law score for City to send United down. It's not a football drama; it's about the era and growing up. I liked the sound of it, the fact it had a bit of comedy, and was my brothers' era rather than mine, and agreed to do it. Immediately I found so much in common with Peter. We have a similar attitude politically, are both runners (he wants to write a cameo in *The A Word* where he overtakes my fell-running character Maurice), and when it comes to football, we love Manchester United but hate the club. We also soon got to know each other well enough not to idealise our dads. We had a shorthand and that allowed us to talk. More than just his background, though, the connection I made was in his ability to sit outside a situation and observe, his incredible ability to capture language. Again, as with Jimmy, I understood the rhythm of his writing, not just the vernacular but the emotional. Peter is a man of immense humour, but it is the humour of nuance, the humour of communication (or lack of), allied to an incredible eye for the interlinked, and more than occasionally broken, chains of human relationship. I could see exactly where he was coming from with *The King and Us* and asked him to bear me in mind for anything else he might be writing. That 'anything else' would turn out to be *Flesh and Blood*, the story of a working-class Mancunian, Joe, adopted as a baby. When, after becoming a father himself, he feels a need to know more about his birth parents, he discovers both his mum and dad have learning disabilities. They'd had sex in a care home and, to cover up the scandal, a nurse had put her name down as Joe's birth mother.

Being part of the BBC's season of disability-themed pro-gramming, it was decided, entirely properly, that Joe's birth mum and dad, Janet and Harry, should be played by people with learning disabilities, the incredible Dorothy Cockin and Peter Kirby recruited from an amateur dramatics group in the north-west. My reaction on hearing about *Flesh and Blood* was immediate — 'I'm in.' That was a decision made as an actor doing a job, but clearly what I was doing was informed by my own lifelong desire to connect with my dad. Equally, clearly what Peter was doing was writing about was any man trying to communicate with his father. There is a universal truth that so many men feel the gulf between them and their dad is way too big to be breached. *Flesh and Blood* was the ultimate example of a man pleading, 'Please, please realise, you're my father.'

So invested was I in this idea of father/son connectivity that, the first time I saw Peter Kirby, who plays my character Joe's dad Harry, I turned to Julian Farino, the director, and said, 'He looks just like my dad.' Peter Kirby looks absolutely nothing like my dad. I was seeing something that wasn't there. Julian was delighted to hear of the resemblance, as, I'm sure, was the producer, for what it might bring to the party performance-wise, but it was simply a trick of an emotionally scrambled mind.

Peter Kirby did, though, become woven into my own life, as I did into his. I felt we had to if we were to make our inter-action believable, to make it work. It was a complex set-up. When myself and Peter were on camera, there were three things going on in every scene – my performance, Peter's per-formance, and my reaction to Peter's performance. At no point could I ever be sure what Peter was going to do or say. I also had to be proactive in keeping the scene going, delivering its nar-rative so it had a dramatic purpose and form. A lot of that was done by talking to Peter about his own life and weaving what I knew into the dialogue, not that he always played the game. Do a second take of a scene that involved asking him a question and there was a good chance he'd look at you like you were daft and say, 'I just told you!' A significant section of the drama was filmed at a social club evening for people with special needs. I was trying to film with Peter and in the background all I could hear was, 'It's him out of *Cracker*. He's in *Harry Potter* now.'

Flesh and Blood ended up winning two Royal Television Society Awards, Peter for best writer, and myself for best actor. Incredibly, I found myself up against Albert Finney, who was nominated for *The Gathering Storm*. When Albert's face came up on the screen, I was convinced he was going to win it. There is part of me that will never quite believe I won an acting award ahead of my hero.

Peter, for sure, deserved his award. He's an incredibly brave writer. He enters areas that others wouldn't even go near, let alone walk away from. He understands the need, not simply to give a voice to those with different lives, different needs, but to reveal them as themselves, not patronised, not moulded to suit preordained and stereotyped ideas of what makes good television. Look at Leon Harrop as Ralph in *The A Word* – the fact he has Down's syndrome is neither here nor there. Neither Peter Kirby in *Flesh and Blood* nor Leon have been defined by 'disability'. That suits me down to the ground. I have always had my eyes open – my mum and dad would always, always, encourage me to see the person first. Inclusivity is a word oft bandied around to the extent that cynics roll their eyes. It should never be seen as something tiresome, a box to be ticked, and then tacitly ignored. It is a real vital thing. If anything, it is me who has been included in Leon's life, not the other way round. He can do 'northern curmudgeon' as well as any actor I've ever known. It is Leon every time who delivers the chemistry that makes the scenes with him and Maurice so memorable. It is Leon who enriches those scenes as he enriches the world he occupies away from the camera.

The A Word says so much to me because it is, at its heart, about northern families and their inability to communicate.

Amid that carnage of stilted conversation, Leon is in fact the most open and honest of us all because he lacks our conditioned inhibition. It's that thing again – the limitations of communication within the confines of masculinity. That is what Peter is so very adept at writing about, the beauty being that he can find such great and poignant humour in it.

I don't have to go far to find Maurice – he is definitely, no shadow of a doubt, 100 per cent, a version of my dad: the unintentional comedy, the brusque insensitivity, the whole 'What? Me?' My dad always did it with a twinkle, and I try to do that with Maurice. He's cleverer than he lets on. There's a knowingness to Maurice.

It's clear I have been extremely fortunate to have appeared in some magnificent productions by some magnificent writers. It's not just me; there are many who recognise a brilliant complexity to those programmes, and that comes from the pen way before the camera. If an actor wants a career in film, they should probably kiss directors' arses a lot more than I have. I want to be successful, but not at the cost of why I started acting, which is to be original. Ongoing relationships with writers have delivered some of my best work on that score. They have delivered my career. Look at *Shallow Grave*. That film wasn't dependent on Kerry Fox, Ewan McGregor and me. They could just as easily have cast Kate Winslet, Robert Carlyle and Linus Roache. Actors are ten-a-penny. My performance in *Shallow Grave* is very well looked upon, but that's because it's very well written. I know, because I have worked in the industry, that there are hundreds of actors as good as me. I got the role, and if you get a role that's well written, basically all you've got to do is use your common sense as an actor and deliver it. The best actors know that.

Somebody came to see me in *Macbeth*. 'You were the best thing in it,' they said.

'Well, I had the best part,' I pointed out.

And I did. Purely because I was on stage so much, people might have made a judgement that I was the best. There's a huge amount of luck to what we do, and I am a good actor – there are a lot of good actors. I am also a good actor who used to have good angles, genetic gifts. And I am an actor who has always appreciated great writers.

There is one I have yet to work with, Mike Leigh. There'd have been a pleasant symmetry since he too was raised in Salford. Mike is another man of high principle. He thinks you have to come from working class to play working class. I think he's right. To have working class play working class makes for a richer performance. I certainly don't like to see middle-class actors playing working class. I always think I can see through it. And I don't like it in principle because they've got enough work anyway. But I do like it if one of us lot acts up a social class or two and really pulls it off. I think of it as revenge.

For me, the connection with a writer goes way beyond a script. I feel I understand writers in a way some actors don't. Or maybe it's just I take an interest in them. It's an immersive experience, which I attribute to my dad, his love of crosswords, books, opening the dictionary, spotting a word – 'Isn't this wonderful?' I can still feel the charged atmosphere of him reading to me in bed, his ability to inhabit those two particular books, *Tom Sawyer* and *Black Beauty*, the colour he brought to those stories. There was a point of connection in that room, as if our souls touched through the written word, and I think that very connection led directly to my fierce adherence to writers. My fall-outs on set have often been about defending the writer and their relationship with the audience. Russell T. Davies, Peter Bowker, Jimmy – I always feel they have a pact with the viewer that 'you are brighter than me'. Run-ins with directors have come when they've been simplifying the script or conjuring up visual clichés and asking me to act them, ignoring the complexity to the writing. Shortcuts. In the early days, Jimmy was always happy if I was on set because he knew if it came to it, I'd be another voice backing his corner, the Roy Keane to his Alex Ferguson. But I was standing up for the audience as well. In the James McTaggart Memorial Lecture that Dennis Potter gave in 1993, he talked about the audience's intelligence. I identified with every word. As a child, I sat in a room with my mum and dad and watched serious dramas and felt just how engaged they were, how concerned, and how complex their reactions were. I always regard the audience as my mum and dad – very, very sensitive, intuitive people.

It saddens me that TV drama covering social issues has slipped so far off the radar, and, no doubt, some remarkable writers with it. Peter Flannery, Peter Bowker and Jimmy McGovern have shown that television that covers real lives can, if written correctly, have wide appeal. Writers like Alan Bleasdale, who gave us *Boys from the Blackstuff*, and Jim Allen, who wrote *The Spongers*, were seen then and are seen now by some as soapboxing. They were doing nothing of the sort. They took people experiencing serious social issues and turned them into real multi-dimensional characters. Bleasdale didn't soapbox. His characters didn't deliver party political speeches. Why would they? That's not what happens in normal houses, normal lives. Instead, Bleasdale pursued the truisms of working-class existence. His characters were on the floor but he, and indeed they, had a fine line in tragi-comedy, and that, better than any big set speech, reflects working-class life. Peter does the same with *The A Word*. He highlights social discrepancy, but politics doesn't come into it. Alan Clarke was the same. He wrote and directed some of the most incredible works of social realism, but he didn't try to come down on left or right. With *Scum* he said, 'Here's what borstal's like.' Same with *Elephant*, about sectarian killings in Belfast. That's the gap he left when he died early. Jimmy McGovern is in that gap, but it's a very small space to get into, and it's getting smaller all the time. TV has become chewing gum for the eyes, all high-concept glossy drama that will fit nicely in a boxset.

Commissioners should credit the viewer with a depth of intelligence, an inquiring mind, and a belief in TV as a tool of awareness, reflection and betterment. Equally, they should recognise that there are incredible writers out there capable of delivering such television as entertainment, not soapboxing, but revealing real life with all its incumbent pain, pathos, ridiculousness and humour.

Our Friends in the North is the ultimate in applying ambition to television. I retain that ambition for the medium, but the truth is there hasn't been a broad-scope social and political drama made since. For years, I've been saying there has to be a black *Our Friends in the North*. Take a 17-year-old disembarking the *Windrush* in 1948 and follow them and their family through the generations. Why has that programme not been made? Trouble is, while the country has changed, the industry hasn't. How many black theatre directors are there? How many mainstream black actors? How many black agents? The industry reflects modern multicultural society in a pittance of ways.

The same can be said for drama school. If I was starting again today, I wouldn't be able to go, full stop. Neither would Maxine Peake and hundreds of others who came through that system. The ladder has been pulled up. Financial hardship allied to a lack of grants means working-class actors are finding it harder and harder to gain a foothold. I've spoken on the subject many times and, as someone who scrambled over the barbed wire to see the problem from the inside, that's only right. Of course I'm going to go out and say, 'Do you know how many of us make it into this profession?' Of course I'm going to go out and say, 'Shakespeare is fantastic but it doesn't have to be received pronunciation and it doesn't have to be white.' Of course I'm going to have that attitude. I think it's perfectly legitimate. Even though I did make it into drama school, I'm pretty sure the likes of me were only there to fill a quota – 'We need eight from Oxford, six from Cambridge, and two scrotes from up north.' Up until about twenty years ago, there'd be one northerner in a Shakespeare cast and they'd play the clown, Autolycus in *The Winter's Tale*, or the fool. That's someone who is white and male. The world is virtually set up for me. The only problem I've ever had is being working class. Try being black, working class and female.

I should be making the kind of programmes that deliver those opportunities. Actions instead of words. Instead, I'm still just an actor. But the time will come. I won't be hiding in a Trojan Horse. I'll be out in the open, and I'll have some incredible writers alongside me.

MAN AND MASCULINITY

'There's going to be girls there, is there?' I was fifteen and going to
Butlin's at Barry Island with school.
'Yeah.'
'Well, you know the score, don't you? Johnnies and all that.' Dad
paused. 'Do you want some more bread?'

Someone asked me recently if my dad ever told me he loved
me as a kid. I almost laughed in their face. It was clear he did
love me, as per the games as a kid, but it was never going to
come out verbally. He wouldn't have done it even if he was so
inclined because he knew he had to toughen me up for what
was coming next. It's undeniable that if you raise children with
sensitivity and introspection, they are not going to survive
very long among heavy artillery or, more likely in my case,
heavy industry.

That right there is the seed of the gender gap, specifically
what it is to be masculine. If a man is to be effective, he must
shut down his vulnerability, a conscious brutalisation process
that goes back years, decades, centuries. Only in 1899, my
grandparents' era, was the school-leaving age raised from ten
to twelve. It was raised from fourteen to fifteen only in the
year of my birth. The message was clear – 'You are only going

to be given the most rudimentary education and emotionally you are going to be raised in an environment that makes you capable of hard, relentless work.' Tough love they call it, and it lives on even now. In my family, it consisted of a lack of physical demonstrativeness and a stultifying dearth of emotional communication, a stoic working-class northernness if you like. Even now there's a part of me that believes we don't have a right to those finer feelings. We don't deserve those emotions as they are the realm of a cerebral class. I was definitely born into that crucible and so was Dad. That's why we had to manufacture closeness. That's why sliding on the oilcloth and grabbing his paper, and his reading to me in bed, were so important to us both. They said 'I love you' without ever having to use the words.

As I got older, we found common ground with a private love of character and words. He recognised a similar appreciation in myself, hence the leaning over the arm of his chair with those fierce eyes reading definitions from the dictionary. That was my window into Dad's soul. While some people may recall lung-crushing embraces from their fathers, or long and complex discussions, for me, and many others I suspect, that closeness came from incidents rather more obtuse. We'd be watching TV together and suddenly, when the Granada logo came up, Dad would reverse the letters and go 'Adanarg'. It sounds so trivial, but actually revealed an absurdist element that contrasted so much with his tension and machismo. It demonstrated a shared love of language even if we were hopeless at expressing its finer emotional forms to one another.

There is no doubt in my mind that I looked to the arts to express what I felt about my family, and not only landed on acting but became the kind of actor I am. It is purely because we didn't reveal our passions and our loves that I am this very physical actor. Some actors, born from a world of openness and considered education, exist on an intensely emotional and intellectual plain. I don't know how to intellectualise a role, but I do know how to physically inhabit it.

The extent of my physicality isn't something I have always been aware of. It was a factor largely learned, again, from Peter Vaughan in a bar in Newcastle while working on *Our Friends in the North*.

'You', he told me, 'need to learn how big you are.'

'That's fine coming from you, Peter,' I said. He was huge – big craggy face, long nose. 'I don't mean your size,' he replied. 'Although you do need to take that into consideration. What I mean is you're a big presence. You need to dial it down because it scares people.'

At first, I couldn't quite reconcile what was being said with who was saying it. Peter was by some distance the most intense actor on *Our Friends in the North*. Forget me, forget Daniel Craig, forget Mark Strong – it was Peter Vaughan. He was the one who you really didn't want to upset. But I soon realised he was telling me, for the sake of my own good, as a person and an actor, to be conscious of my impact. I loved Peter. He took a paternal and professional interest in me.

That presence, that intensity, that some people, not just Peter, have identified again comes from growing up, like most working class children, with the institutional message, 'You're stupid', as did my father, as did my brothers. If you're working class in this country, you may be able to shovel shit or push a trolley, but, 'You are thick. You do not emote.' 'You are thick. You are not worthy of a decent education.' Those central messages of unworthiness become so ingrained that they are self-perpetuating. Come up with a big word and not only are you mocked – 'Oh, where did that come from?' – but you mock yourself. So yes, I am intense, and that's because there's a lot of fierce concentration on trying to be articulate, rather than that laid-back public-school attitude to intellect that some people seem to have.

Possibly I do also intimidate people because of my size. I'm actually under 6ft, 5ft 11¾, but people always think I'm 6ft 2. I've always had a physical presence, broad shoulders, wiry, good hand–eye coordination, but it is how you make that presence felt. Dad's skill in that department, that quality of presence and intensity, unwitting as it was, has come to me. Peter, I think, had clocked that and wished to alert me to it. I think perhaps the same thing had happened to him. Sometimes on sets you see actors far more busy trying to lay down the steps for their next job than doing the job they're actually there for. I'm from Salford – 'Right, what am I here to do?' That whole ethic of 'let's get on with this' definitely comes from my dad. A million-mile gap, you might think, would exist between the Colgate-Palmolive factory and a TV set, but actually me and Dad operated in a very similar manner. Dad was a shipping out foreman. A massive flatbed lorry, a 'wagon' as he called it, would come in and my dad's team of stacker truck drivers would load it up. As foreman, he made sure they did it pronto. He too would get very adrenalised from his job. He worked with a physical and emotional intensity, exactly the same labels attached to me. I like that straightforwardness, and also there's a lot of technicians who don't need me floating around going,

'What's my motivation here?' Get on with it – it's a job of work. Peter admired that attitude, but he was also referencing that others don't always view a person in the same way they view themselves. If I walk through a door, I'm walking through a door. To others already in that room, me walking through a door wanting to crack on might be a little more unnerving. My intensity might be a little overwhelming. He wasn't wagging his finger; it was a lesson from an older actor to a younger one. Peter had bigger shoulders than me and I listened.

My dad had definitely shared with me a very visible masculinity. His appearance and actions shouted standard maleness, but the way I viewed him was different. It seemed obvious to me that, at his core, causing his outward behaviour, was a great femininity and vulnerability. My view of maleness was formed from how tyrannical my dad could be and yet how gentle. Through him, I learned to accept that the two things could coexist. I too have a masculinity allied to an intensely female side. Perhaps the difference is I'm aware of it. Dad, I think, found his sensitivity a source of conflict. For many years, I was the same. I resented it. I resented the part of me that made me different. If you are a late-twentieth-century male, traditional working-class, you are not going to like that side of yourself. I wanted to be black and white. I didn't understand that it is the sensitive side that offers true insight in life – intuition and empathy.

I think there were times when Dad felt acutely different and needed to escape. At work, for example, he withdrew at lunchtimes. He never told me that, but it was obvious. When I looked at my dad's paper in the evening, all the crosswords would be done (all the races would be marked, too – but my

240

mum wouldn't know about that). Dad, like any working-class man, had to take in the world around him, make a lightning-quick assessment of how to survive, and get on with it. His love of his dictionary was apparent in the house, but he wasn't likely to go to the boozer or the factory and speak about it. Chances are he'd have been mocked, so he kept his mouth shut. The nearest he could get to his real character at work without sticking out was the crossword.

For the modern man, masculinity comes from within. For the working-class man, it came from without. I believe Dad came into this world caught between the masculine and the feminine. He was innately a very, very sensitive bundle. But his default way of behaving was learnt, laddy, an act, a character he took on to survive. You can't go into Colgate-Palmolive on a stacker truck spouting the sonnets of Shakespeare. Would you want to be the one examining your deeper feelings, in depth, in a factory or pub full of men? Working-class life, in my dad's day, was about survival. Those survival chances would not have been helped in any way by opening up regards your doubts about your own masculinity or how it was defined in society in general. Men might admire one another's skills – 'You want to see his joinery' – but there wasn't enough time, learnt freedom or communal will for any deeper examination of one another's feelings. Dad certainly didn't have the luxury of being able to explore his masculinity through being an actor. His wasn't a bohemian life of self-analysis and pondering the relevance of classic stage works to an imagined 'man of today'. His male peers were present, real, as was his life. There were other more pressing matters than a discussion about the Lakeland poets.

When, after Central, I had felt totally lost, detached from

the industry I was trying to operate in, with pressure closing in from all sides, and developed an overwhelming need to speak to someone about it, I began seeing a therapist. Back then, to walk into somewhere and try to get therapy very much wasn't the done thing. Yes, everybody does therapy now, but this was the '80s and I was a hairy-arsed northerner. What took me there was the line from Grandad Pop to my dad to me. The difference between me and them was that I was living in the modern world and I was not going to deny quite how vulnerable and feminine I was, something they had to do out of necessity. Therapy wasn't an option for them. Dad was working in heavy industry. He'd go home and read his dictionary, but when he went out the door to Colgate-Palmolive, he put his work face back on. Talk about acting. He did that five days a week for year after year.

Dad was, however, in private at least, allowed to be more flexible, albeit with a good measure of conflict and contradiction. To show weakness in a platoon is to let the platoon down. I wouldn't want to be the one who did that, but I also wouldn't want to be the one who vilified the man who revealed it, and, while he'd lived in much less reconstituted times, I saw the same in my dad. I remember him once sat on his throne very uncomfortably watching John Hurt all tarted up as Quentin Crisp in *The Naked Civil Servant*. There's one scene where Crisp walks round a corner only to see a load of soldiers outside a pub. He knows he's going to get beaten up, but he makes a decision, setting himself and walking through them – 'Confront your enemies, avoid them when you can.' The soldiers don't hit him because they're too consumed with bemusement at the audacity of what he's done. While this was unfolding on screen,

I was watching my dad out the corner of my eye. I could tell he admired Crisp, and I knew, because of the world of strong masculinity, and indeed casual homophobia, he occupied, that the emotions he was experiencing confused him. He also loved Patrick McGoohan as *The Prisoner*, a male in crisis, trapped and emasculated, an antidote to Bond, and with more than an element of homo-eroticism.

Dad asked me once, 'You're not a gristle-twister, are you?', because I'd told him I didn't have a girlfriend.

Much more preferable to be 'podgin'' – shagging. I'd been doing exactly that when I came home one Sunday morning and my dad was outside working on his car.

'Where've you been?' He eyed me up and down, those blond streaks in my hair, Paul Calf meets Kenneth Branagh. 'Have you been podgin'?' I blushed and half indicated I had.

'You can make yourself bloody ill, you know,' he said, and went back to his car.

It was the same with other prejudices. The racism he saw on *Roots* would make him seethe, and yet he himself would use racial epithets. This man who admired Paul Robeson so much would, in clear opposition to that fascination, use terms that were wholly unacceptable. I believe that came from two things – wanting to be one of the boys and fear of the unknown. Again, we get back to the rudimentary education he was given. When I came back from drama school, your classic Rik Mayall student, I berated my parents about racism and my dad commented, 'I have to say, my doctor's Indian but he's a nice fella.' It was said in all innocence. I know had he seen a black man being racially abused he'd have found it intolerable. He hated bullying. To be a bully was not to be a man. Had he walked down a street and seen two white men dishing out a hiding to a black bloke on his own, he'd have pasted the pair of them.

Dad's masculinity, therefore, was oblique. It wasn't straightforward. His attachment to the underdog meant he understood the many shades of right and wrong, strength and weakness. And yet as much as he respected the voice of the oppressed, the minority, he was also informed, as is so often the case, by that desire not to stand out. He was an individual who, on occasion, felt, due to decades of social engineering, compelled to go with the crowd. To show a sensitive side was to invite homophobic abuse. I'd done it myself. There were a couple of lads at school we called 'puffs', 'faggots', 'queers'. I became just like one of the other apes. Racist terms we used as well. That's what happened in white working-class backgrounds in the '60s and '70s, especially in my area because it was all white. That was something else I rejected. I came to London and started mixing with people of all kinds of sexuality and race.

Equally, to be masculine was not to show overt sensitivity in a relationship. Dad loved my mum very, very deeply, but I wouldn't see him being romantic or showing obvious displays of affection. I never saw them holding hands or kissing, but then my mum's not that physically demonstrative either. You could say she's of that era, but none of us have broken that barrier, so maybe it's just in the genes. With the Ecclestons, we communicate how we feel with our eyes. If you want much more, forget it.

Similarly, there'd be no bunches of flowers from Dad – none of that – and he didn't like dancing – he was too self-conscious, too embarrassed – so Mum would always dance with somebody else.

I once went into my mum and dad's room and saw a book, *The Sun is my Tormentor*, a *Mandingo*-esque novel of love and adventure, by Mum's side of the bed. Seeing my mother in middle age and her desire for romance moved me deeply. It made me cry. I felt for her emptiness and also because I knew there were greater romantic novels that, because of her conditioning as being unworthy of such literature, she perhaps felt she couldn't venture into.

Who knows how the physical side of their relationship expressed itself? As anyone of my generation knows, there was rarely, if ever, any discussion about sex. It was bad enough if it happened on the telly, let alone in your own house. On holiday, because of money, I would share a room with them. That's when most couples might finally relax. And there was me on a camp bed. How did they handle that?

I feel I am caught in a dichotomy with masculinity. I understand its crushing historic negativity and the untold damage it can cause as it cascades down through the generations, and yet I cannot deny that it has an importance, a resonance, with me, which makes me reluctant to throw out a lot of masculine tropes. I genuinely like the physicality of males. It's part of us, and I love it. The question, then, is whether physicality is the same as masculinity. For me, the difference is that to be a man does not mean to be in denial of one's feelings; it does not mean a stultifying lack of communication and adopting the mental and physical mannerisms of the traditional alpha male. For myself, there are roles I feel that have suited me as a man better than others. I was reminded during the rehearsals for *Macbeth* that I can't work intellectually. The director kept telling me, 'We just want to see you thinking.' I don't know what thinking is or means. I don't trust my mental ability and I come from generations of people taught not to trust theirs, to regard themselves as not having an intellect. The way I play any role is physically and instinctively and intuitively. Sounds a bit grandiose, but that's just the way I am. I don't play any part with my head; I do it with my heart and my body, exactly how I would on a building site or in a war zone. Macbeth is a person of the body, a soldier, which made me feel qualified to play him in a way that I'm not qualified to play Hamlet. I needed to play Macbeth by saying the words and then on some emotional, intuitive level get into his head. Now I have landed on words in a book, but again this memoir is hewn predominantly from what happened anywhere other than in an intellectual, or even plain academic, environment. I would find freedom of inner expression through anywhere other than education.

As quite a physical actor, the physical performance of Macbeth was well in my ballpark. But truly to reflect him as a fighting machine, I had to look like one. People go out and play Macbeth and perform as if they're reading poetry. Wrong. He's a warrior, and I went to work on the weights to make myself look like one. When I played Hamlet, on the other hand, I never thought anyone could believe me in that role. It wasn't so much the less defined physicality; I simply never thought anyone could accept me as a student of philosophy at Wittenberg. But I believe, and I think others would too, that I could be a soldier and cut someone's head off. Hamlet has an intellectual complexity. Macbeth? By killing, he just becomes confronted with his self. At that point, he's basically a grunt, and I can do that. But is one less of a man than the other? Shakespeare's brilliance was to take a character like Macbeth, the 'grunt' of my own description, and then add layer after layer of complex internal and external emotional questions. A man asking, as all men are forced to at some point, several points, 'Who am I?' I'd noticed it before when I was playing smaller roles in the play, such as the Bloody Sergeant. From my vantage point, I'd watch, fascinated by what Shakespeare was doing, taking somebody who has killed children, killed an old man in his sleep, and making us feel sympathy for him. How? How can we be sympathising with this monster? At the same time, Macbeth is experiencing serious mental torture, a breakdown in modern parlance, as he tries to reconcile the man he is with the man he wants to be. The genius of Shakespeare is that he wrote *Macbeth* in 1623. He was sparking conversation about masculinity centuries before they started discussing it on *Newsnight*. I wonder how he'd feel to know that the masculinity debate would still be raging 400 years later. But Shakespeare was far from the initiator of that debate. Sophocles' tragedy *Antigone*, in which I starred at the National Theatre, was written in 441 BC. Then I played Creon, a man whose intractability is his weakness and yet he is blind to the failing. Absolute masculinity. And again a state of mind I felt compelled to inhabit and explore if I was going to deliver the role to the best of my ability.

It's important to recognise that, while my mum appreciated Dad's gentler side, she enjoyed the alpha side too. Having Dad in the house made us all feel, I'm sure her included, that nobody was going to cross us as a family. I was once hit by a metalwork teacher at school so hard that I flew across the room. I was messing about and he saw me. A huge bloke, he got up out of his chair – it was the suspense that was most horrible – and walked slowly across the classroom. And then it came – *wallop!*

I told my mum and my brothers and they were adamant that Dad shouldn't find out. He would have been straight up there and filled him in. I didn't need telling. I knew to avoid revealing matters of emotional import to my dad because I wouldn't want to distress him. My mum and my brothers were the people I went to. My brothers were unusually feminine and would give me the support I needed. Keith echoed my dad, a gentler version. Alan was maternal and echoed my mum.

Mum also saw a man who got his hands dirty and grafted, a man who was never late for work and never had a day off sick. Dad did what the man did – he provided. The adjunct to that, the bolt-on extra, was that he was smart, considerate and polite. I saw every side of Dad as she did, which opened my eyes to an unspoken, barely recognised form of maleness. At the same time, my mother's personality – equally strong, but more predominantly calm, loving, open – delivered an intensely female side to me. So maybe I am more like Hamlet than Macbeth after all. Asking that essential question, 'Am I my mother or am I my father?', in the end Hamlet concludes that he's neither, he's actually himself – 'I love them both and they're part of me, but actually there's a me.' I have yet to reach that level of certainty. It feels there is too much of Dad in me ever to claim independence. Our identities are knotted too intricately together, which has meant some quick and highly necessary realignment at times. When I came to London in the early '80s, it might as well have been in the form of a dinosaur plodding down the M1. That dinosaur had to learn quickly. He had to deal, quite rightly, with the third wave of feminism. The women I went to drama school with were going to Compendium bookshop in Camden Town and reading Angela

Carter's *Nights at the Circus*. I was raised by a bloke who came from a very male environment and my male role models, Sean Connery in *James Bond* and Clint Eastwood as *The Man with No Name*, were so far pre-#MeToo they may as well have existed in the Palaeolithic period.

Through the arts and acting, I found a way wholly to be myself, unashamedly, while remaining male. I could love football as well as poetry. Society didn't allow Dad that luxury. I have represented that working-class position so many times on screen, men who are, both physically and in terms of their employment, archetypally masculine, but are enduring personal crisis, a tension between how they believe they should project themselves and how they actually feel. It feels as if I've played dozens of incredible and emotionally complex men, and yet at the same time always played my dad. It's as if I, and the writers I have encountered, have always known the fascination with Dad that churns inside me, possibly because the same obsession churns inside them with their own fathers.

I've spent my entire life trying to hook the best bits of my dad and throwing the worst bits back, and that tension has given me a career. Look at Trevor Hicks – dignity at all times. I understood that because I'd seen it in my dad. Drew McKenzie – huge potential stymied by institutional self-preservation, blindness and bias. Again, Dad. I could go on – and on.

Robert De Niro once pointed out, 'You know actors win Oscars for crying? Human beings try not to cry.' He's right. I've played lots of characters who try not to cry. I studied at the master. I saw how he reacted when he heard the news that his best friend Larry Morgan had died. It was as though he went into shock. He was fighting the emotion. As much as it tried to get out, he was pushing it back down again. He was physicalising the pain. 'He was my best friend.' Feet treading on the spot. 'He was my best friend.' Arms up and down. Fighting, fighting. It was like the horse had got out of control and he was trying to rein it in. I know, in the same position, my mum would unashamedly have quietly wept in front of us.

I only saw Dad cry once. In 1976, he managed to get hold of tickets from a lorry driver for the FA Cup final between Manchester United and Southampton. I'd completely fallen in love with the Tommy Doherty United and been to every game home and away in the run to Wembley. I couldn't have been more excited – except, of course, the tickets he'd got hold of were from a Southampton lorry driver. We emerged from the stairwell slap bang in the middle of the Southampton end. I burst into tears, so upset it made my dad cry too. A Southampton dad consoled me, which my dad really appreciated. Thankfully, the deal Dad struck next year for the FA Cup final against Liverpool, tickets that were like gold dust, saw us well and truly ensconced in the United fans.

Maybe Dad cried when his sons were born, although when the twins came into the world he wasn't even allowed to be in the same room. Hospitals made no provision for men to be present. Even to enquire would have been deemed an oddity. Word was he was so consumed with anxiety that he ripped up his cigarette packet and book of matches while he was waiting outside. Thankfully, attitudes changed between 1956 and 1964, which meant he was present when I made my entrance.

'I will never ever forget the look on your mother's face when she first saw you,' he used to tell me. Again, he lived that moment vicariously through her. His fascination, his satisfaction, was in witnessing a woman see her offspring for the first time. From that moment on, he saw Elsie Eccleston through the prism of childbirth. It changed his perception of her and heightened his respect to see her go through birth and bring another human being into the world.

There was something about birth in particular that caused absolute wonderment in Dad. If it was featured on a documentary, he would get emotional. 'Isn't that marvellous?' he'd say. 'Isn't that marvellous?' Over and over again. He would watch all the viscera of it and be amazed by it, whereas some men, especially back then, would have been, 'Turn it off!'

It's one of the reasons Mum fell in love with him – she knew the tenderness was there. Behind those four walls she encouraged it to come out. When she had children, she was telling him, 'This is in you. They need you.' He didn't need asking twice. He was already versed in strong emotional attachment. He had a very paternal side when it came to his own family, always there for his brothers and sisters if they had a problem. My mum always said how marvellous he was when his own dad had dementia. He didn't need to be asked; he wanted to be right there caring for him. He'd go round straight from work. He was very nurturing, not a word some might expect to see in an examination of working-class masculinity. And right there is the crux of the situation – masculinity is just as subject to idle stereotype as femininity. I have been as guilty of that as anyone at times, but the more I have stopped and sought to understand masculinity, the more I have learned that really there is no simple definition. I set out to understand the line of men I come from and my place in it, only to find that perceived uniformity, that line, is actually non-existent. Each and every one of those men will have been wildly different, leaping from one generation to the next, shedding and accruing baggage along the way. Everything in common and nothing in common. As individuals, how could it be any other way? What saddens me is that their uniqueness was so abjectly dismissed. To the factory owners, the politicians, the generals, they were anonymous. Their lives were purely functional, utterly unimportant, and within that skewed dynamic a masculinity based wholly on survival thrived.

I'm glad my dad had the domestic life that allowed him, and us, at least a glimpse of his true self. In his house, on his throne, for a few hours a day, he was the man he wanted to be. The tragedy is that there are still millions of men doing the same: shielding private versions of themselves. In the wider world, they are uncomfortable opening up, and with that comes tremendous pressure, potentially breakdown. Honesty about masculinity is the way forward. But how can that happen when it suits every controlling interest to present vulnerability, sensitivity, independence of thought, in the working class as something to be swatted like a fly? There will, I fear, be stacker truck drivers with a dictionary by their armchair for a good few decades yet.

2 0

MACBETH

'Oh, yet I do repent me of my fury.'
Macbeth

The trigger for my obsession with Macbeth was obvious. It went beyond simply wanting the part; I needed it. I knew my dad had given me the ultimate preparation and permission, an intimate knowledge of both Macbeth's mental and, equally importantly, physical state. Macbeth is a soldier bred for brutality. Alone, I couldn't put myself in that position, but with my dad alongside me I could. A soldier? My dad? Oh yes, he could easily have done that. He might have been a student of philosophy like Hamlet if he'd had a public-school education, but he could definitely have been a soldier. He had loyalty, bravery and purpose – and he could more than look after himself. You wouldn't want to get in a boxing ring with him, or an argument in a pub, any more than you would want to face him on a battlefield. More than anything, Macbeth had the ability to frighten. And that, for years, was the dominant emotion I felt from my dad.

Ronnie was Macbeth, he just never knew it. Within all that ornate and extraordinary language, Shakespeare presents to us a man who knows, 'If I do this, I'm going to mess myself up' – and then does it. My dad was the same, capable of wilfully destructive behaviour that would ultimately damage himself more than anyone else, letting himself down, betraying himself, and then, also like Macbeth, experiencing great remorse. 'I know this isn't right but I'm going to bloody do it.'

If he really lost it with me, an hour later he'd be mortified. Even as he was losing his temper there was self-hatred in him. He knew it was wrong, that he would regret it, but he was going to do it anyway. Whatever age I was, I recognised that mental process. There was a self-lacerating quality to it, an almost Catholic conscience that would churn and churn. He'd brood, and you could feel it. Of course, with Macbeth, the loss of control, with deep ramifications, is amplified many times over, and yet it still felt so close to home, the reason being Macbeth is not ethically deformed, he is a decent person. Allied to his overt masculinity, albeit rarely made visible, he has a tenderness, a gentleness, and a vulnerability. With typical astuteness, Shakespeare takes an everyman character, like my dad, who's good at life, and his job, and has many sound and positive characteristics, and has him destroy his own morality and, therefore, his own sense of self. It sounds extreme, and it is extreme, but I could imagine my dad, not like Macbeth because of his ambition, but because of his extreme frustration and passion, killing somebody in a rage, just the same as I could imagine myself killing somebody in a rage, and I could imagine how that act would consume and eventually destroy him, and me.

My dad informing, inhabiting, Macbeth – that's what happens when you invest in these amazing Shakespearean parts, these works of genius. For the first three months, all you are doing is remembering the lines. Slowly, however, the character soaks in and you get an aerial view of their journey, the pivot points, and what's elemental to their personality. By osmosis there's then a drip, drip of your own past experiences into the portrayal. The result is that, with all the major Shakespearean roles, Hamlet, Macbeth, even the vain and pompous Malvolio in *Twelfth Night*, what you end up doing, through the filter of the character, is becoming more and more yourself and those around you. That's possible because Shakespeare's plays are about very elemental and primal things. He writes about blood and bone. On so many occasions, he invites us to imagine what it would be like to be a person not so very far removed from ourselves. With Macbeth, he delivers the same invite as Raskolnikov in *Crime and Punishment* – 'You've all imagined killing somebody and what it might feel like. Now I've done it for you. Come to the theatre, here's your worst nightmare, taking another human life.' The point is that actually both Macbeth and Raskolnikov are decent people.

I wrote to the Royal Shakespeare Company and asked to play Macbeth. I then failed badly at the beginning of the run, and that was hard. Professionally, and just two years out from a breakdown, I had determinedly sought out the biggest test I could possibly have taken on, the defining role in British theatre, at the RSC, and I wasn't getting anywhere near it. A lot of the reviews, quite rightly, reflected that distance. The most devastating was Michael Billington in *The Guardian*. 'His speaking of the verse lacks irony or light and shade,' he commented. Those words devastated me. I read that review and then had to go on stage that night. I respect Michael Billington, which was why it hurt. It stung also because early on he was right. I was dreadful. I was down for 120 performances, but what could I do? Again, my dad was in my head. If I'd said to him, 'I'm not doing this anymore,' he'd have kicked my arse from Stratford to Salford and back again. As it was, I did numerous performances where I didn't want to be there. Friends were saying, 'What's wrong with you? You were born to play this role.' But if you don't feel the part, then such words, appreciated as they are, become meaningless.

Why read reviews? I had this exact argument with Niamh Cusack, who played Lady Macbeth. Thatcher must somehow have worked her magic on me because I see it as though I'm running a business. I've run it since 1989 when I started working and if I'm making a product I want to know what people think of it. Avoid the reviews and you're trying to guess. You are left looking for little signs, how people around you, actors, directors, family, friends, agents, are behaving – 'Has he read the reviews? Has he not?' 'Does he know what's been said or hasn't he heard yet?' – trying to decodify their language, their expressions. There's another thing: I'm an egomaniac. I'm convinced the reviews are going to reveal me as the greatest actor of my generation, which, of course, they never do because I'm not. In seeking that high, I risk the low. A bad review takes me right back to that young lad who thought he should never be an actor in the first place. It tells me what I've known all along, that I don't belong, a feeling I carry to this day. With *Macbeth*, I'm proud that I read those reviews and kept going. Eventually, I reached a point where I felt I did belong. The confidence came back and, by the end of the run, I believed I had the right to play the part and was a better actor for it. I also understood that if you want to be a great theatre actor you have to spend your life doing it, and I haven't. I've spent my life being a TV actor, and I got exposed. My ambition tripped me up – literally when I ended up in front of the stalls. 'TV actor falls off the stage' – says it all.

Hubris – so often a visitor to my door. I'm honest enough to say, in my career as a whole, I thought I was going to change acting, like Olivier changed acting. I thought I was going to surpass Robert De Niro and Gary Oldman and be up there with the best. If you don't think like that, what are you going to do? Head out saying, 'I'm just going to be middle of the road'? As time has gone on, I've understood I wasn't going to change acting, I was just going to be an actor, sometimes good, sometimes bad. In a business that doesn't always reward talent, it's difficult ever to know where you fit on the scale of acting ability. You don't always reach the top on merit, which is why sport appeals to me. Fastest, highest, strongest. In my industry, as I know, you can be rewarded for being in the right place at the right time, getting a role above an actor better suited because you are perceived as being box office or having a higher profile. It's hard to get a measure of self-worth in an industry that operates like that. I get my self-worth elsewhere. The mere act of sticking myself up for judgement allows me to draw a certain value. It's an industry where somehow you're always disappointed, but I've learned to take the positive from that, which is: 'I gave it a go.'

With *Macbeth*, I transformed a bad experience into a good one, which ultimately made it more satisfying. I've been acting, one way or another, for almost forty years, and I learnt more in those six months in Stratford – to fail, to fall, to be reviewed so badly, and yet recover – than perhaps any other period in my career. There is actually something truly fantastic about entirely losing your confidence. If it vanishes, and then you get it back, you know you'll never lose it to that extent again. An actor has something in common with a sportsperson in that a bad performance is always a possibility, but soon enough there'll be a good one to counteract it. I see a parallel with my mental illness. At my most fragile, I felt genuinely suicidal, and yet I managed not to give in to that desire to harm myself. What doesn't kill you makes you stronger. It's a terrible cliché, but it's true.

I learned in the end not to fixate with *Macbeth*. When I play a character, I can become very obsessed, a drive, an attention to detail, an intensity (that word again), which I know absolutely started from trying to work out my dad. Sometimes, though, as an actor, it's better to step back. At the start of the run, when I was struggling, I knew exactly what the issue was – relaxation, or rather a lack of it. In order to find variety – vocally, physically and psychologically – in performance, an actor has to be relaxed, and in order to be relaxed they have to be confident. My confidence was on the floor with the rest of me. And when you're not confident you become stiff, not just in delivery but physically and imaginatively. At that point, the audience knows you're not getting it. And you know they know you're not getting it. That's the flipside of my job: I succeed in public, but I fail also.

Sounds pretentious, I know, but Allen Ginsberg once reported how he saw Dylan in the early days and found him wholly inseparable from his songs. He didn't know whether Dylan was the songs or the songs were Dylan. Ginsberg put it that Dylan became basically 'a column of air'. I remember puzzling over that comment and asking myself, 'Should that be my aim when I'm doing Shakespeare?' To almost remove myself from the process? There's something to be said, when playing Shakespeare, in not imposing too strong an intellectual idea or emotional colour. The language is so rich anyway. Throw more at it and it quickly becomes too busy. I feel like the job is actually just to say it. Don't try to hammer it into a particular intellectual or emotional shape. Let it flow through and past you. Be in the moment and just let it come out.

The same can be said of any performance. As an actor, to move an audience, you need an element of detachment. It's not important what the actor feels; it's important what the audience feels. There's something surgical about acting and I don't think actors should be ashamed about admitting it. Playing Derek Bentley, with the bones I had, I knew the best angles to make the most of them and, in purely practical, technical terms, those angles worked brilliantly. There are far better actors than me, but something can happen to their features so that what they are trying to convey doesn't come across. I knew my angles because I'd spent so much time in the mirror as a child and had an instinctive understanding of their relationship to camera. I'm afraid it's not some extraordinary alchemical thing going on inside, it's just I understood that if I adopted a certain look at a certain angle, an audience would feel more sympathy than if I lifted my face five degrees and did it another way. If I did it one way, it was Derek, if I did it another, it wasn't. That's mathematics. I was a bit disappointed an actor could achieve so much technically, because my gods were Gary Oldman and Daniel Day-Lewis, who seemed to fashion their accomplishments on a much more cerebral basis, but, believe me, they'll understand the laws of mathematics too. Angles were my ally. I also had a great deal of neurosis and self-doubt. Put a camera on that and something happens. The clinical nature of acting appeals to me because I come from tradespeople. Yes, there's something mysterious that goes on between actor and audience, but basically it's a trade. My brother Alan makes beautiful furniture. My aim has always been to make a beautiful performance that, practically, does what it should. I would argue there is no more virtue in a beautiful performance than in a beautiful chair that has been made by hand. They are both there to create a feeling, not in the creator, but in the receiver.

The challenge with stepping back from Macbeth is that it's a role played on the inside as much as the out. It's not easy to untie the binds, and there are times when the character can feel like a burden, an awful thing to say for a role that most actors would die for, but reflective of the fact that he brings with him a terrible discomfort. In my case, all my worst nightmares are about killing somebody, changing my life for ever and never being me again. That's what Macbeth does and that's what I did night after night. The remarkable thing is I grew to relish the experience. The way I played Macbeth at the end was so different to when I started out. I learned things about myself, and him, in that time. But how can an attitude to a character *not* change? Forget stage fights; actors have days when they must face their own battles before they arrive at the stage door. I've had those days, and the subsequent performance may see the surfacing of that sadness or anger. The beauty of theatre is you are living, and you bring that to the performance. You have to tell the story, you've got to be true, but your own existence is unavoidable. The two are interlocked, physically as well as mentally. When I had a three-week mid-season break from Macbeth, my psoriasis, generally an infrequent visitor to my scalp, ears and elbows, spread to my shins, hips, knees and backside. I was doing a weird and highly adrenalised job. Once I relaxed, the psoriasis shouted up to tell me, 'This is what you were feeling like on the inside.' As much as I had grown to love Macbeth, I needed a break from him. Through the character you gain knowledge, good and bad, about your own humanity. I needed that time to escape the microscope I was pointing at myself.

I'll never be the Macbeth I thought I could be, but I did it, at the RSC, and without doubt it's the biggest achievement of my career. For my generation of actors, playing a major Shakespearean role is the top of the top. But it's about more than just me. Back in 1961, when Albert Finney depicted the life of Martin Luther in John Osborne's play at the Royal Court in Chelsea, and his name was in lights above the door, he invited his mum and dad down from Salford. He took them for a meal on the King's Road and then walked them to the theatre in Sloane Square.

'There you are, Dad,' he said. 'What do you think of that?'

'Hmm,' pondered his dad, 'doesn't my name look good in lights?'

That's how I feel. My entire career has been aiming towards performing at the RSC and that's where I reached. But what's genuinely wonderful is that it was an Eccleston at the RSC, not me. If any of my grandparents were still alive, the idea that an Eccleston could play Macbeth in Stratford-on-Avon? Unheard of. I see that achievement as my dad at Whiteacre, my mum cleaning toilets at Worsley Baths and working at the launderette for the council. That's what I took on to the stage, because everything I've ever applied to my acting comes directly from what they taught me about concentration and hard work. A group effort of my mum, my dad, my brothers, and me. When it came to me doing any landmark production, a little moment of contemplation was very important. 'This is for the Ecclestons.' I'd felt exactly the same when with *Jude* I went to Cannes.

There's an important caveat to that statement. If you're from Salford, or any working-class area, and you find yourself on stage in a dream job, yes, you can be allowed a moment of 'I made it – who would have thought?', but that should never mean there's a surprise in someone from that background having the ability to do so, or that they wouldn't be encouraged by their family. I was approached for the role of the dad in *Billy Elliot*, but to me it was just a cliché, the working-class father who can't comprehend that his son wants to become a ballet dancer. I never saw any of that and I don't believe a lot of other working-class kids do either. Forget *Billy Elliot*; the minute I said I wanted to go into acting my dad was right behind me, as was my mum. Yes, she had the fear of 'I'm going to lose my lad', but she was just as supportive. The same assumptions are applied to friends, that when I chose acting as my path in life a lot of them would have been sneering – 'An actor? What?' – again, the *Billy Elliot* cliché, a middle-class view of working-class people.

In all those performances for the RSC, be it the better days or the more turbulent, I carried my family's communal belief that we, I, could do this. When I got that part, I had no sense of personal vanity. All I could think about was their hard work. They had brought me up to have such a sense of belief in myself – positivity and possibility – and the Olivier Theatre at Stratford was the result.

Ayub Khan Din was in that mix too, the same brotherhood with him as back in the day when we both chose to follow an unusual ambition alien to our families. Ayub had normalised the desire to occupy Macbeth, to speak those same lines, feel those same emotions. If he'd come from two people who owned a chippy, and I'd come from two factory workers, it was OK to be us. On stage at the Royal Shakespeare Company, thirty-six years after we'd toured the play with Theatre Beyond the Stage, with my head now beneath the crown, I would have flashbacks to Ayub and what he did with the role. But always there was someone of even greater significance in my mind – Dad. Back in 1982, I had become fascinated with Macbeth because I so recognised him as the man I lived with. I decided there and then I wanted to be an actor. That triangle – myself, Macbeth and Dad – has made up the three corners of my life and career ever since.

2 1

A MIND DISEAS'D

When I first went to Old Trafford with my dad, he would put his hands on my shoulders to guide me through the crowds. In the last few years, I did the same for him.

I'd keep talking to him. 'All right, pal?'

'Yeah, yeah, I'm good.'

'Can you see where you're going?'

'Yeah, yeah.'

Dad crashed his car, a bad accident, straight into the back of another vehicle. To this day, I don't know how he walked away. As it was, he was taken to hospital, and I was first there.

I rushed in. 'My dad's been in a road accident,' I told the receptionist. 'He's just been admitted.'

He looked at me, twigged who I was.

'Can I have an autograph?'

I'm pretty good with autographs on most occasions. This wasn't one of them.

'Not the time, pal.'

With his cuts and bruises patched up, the next step was to find out what had happened. Dad was diabetic, so there was a possibility he might have gone into a hypo at the wheel. Equally, he might just not have been concentrating. Subsequently, Dad went back for CAT scans, and that's when the doctors told us they'd found evidence of vascular dementia, where blood supply to the brain becomes reduced.

Dementia is a very recent acknowledgement within social and medical circles. The word rolls off my tongue now, but initially when doctors used it in terms of Dad, I had so little awareness of either it or what it meant that I had to go home and look it up on the internet. I sat with a laptop on my knees and read about the seven established stages of dementia. I investigated the illness like I would a character until it too became a living, breathing entity. I chose not to share the seven stages with my mum and brothers. Alan and Keith could find out for themselves and I didn't have the emotional stability to tell Mum.

From what I could work out, Dad was at stage two, described as mild cognitive decline, forgetfulness, while still able competently to go about life. I looked down the list to stage seven – incontinent, incomprehensible – and it frightened me. But there was no great exhibition of anguish, from myself or anyone else. The way the family looked at any challenge was with a classic working-class stoicism – 'We just have to get on with it.' The diagnosis also made sense and I felt very, very stupid for not realising earlier. Behaviours started to slot into place. Looking back, my mum, my brothers and myself could see the condition had been revealing itself for the previous three years, sometimes subtly, as in a growing inability to concentrate, sometimes rather more obviously, the grass in my garden being a case in point. Dad became fixated with it and kept going on about how long it was, telling me to get it cut. In the end, I lost my temper and snapped at him about it. There's some associated guilt and shame about how I spoke to him, but I can give myself a modicum of leeway because I didn't know there was an issue.

A little earlier, I had been filming *Cracker* in Manchester, while living at home, when Dad suffered a medical emergency. He went temporarily blind – the result, we discovered, of a blood clot. He also had some mini-strokes. Together, I think they marked the real beginning of his slide into dementia. The damage took a good few years to manifest itself, but from that point on there was a softening in his nature. I found him much more relaxed. I can remember feeling how the spike had been blunted in his character, a spike that itself had more than likely been a contributory factor. Anger, in the short term, can be a good feeling; it makes you feel empowered. In the long term, it makes you ill. In Dad's case, it sent his blood pressure hurtling, a factor shown to damage and narrow blood vessels in the brain, which is, essentially, vascular dementia. His late onset diabetes, a disease of the circulatory system, only worsened an already delicate situation and was almost certainly another huge contributing factor. He'd been told to change his eating habits. There was a chance, if he did, he could put the diabetes into reverse, but he wouldn't do it. My dad's complex relationship with food meant he wasn't willing to compromise. He comfortate. Remember, this is a man who spent much of his early life being denied the pleasures of food. And now he was being asked to do so again? He just wasn't having it. Perhaps also, on some level, his self-esteem and confidence, dishevelled from the emasculation of breakdown and redundancy, meant he thought himself unworthy of saving. You can add into that a healthy dose of 'What do they know?' His idea of what and what didn't constitute an issue differed somewhat from the medical profession.

One doctor said to my mum, 'I've done a questionnaire with Mr Eccleston and he tells me he doesn't drink.'

'I beg your pardon?'

'Mr Eccleston has told me he doesn't drink alcohol.'

'Doesn't drink alcohol? He drinks six or seven pints on a Saturday and Sunday, sometimes on a Friday as well.'

She quizzed Ronnie about his response.

'I know I drink,' said my dad, 'but I don't *drink*. I'm not a drinker.'

To him, the question 'Do you drink?' meant 'Do you go to the pub every night?' The answer to which was 'No, I don't.'

Smoking can also be a contributor to dementia. Dad had started smoking again on the Saturday night of his and mum's silver wedding anniversary, stressed because the coach we were all travelling on to the restaurant was late. From that point, he smoked really heavily again. Dad didn't want to deny himself the pleasures of life. What he was unable to see was that the pleasures of life can alter.

Had Dad's diagnosis not been made after the crash, which in itself may have been caused by the onset of dementia, it surely wouldn't have been long in coming. His behaviour quickly became increasingly erratic. In late 2002, I played Hamlet at the West Yorkshire Playhouse. Keith and his wife Ann were driving Mum and Dad there, 70 mph down the motorway, when Dad opened the door and tried to get out. Keith slammed the brakes on, quite literally putting a halt to the situation before it went too far. Dad wasn't stupid. He may have been in the foothills of dementia, but that doesn't mean he was totally devoid of self-awareness. He knew opening the door of a moving car wasn't a great idea. He also knew his mental faculties were disappearing and, as he never had done, wasn't going to allow himself to be steamrollered. There was a lot of life to be lived and he fought to hold on to his old behaviour. On one occasion, as he'd always done, I saw him reading a book. But I could tell from the way his eyes were moving across the page he was retaining nothing. He was completely in the moment. Picking up a book was about trying to maintain normality, nothing more. It was about resistance. Except this time, the opponent wasn't an all-elbows defender on a football pitch, a know-it-all manager at work; it was himself. And it was a fight he could never win. Once that realisation came, it could deliver a devastatingly hard blow even in the most benign of circumstances. Dad once knocked over a cup of tea at Keith's house. 'No bother,' Keith reassured him, 'it's fine.' But it was far from fine to my dad. He was consumed by embarrassment and anxiety over what he'd done, to the extent he was down under the table on his knees trying to mop it up.

'What's happening to me, what's happening to me?' he kept repeating. 'I am Ronnie Eccleston.' Horrendous to experience. Perhaps even harder to watch.

Other times, thankfully, there'd be an element of humour to Ronnie's changing state of mind. Once he came downstairs with a shirt and tie on – and another shirt and tie on top.

'Ronnie,' my mum pointed out, 'you've got two shirts and two ties on.' He looked at himself and laughed. She had a stock phrase when mix-ups like this happened – 'Confused.com'. Beautifully, and movingly, I experienced, on occasion, a phenomenon that sometimes happens with those with dementia where reserve is wiped out. One night, as he walked me to my car outside their house, he turned to me.

'I love the bones of you,' he told me.

It was wholly unexpected and, at that moment, I felt embarrassed. 'All right, Dad!'

Dementia had removed his inhibitors and allowed him to tell me something so intensely emotional.

As an actor, I became aware, right from the start of Dad's illness, of life imitating art. *Flesh and Blood* was a case in point – eight intense weeks playing a character desperately trying to gain recognition from a father who doesn't recognise him, as played by an actor who himself isn't wholly cognisant of the process. There's a scene where my character shows his dad a picture of himself as a baby.

'Do you know who that is?'

'No, no, yeah, yeah, no,' says Peter Kirby.

'That's me.'

'Yeah, yeah. I know it is. I know it's you. Yeah, yeah – do you like *James Bond*?'

There is, of course, no reconciliation at the end of *Flesh and Blood*. There is no scene where father recognises son and everyone skips off into the sunset to live happily ever after. Joe reaches another destination, and that is to realise, 'There's a biological connection that this man can never comprehend. I've got to stop thinking about myself and celebrate him for who he is, because actually he's a great positive in my life. He's never going to know who I am. But I know who he is, and I can have a relationship with him and accept him on his terms.'

Accepting a father on his terms. Hmm. We wrapped the production on Friday, had a party, and then on Saturday morning I'd arranged to go to Old Trafford with my dad. I was really looking forward to it – and he turned up with the season tickets from two years before. I'm disgusted with myself thinking about it now, but I gave him a bollocking. I was pissed off because I couldn't go to the game. More than that, though, I was pissed off because he had dementia. That is shameful on my part, but genuinely that is the case. Maybe that shame is something others in the same position will recognise, an occasional presence of a selfish internal voice, one that so desperately craves 'normality'.

I put my anger at his illness down to coming straight off the back of *Flesh and Blood*, with its fictional narrative so unflinchingly similar to my own non-fiction life. Amid that emotion, present as he always was whenever me and my dad knocked heads, was that little boy who was frightened of him. I definitely harboured residual anger towards him, a straight reflection of the anger he'd exhibited towards me. Sounds harsh, but he was getting back the temper he taught me. I was in control now. I'm not proud of that, and I'm not saying it's right, but that's how I justified it to myself.

I looked into his eyes and could see him trying to process what was going on. He was staring at the season tickets, semi-computing that they were the ones from two years ago, while trying to work out what the situation meant, and what should happen next. For ten seconds, my peripheral vision was blacked out, blinkered. All I saw was this big, fierce bird-like face looking around lost in confusion. I put Dad on the bus home, the route being familiar to him, and walked away. I rang later and explained to my mum what had happened. And then I started crying. I cried for four hours. That night I had a date with my girlfriend. I told her about it and cried all over again. I broke my heart like I've never broken my heart since. That moment of seeing his confusion had left a mark – not a bruise, but a deep, lasting weal. Until that point, I'd understood intellectually that my dad had dementia because we'd been told. But emotionally I hadn't understood it at all. And then there, in the street outside Old Trafford, I'd been given a window into somebody going mad. Becoming demented. That's the truth of it – demented. It's a shocking word. We used to talk about demented dogs, and we shot them. When we say dementia, there's no hiding the truth. It means people are demented. We can dress that up however we want, but there's no denying the naked reality beneath. That day I had been presented with the stark vision of a man floundering in a maze of his mind's own making. Not knowing who and where he was. And I'd just been horrible to him. And he was my dad.

Progressively, Dad's independence of action and thought was being taken away. On one occasion, he went for his paper and an hour later wasn't back – from a newsagent that was a five-minute walk away. Two hours later, he still wasn't home. Mum had to ring the police, and Ronnie was eventually spotted and returned. That was the end of him going for his paper on his own, although Mum never couched it so obviously. Pre- or post-dementia, you never told my dad anything – you cajoled him. After his disappearing act, whenever Dad announced he was going for his paper, Mum would say, 'I'll come with you.' That way they could go for the paper together. Without admitting it, I expect he was relieved.

A couple of times the bookie knocked on the door. Dad had always loved a bet – it delivered an adventure, an element of excitement, the unknown of what was going to happen – and he still liked to go to the betting shop even when he had dementia.

'Elsie,' the bookie would say, 'Ronnie's had a win but he's not come and picked it up.' I still find that touching. They'd known Dad in the bookies for years and were looking out for him now he was ill.

Occasionally, Mum left Dad at home and went out to do her own thing. It wasn't often, but every now and again she needed that bit of space. He knew she was out, but if I asked him where he didn't know. He'd keep looping back to it – 'I don't know where your mum is' – to the point where he'd stand by the curtains until she came back. His life was dictated by whether Elsie was there or not. To a certain extent that was true before dementia. She was his anchor and his touchstone and his lynchpin, much more than his children were. He loved his children, but Elsie ran everyday life and the house. He was familiar with that arrangement, and for those with dementia, familiarity is everything. When I had a bit of success, I enjoyed taking Mum and Dad out to posh places, splashing out a bit. One time they came down to London to see me deliver Robert Laurence Binyon's war poem 'For the Fallen' as part of a Remembrance event in Leicester Square. It was live on television and I was asked to take part as my stock was high as the Doctor. Afterwards, we went to an upmarket fish restaurant, J. Sheekey, in Covent Garden, a place a lot of actors go after West End shows. On the menu, Dad saw fish and chips. Great, one of his favourites. Then he saw the price of it.

'How much? For fish and chips? I'm not bloody paying that.' He was kicking off, trying to leave the restaurant.

I tried to calm him down. 'Dad, Dad, it's fine. I'm getting it.'

'I know, but look at the price!'

The dementia was already feeding him a great plateful of

anxiety. He was in a place where he had no control over what was happening – and that was a big thing.

This was a man floundering, becoming submerged beneath wave after wave of affliction and change. He was diagnosed with oesophageal cancer and had to have a total gastrectomy. It wasn't an easy conversation to have with a man with increasingly little understanding of his own being, let alone the intricacies of his health.

I was walking up Coniston Avenue with him to get his paper. 'Now, Dad,' I looked at him, 'you know you're going in hospital tomorrow?'

'Why? Why am I going in hospital?'

'Well, Dad,' – and this is hard to say to anyone – 'you've got cancer.'

'Cancer? I've got bloody cancer?' It was as though it was the first time he'd heard. He was having none of it. 'Look at me, Chris! Look at me! I can run. I can jump.' He was actually doing the actions. 'What are they talking about?'

He was scared, as we would all be. Scared of cancer, scared of being in hospital, scared of being away from Elsie.

Dad had been told from the off about the size and potential ramifications of the procedure. 'Mr Eccleston,' stated the surgeon, 'it's a very risky operation.' It wasn't that Dad's confusion cleared at that moment, but he appeared to comprehend the urgency, the seriousness. He somehow recognised the doctor's emotion.

'Listen,' he said, 'you have got to do it for me because otherwise it's nowt down for pal.' Dementia took a lot of things, but it couldn't take the Salford out my dad. 'Nowt down for pal' means you're dead.

'If it goes wrong,' he also told the surgeon, 'it's not your fault.' To see my dad, in the state he was in, mentally and physically, give that to the doctor, to show such empathy with him, I don't think I had ever been prouder. But there was an unspoken truth about what was happening in that theatre. They were operating on a man in the mid-stages of dementia. They were saving his life so he could go mad.

Dad was taken to critical care after surgery. It was the same hospital, Hope Hospital, now sadly renamed simply as Salford Royal (what better name for a hospital than Hope?), in which he was born. For his complete helplessness, his naked reliance on others merely to exist, he might as well have been a baby again.

I would sit with him in recovery, my job being to make sure he didn't pull his catheter out. He had dementia, but he also had an almost allergic reaction to the anaesthetic. It scrambles everybody to some degree, but especially so if you have dementia, and he was in an abject state of physical and mental confusion. It was an incredibly difficult period, so much so that Mum stopped being able to go to the hospital. Dad turned on her, giving her a hard time, as if she was somehow to blame for his predicament. It was just too much for a wife and mother who was already physically and psychologically exhausted. She didn't miss many visits, but me and my brothers would always make sure one of us went so she knew he had somebody there. He'd have sat by that bed for us. No better man to have in your corner than my dad.

As well as preventing him tugging on his catheter, I felt my visits were there to protect his dignity. He had pyjamas on, but his constant movement, some innate recognition of a foreign body, the catheter, being inside him, meant he was pulling at them, exposing himself without knowing it. I'd seen his penis about twice in my life and now suddenly it was there. Somewhere inside me, while I was acutely aware of my dad's condition, where so much similitude to the father I once knew had been ripped away and tossed aside, was the son who recognised that to see his father's penis was at odds with every ingrained element of that relationship. Again, an emphasis on how far we had travelled. A man with such pride. The operation hadn't killed him, but surely, had he been aware of it, the thought that his son was now seeing him in a way that, in any semblance of normal life, he never should, would have been the final blow. All that was going round in my head as I desperately attempted to avert his hands, tried to stop him inflicting pain and damage on himself.

He's shown me what it is to live, I thought, *and now he's showing me what it is to die.* That may sound pretentious, I don't know, but as I looked at him I couldn't help but think, *You taught me how to kick a ball. You taught me how to be, how not to be, and now you are showing me what it's like to die.*

He was thrashing around. 'Dad, Dad, please stop this, Dad. Will you please stop doing this?'

He did just that and stared at my face – 'You look just like my father.' I was taken aback. He was suddenly lucid.

'I look like your father,' I told him, 'because I'm your son, and I love you.'

I kissed him.

'Ooh!' he went, and smacked his lips. Even in his dementia, he had to make out like I was being queer.

It was one of the most vivid moments of my life, so much emotion instilled in it. It also made me think of his father, a hard man, fierce, like him. The bone structure, the big nose, the piercing eyes. At that minute, all three of us were in that room. It felt like any of us could have been in each other's position.

Dad, for certain, had seen this set-up from a different angle. His father had a tumour on the brain and my dad's belief was that doctors had experimented on him with LSD. In the end, he went what was described simply as 'mad'. Whether it was dementia, I don't know – conditions weren't termed the same as they are now – but the symptoms sound rather too similar for it not to have been. At night, his sons would take turns in heading round to their mum's house to help her look after him. One night he pulled the wardrobe over on himself because he believed there were things, alive, coming out of it.

Nana and Grandad Pop had moved from a family house on Summerville Road in Salford to a smaller house on Tenby Drive, from where they could see their old house. The move, understandably, had caused some confusion with Grandad Pop. 'I don't live here, this isn't my house,' Grandad was telling my dad, which prompted Ronnie to take him for a walk.

'I took him out the house,' he told me, 'walked him down to the bottom of the road, crossed over, walked back up, and went back in.'

Granddad Pop looked at him. 'You think I'm bloody stupid, don't you?'

Dementia is all over Dad's side of the family. He had seen his mother go the same way. Among other signs, she'd started accusing my Auntie Amy of stealing from her. He'd seen that happen to his mother but would never talk about it. To talk, as we know, was bred out of him. The descent into dementia happened also to one of his brothers and his sister. None of these occurrences was ever described as 'dementia'. People in those days – and we're talking as recently as the '80s and '90s here – went 'doolally'. People would say, 'Oh, he's got old', or use the term 'senile'.

Eventually, the time came when I stopped calling him 'Dad'. I had to. There'd been an incident while we were on holiday. It was very, very frightening.

I'd rented a cottage in Cornwall with my girlfriend and invited my mum and dad to stay. Initially, all was fine. As ever, me and Dad spent a lot of time doing the crossword, with the paper laid out on the kitchen table. 'Dictator' was the clue. Six letters.

'Despot,' said my dad.

'Cop for that!' I cried – we had phrases we always used when doing crosswords. I was so happy. I was spending time with Dad, Mum was having a holiday, everyone was relaxing. And then I could feel him looking at me. Feel him, right there, inches from my face, staring, his eyes boring into me.

'Are you related to me?'

I looked at him. 'Yes, Dad, I'm your son.' There was a little bit of contained anger in my voice. How could he not know who I was?

I repeated, 'I'm your son.'

And it just went off.

'Does she know that?' He was agitated, gesturing towards my mum sat in the other room. 'Does she know you're my son?'

'Yes. That's my mum.'

We walked into the other room. He pointed at me. 'He's just told me that he's my son.'

'Well, yes,' said my mum, 'that's Chris. He is your son.'

'Well, I don't know anything about that.' He was shouting now. 'I don't know bloody anything about a son.'

It escalated, until Dad was consumed with a truly desperate rage. Somehow, my mum managed to shepherd him upstairs into their bedroom. I couldn't help – the mere sight of me was enough to send him into full-on hysteria.

Me and my girlfriend got out of the way and went to our bedroom. All we could hear was Dad shouting. 'He says he's my son. I haven't got a son. I don't know who he is.' He was going and going and going. In his head, when I'd said, 'I'm your son,' I was telling him he had a child that his wife didn't know about. His illegitimate offspring had appeared out of nowhere. Effectively, the way he saw it, he'd been caught out playing away. He thought he was in trouble. He'd been emotionally reliant on my mum throughout their marriage, which had morphed into her becoming his carer, and now he thought he'd been fingered for a past indiscretion.

It was the middle of the night and we were in the middle of nowhere. As I lay there, I had no inkling what might happen. I didn't know whether he was going to become violent, walk out of the cottage, challenge me, my girlfriend, anything. We were all adults with him in that house and yet we were all scared, because the other side of Ronnie is that thing I do on screen. Volcano.

'This is all my fault,' I kept saying over and over. I'd made a mistake in taking him to Cornwall. He wasn't in his own environment, there was nothing familiar, and then here was this guy, very like him physically, telling him he's his son, using all his language – 'What a player! Cop for that!' He was confused. Mentally, it had thrown him. 'I used to do a crossword with . . .

I did it with . . . who's this? . . . I don't know who this is.' The distress in my father was incredible. And that came from him not knowing such an obvious thing. 'Son? Son?' That surely then leads to a question he didn't, couldn't, or wouldn't vocalise. 'Who am I? WHO AM I?'

The bald truth of the matter descended on me. My dad does not know who I am. I am Chris, his son, and he thinks I'm a stranger. And that was it. End of. I never ever went down that route again. Because it's not about me, is it? It's at that point you start dealing with the dementia rather than the person. An insistence in carrying on the old way – 'Dad', 'son' – would distress him and endanger my mother.

Next day, Dad had the emotional residue of the strain and the rage. He was confused and pale. The rest of us were shaken and everything felt eggshell fragile. I felt ashamed of myself for my clumsiness in taking him to Cornwall. I was also questioning the neediness in me that, when he had asked who I was, meant I'd not stopped and thought about the situation, but, without hesitation, blurted out, 'I'm your son.'

I realised it had taken me five years to stop hoping the dad of now was the dad of then. I couldn't talk to him about it, so I would have to have a conversation with myself instead. 'Forget it, pal. Store all that up, love all that about him, but deal with the now.'

I was slow to make that realisation, hence my desperation for him to recognise me as his son. I'm sure that's a common error. My wake-up call was that day in the cottage. That, you could say, was my Damascene moment.

At home, we'd learnt how powerful music was in calming Dad, how deeply soothed he was by it. In the '60s, Frank

Sinatra had filmed a series of concerts that had been released under the title *A Man and His Music*. He recorded a number of performances in the collection, but there was one that my dad watched on a loop. Mum would put it on so she could get on with her housework. If I was round, Dad and I would sing the songs together – 'Nancy (with the Laughing Face)', 'I've Got You Under My Skin', all sorts. For a long time, Dad remembered the lyrics, then they went and he'd sing the tune instead, slightly behind, but still there. Music had always been massive for my dad and continued to be so well into his dementia.

But Mum needed a break, and occasionally the three of us would go to the Trafford Centre and I'd take Dad off to Starbucks.

'Go on, Mum. Go and have a mooch on your own.'

I'd turn to my dad. 'Shall we go and have a coffee, pal?' In his mind, I was a friend, someone he'd just met perhaps, so I'd call him 'pal' or 'mate'.

He still recognised my mum as Elsie, though. She was the last person he forgot.

'Where's Elsie going?'

'Just to get a few bits. Come on, let's go and have a coffee.' Father and son but not father and son.

Dad would always have a latte and the conversation was just as familiar. I'd remind him of himself, his history, his life, and then he'd start to talk. As he spoke, he'd get comfortable, because he had something to offer, he was part of the moment. He'd talk and talk, and then he'd say, 'How do you know all this? How do you know all this about me?'

'Well, I've known you a long time, pal. I'm your friend.

I know Elsie, and I know you've got two sons, twins, Alan and Keith.'

'Yes, that's right.'

'And you've got another son, haven't you? He's the actor.'

'Yes, he's an actor. He does a bit of acting.'

There's a dark humour to this. I recognise that.

Occasionally someone would come up to me. 'Excuse me, sorry to bother you, can I have an autograph?'

'OK, no problem.'

My dad would sit there watching. There'd be a flicker of recognition at this unfolding scene.

Occasionally, I'd change things round by telling him what I did.

'Oh, you're an actor, are you? You do a bit of that, do you?'

I'd drag up his old saying from the play he'd done at Whiteacre.

'Cor, stone the crows, if it ain't Charlie. Move another inch and I'll blow your bleeding head orf.'

He'd start laughing. 'How do you know that?'

'It's one of yours. You did a bit of acting, didn't you, at Whiteacre?'

'Oh, I did, yeah. I was very happy at Whiteacre, you know.'

'What was the headmaster's name?'

'Mr Targett.'

'Mr Targett, that's right. And what was the name of your dormitory?'

Give it time and it would come.

Occasionally, I'd see anxiety in his eyes, a discomfort with this stranger talking to him, or the unfamiliarity of the surroundings, in which case I'd draw on speeches from Shakespeare:

To be, or not to be, that is the question:
Whether 'tis nobler in the mind to suffer
The slings and arrows of outrageous fortune,
Or to take Arms against a Sea of troubles,
And by opposing end them: to die, to sleep
No more.

He'd listen, agog. The words would settle with him for a few seconds.

'Bloody hell! Where've you had that from?'

'It's *Hamlet*.'

'Bloody good that. How do you remember all that?' He was amused, intrigued.

By that point, I'd made my peace with being anonymous to Dad. It might not have been perfect but, like the boy in the cinema watching spaghetti westerns all those years previously, I was just enjoying the closeness I'd always wanted. More than anything, I enjoyed it because I felt I was giving my mum a break, and I knew she needed one. My brothers would do the same. When I was with Dad, I was doing it for them and my mum, and whenever they were with my dad, they were doing it for us two. All three of us were so versed in Dad's history that we knew how to hand it back to him and make him come alive.

I'm not saying it was easy to interact with Dad on the basis of being unknown to him. How can that scenario ever lack a certain amount of pain? But, as awful, as gut-wrenching, as devastating as it was, we all came to understand that for us to have a relationship with him, we had to stop looking for recognition as ourselves. There's only one real path towards acceptance of dementia – take your ego out of it. Once you've done that, it's fine, because you can still love the person who's there.

That reconciliation with the situation, though, was ours, not his. Issues could still blow up from nowhere. There were times when he definitely saw me, this person who he didn't know, as a threat. Occasionally, I could feel his anger if I was driving him and Mum somewhere. Who was this stranger driving Elsie around? *He* drove Elsie around, that was his job.

Other times in the car he'd suddenly panic. 'I don't know where I'm going. I don't know where this place is.'

'It's OK, pal, I do,' I'd calm him, and eventually he'd quieten down. He needed someone to be firm, to ease his frantic mind.

He developed a nervous tick where he'd slap his legs – *rat-a-tat-a-tat-tat* – *tat, tat*. He'd never done it before dementia. It came, I think, when he had an intrusive thought – 'Who is this bloke driving me?' – physicalising it, an internal and unwitting coping strategy perhaps.

I would be reminded as he sat in the passenger seat how, when I was younger, and the roles were reversed, he would give my knee a squeeze as he changed gear. He did that from when I was three right up to my mid-thirties. Without thinking, one day, as I was driving him, I did the same back to him. He turned and looked at me, properly staring me down, as if I'd done something a bit queer, overstepped his boundaries. It was awful. He did that because he was frightened. The same man who had frightened me was now frightened himself because I had squeezed his knee.

That same perception of me as a threat also saw him practically kick me out of the house on Christmas Day. We'd had Christmas dinner, after which, traditionally, Dad had always washed the pots, his contribution to the day. As the dementia took hold, however, he'd done less and less around the house, and so I went into the kitchen to do the washing-up instead. He followed me. I tried not to make eye contact, but I knew he was staring at me. He walked out. I could hear him having a word with my mum. Then back in. Looking at me, a dirty look, trying to intimidate me. I knew I had to say something.

'Are you OK, pal?'

'Yes,' he replied, 'I'm all right. I'm OK.' The emphasis was very much on the 'I'm'.

He went back into the front room. I gave it a second and followed. Mum was sat there looking uncomfortable.

There was only one thing for it.

'Right, I'd better get going then.'

I put my coat on – 'See you both soon' – and left. He didn't want a stranger in the house; it was winding him up. The best way to deflate that situation was for me to leave, and that's exactly what I did.

I rang Mum the minute I got home. She got very upset, angry even, about Dad's behaviour. 'I'm annoyed with him,' she said. 'How could he kick his own son out the house on Christmas Day?'

'Mum,' I told her, 'Dad didn't kick me out the house. Dementia kicked me out the house.'

She knew that really. Kicking his son out was the last thing he would do.

Thankfully, there were other Christmases that delivered memories I treasure still. One year I got us a bottle of Amarone to have with our Christmas dinner. I poured three big glasses. Me and my mum sipped ours. My dad still hadn't touched his by the time he'd polished off his dinner.

'Ronnie,' my mum said, 'you haven't gone near your wine.' Ronnie was more of a beer man. He picked up that Amarone and sank it like a pint. That manifested itself a little later when the three of us ended up in the middle of the living room dancing to 'Saturday Night at the Movies' by The Drifters.

'Come on,' me and my mum were urging him, 'it's Christmas Day, we can still have a laugh.' He was very childlike, he was very happy. It was a lovely ray of sunshine through the gathering greyness.

Dad's reduced world was ever shrinking, and the evidence was visible not just in his relationship with his family but also in more everyday ways. This man who once had been so selective about the television he watched had now become someone who had it on all the time. He would sit in front of anything. Sometimes the TV took on an entirely new dimension. He really liked the sitcom *Miranda*, for instance, the reason being Miranda Hart talked direct to camera. My dad would talk back, agreeing with her – 'Yeah, yeah, oh yeah' – laughing. He thought she was in the room conversing with him. I nearly met her once and was disappointed when the chance disappeared. I wanted to let her know about my dad, because I suspect she was, without knowing it, connecting with a lot of people with dementia. There was almost a joy in seeing that relationship. It offset the more disturbing moments, like watching him scratch away at the carpet with his fingernails.

'What are you doing?'

'There's black pieces in this carpet.'

To see that was hard. This was the same man who had previously reached down from his chair, not for a non-existent presence in the carpet, but for a dictionary, a source of wonderment and surprise, shared with his wife and sons. Dementia had stolen that solid, purposeful, imaginative personality and replaced it with something random and unrecognisable.

It was also increasingly stripping his dignity. He'd get desperate for the toilet. I'd go into the gents at the Trafford Centre with him to make sure he found a cubicle, something he wouldn't be able to do on his own. Often then he wouldn't be able to go. The dementia meant he hadn't correctly recognised the signals from his brain. I'd be waiting by the door of the cubicle, listening. This was the same man, the same flesh and blood, who named all my Indians.

It was my mum who preserved my dad's dignity. She was his carer. I just occasionally looked after him. The quality of life Mum gave him was beautiful. He was never turned out anything less than immaculately. Changes that were made were incremental. Nothing that would ever upset his routine. She tried to keep their habits the same, so they ate together at the table – again dignity. Always dignity. We were never a dinner-in-front-of-the-telly family, only latterly did it become easier for her to let him eat like that. Those kinds of changes were never made blithely. And the emotional weight of his inability to act in a certain manner any more was never easy to deal with. My dad had very beautiful handwriting and would write all the Christmas cards, a challenge for my mum because of her dyslexia. His attention to detail even extended to the envelopes, which he would address with a great geometry by writing them parallel to the lines of the phone book. One year my mum said to me, 'I asked him to write the cards and I did get upset. I looked at the writing and it had really deteriorated. He was getting awfully mixed up.' That sounds like nothing, but when you've spent a life together, it's everything.

The carers should be writing these books. They know the truth of dementia better than anyone. And all too often, as they look after people who have forgotten themselves, so their stories, too, are forgotten. It would bring me up short sometimes to think of Mum and how every night she would lie in bed next to a husband to whom she was now a virtual stranger. How much must she have wanted to reach out for some comfort? How much in everyday life must she have yearned for a hug from him? How much must she have wanted, just for thirty seconds, for her Ronnie to come back?

She wasn't alone. There was always that little vestige of blind hope that some way, somehow, the old Dad, or something akin to him, would miraculously return. At one point, it did actually appear to have happened. Keith rang me up. 'Chris! He's come back!' I realised from Keith's tone his desire for it to be true.

I spoke to my dad on the phone.

'Hiya, cock, you all right?'

'Yeah, great.'

'You in London?'

'Yes, I'm in London.'

'Well, look after yourself, cock.'

Something had briefly realigned, and Dad was indeed, as Keith had indicated, very articulate. He seemed actually to know who I was. In the end, it turned out to be nothing more than a fleeting moment on a different drug.

Another time, Mum and Dad were watching the telly. Ronnie turned and stared her straight in the eye.

'What happened to me?'

'What do you mean, love?'

'What happened to me?'

My mum couldn't quite believe what she was hearing. It was 2010. Ronnie had been diagnosed with dementia for a decade. He hadn't asked anything of this nature, shown any recognition of his condition, for years. And then, suddenly, an eruption.

Mum was quick. 'Well, Ronnie,' she told him, gently, 'you've been having trouble with your memory. You're finding it hard to remember things.'

And then, in an instant, he went back to his previous self. That was it, done. The genie was back in the bottle.

When my mum told me what had happened, I found it immensely moving. Not just for my dad, and her, but as a human being. Ten years on, and smothered by medication, somewhere, somehow, Dad had managed to ask, 'What happened to me?' It was as though a spark had gone off in his mind – 'I've been living this life unconsciously and now I'm conscious – wow.' He was a shadow of his former self, and yet, from that darkness came a lightning flash of awareness, of enquiry. In that brilliant illumination was exhibited the strength of the man. Even at this point, so far down the line, there was something still happening inside, a semblance of Ronnie, a semblance of a man with an incredible mind attached to an incredible memory, a phenomenal memory. This was, remember, a bloke who had run warehouses as big as football pitches. If somebody came in looking for a particular box, he'd be there straight away – 'Aisle 85, pallet 61.' When he started going to Whiteacre reunions, his memory became a running joke. 'Right, Ronnie, who's this?' someone would ask, shoving a photo under his nose. 'And what dormitory was he in?' It became a party trick. I think he passed that skill on to me. I am in the memory game after all. More than lines, though, I remember things about people. He had a memory that threw its cloak wide, and I have that too. When Dad's memory started disappearing, however, that cloak turned to a straitjacket.

Thankfully, as the dementia worsened, there remained the odd chance to cast off the shackles. We would, for instance, go to Old Trafford a few more times. There remained in him some recognition of what was going on. The club would play the Matt Busby song 'United Calypso' over the PA system before the game and he would start singing it – *'Manchester, Manchester United; A bunch of bouncing Busby Babes; They deserve to be knighted!'* – later forgetting the words and filling in with the tune instead – '*da-de-da-de-da*'.

There is one goal that sticks in my head. Ruud van Nistelrooy ran half the length of the field with the ball and stuck it home. 'What a goal!' my dad was shouting. 'What a goal!' He was absolutely electrified. Whenever I see that goal, I think of him.

There was another unforgettable incident at Old Trafford. Me, Keith and Dad were walking round the ground and there was a car trying to get through the crowd. In it was the United defender Denis Irwin.

'Denis Irwin!' stated my dad. 'One of the best!' He said it, deliberately I think, in a very straightforward, parodic way, like an announcer, to the extent Denis himself started laughing and so did some of the blokes around us. I love that memory.

Eventually, however, Old Trafford became too much for him. Nearly seventy years after he first went to watch Manchester

United, we left his final match together before half-time. Sat in between me and Keith, I'd noticed he wasn't reacting to anything about the game. I think he became acutely aware that he wasn't at home, was in a place he didn't recognise, with lots of people he didn't recognise, possibly including us.

He got up. 'I'm going home.'

'It's only just started.'

He wasn't having it. 'I'm going.'

Lovely thing is he made us leave a game early that we were losing badly to our worst enemy. It was 14 March 2009, United v Liverpool. I have very little to thank Dad's dementia for, but I'll thank it for that.

Again, there was a synergy. Thirty-seven years earlier, on 11 October 1972, he'd taken me to my first game, Bristol Rovers at home in the League Cup – we'd lost that too. I didn't care. I was eight years old and with my dad. We had amazing seats, in the South Stand Upper, above where the manager sat, at that point Tommy Docherty. George Best and Bobby Charlton played. But none of that mattered. Like the cinema and TV, football, ever allied to the romantic idea that my dad could have been a professional, was a bond between me and him. On the way out at the end of the game, one of the Bristol fans was dancing on a trestle table with a big tall cardboard hat on his head, and all the United fans, including my dad, were laughing at him – none of that incessant abuse you get today. As ever, the fact the guy had the hutzpah to get on the table really appealed to my dad.

Recently, I took Albert to his first ever game, the FA Cup final. Chelsea beat us 1-0. At the end, he put a giant popcorn box over his head.

Memories.

2 2

THE RAVELL'D SLEAVE OF CARE

One time, Mum found Dad sat in the communal area.

'Come on, love,' she said, 'shall we go to your room?'

They walked in and she shut the door.

'Shall we have a dance?' he asked.

Mum was a little taken aback. Dad, after all, had never been one for dancing.

'Yes, we can have a dance if you want.'

They held one another and, as they did so, he tried to kiss her, gently pulling her down on to the bed.

For my mum, the sheer emotional stress, turmoil and soul-destroying dismay of the day Dad entered the home, the decanting of sixty years of immeasurable closeness and bound personal experience into an empty vessel of unknown strength or fragility, is beyond imagination.

As is the stark reality of the long hours of the night before as she lay in bed beside him, and the torturous conversation in her head – 'The man I've known for sixty years is right here next to me. And then tomorrow night I'll be here and he'll be in a home 8 miles away – and it's all my fault.'

Which it wasn't, of course. This wasn't the same man she'd known throughout those decades. His personality had been dismantled and dispensed with. It was physically him, but otherwise, the man she knew, and who knew her, had disappeared.

For eleven years, she had lain next to Dad as the dementia took gradual hold before she finally took a look beyond the boundaries of her own adoring arms and into a care home. Me, Alan and Keith, on the other hand, had long been thinking that Dad's care was becoming too much for her. Eleven years? There was no doubt in our minds that it was the right decision. The burden of care on her was immense, so intense as he got older, that we genuinely thought it might kill her. The effect on any carer can never be forgotten. There were two people in that relationship, not one. Mum wanted nothing more than to look after the man she loved, but 24-hour care is hard both physically and emotionally. Dad was never a benign presence. He still had the propensity to blow up. Anyone who has seen the effect of dementia knows it can make people unpredictable. I'm not sure any of us knew the real extent of what was happening behind that front door, day in, day out. I'm sure there were things she never told us, that she became quite adept at covering for him.

Mum had enjoyed some respite when Dad briefly went into care while I took her on holiday or she went away with friends. While never finding it easy to be separated from him, those breaks would deliver a visible improvement in her health, returning much less tired and stressed. Those short periods also provided a small degree of preparation for when he went into full-time care. When she did finally make that decision, it was a move, as ever, born from a place of utter unselfishness. Mum's attitude was simple – 'If anything happens to me, and the lads have to deal with it, it will be awful for them. So I'll do it.' She was nullifying the hard questions before they could ever happen. Would I come back from London and look after him? Would Alan or Keith take him into their families? She put all that to bed by making her decision. It was a perfect example of her emotional generosity and sense of maternity.

The day she left him at the home, Alan went with her. I rang her later. She was devastated. Just devastated. 'The worst day of my life,' she would always tell me, 'was not when your father died, but when I had to put him in a home.'

More than anything, Mum wanted to know Dad was being well looked after, cared for, treasured, as he deserved, but sadly it wasn't a good place. The respite home, where Dad had stayed while Mum had the odd rest, would have been perfect. Not only was it at the end of their road, but it offered a close and welcoming environment. Disappointingly, when the time came, they couldn't take my dad permanently because his level of dementia was too great. Ronnie being in a different home further away meant Mum would suffer when they were apart, wondering whether he was eating, or if people were being kind to him.

The home could definitely be chaotic. One night I went to see him and initially couldn't find him. He wasn't in the main space, nor the side room, but a smaller room I'd never seen him in before. As I sat with him, an elderly man got up and punched a frail and greying old woman in the face. My immediate reaction was to look at my dad. I saw him flinch. 'Oh. Eh. Don't do that,' he told the man. Twenty years previously, he'd have flattened him. The woman had been laughing, now she was sobbing. 'No!' I said to the man who'd attacked her, and took my dad out. Seeing my dad in that environment, and his sense of distress and confusion, was shattering. I was the only person of sound mind in that room. It was like a roomful of children with no one in charge. I was only in the home for the odd hour here and there. My dad was in there twenty-four hours a day. All I could think was, *What the hell is happening to him? What are they doing to each other?* These places, farcically, are called care homes, when the actual carers are nowhere to be seen. The only ever-present at Dad's care home was the smell of urine and excrement, shrouded in air freshener. That, no doubt, comes down to a lack of money. We have somehow turned care of those with dementia into a business where patients aren't cared for but managed. The care is for the balance sheet. My belief is we don't know the half of what goes on in care homes. When we're told what dose of medication our loved ones are on, can we really be sure that is the case? If there are forty or fifty people in one place with dementia, are they not being given more sedatives to keep them just so? If people in homes are invisible, how do we know their care isn't too?

Mum certainly was vigilant. She was distressed once when she turned up to find Dad in someone else's pyjamas. As she had done at home, she tried to ensure he was well turned out, taking clothes in for him. Dad also suffered from badly split feet, which gave him great pain, so she'd attend to them as well. She'd do very practical things to make him feel comfortable. Mum won't want me eulogising what she did because she'd say, 'He's my husband. I was married to him. He'd have done it for me.' And she was right, he would. But when you see carers, and I'd see many of them at the home – sons and daughters with their mums, blokes like me and my brothers sat with their dads – the beautiful lightness of their love is doubtless combined with an immense weight of guilt, tension, loss and sorrow.

Generally, Dad would sit in the main room where there'd be a lot more residents. The routine became familiar. I'd walk in, see a nurse calming someone down – 'Now, now' – look round and there'd be Dad. I'd walk over. 'Hiya, pal!' He'd make a noise – 'Uh, uh.' If Mum was with me – 'Hello, Ron? Are you all right, love?' – there'd be little bit more coming for her. He didn't hold on to Elsie as his wife; he held on to her as someone benign and nurturing. She gave him a comfort that I couldn't. When he was with Mum, I could see and feel him picking up love. He'd look up and smile because the love was just there. It truly existed, as tangible as the carpet under his feet, the noise from the telly.

Dad's speech disappearing didn't distress me as much as the visual cues, the expression in his eyes that revealed the loss of himself as Ronnie. What he was saying made sense to him, even if he wasn't mechanically able to shape the words. While there was, naturally, an overarching sadness at his predicament, just being in his physical presence was lovely. The smiles I got, or witnessed, were worth millions to me. When they came, I'd feel a rush of emotion.

To maintain an air of normality, I might tell him the United score. I was there once when they were actually in action – 'United are playing, Dad, and they're winning.' An 'Uh' of recognition.

'I remember you telling me about Duncan Edwards,' I'd say sometimes, prompting a short flurry of noises, completely incomprehensible. I had a feeling at the root of that utterance was his stock phrase – 'Amazing – legs like tree trunks.'

Mentions of Elsie, Duncan Edwards, Whiteacre or Colgate-Palmolive would generally generate a reaction. What I would want to do but always held back on was mentioning the twins, because of my own experience of him not knowing who I was. There was a very good chance he would remember he'd had identical twins, but at the same time the concept of being a father had gone. I felt maybe I could mention them, but the Cornwall experience prohibited it.

What I really wanted to do was bang on the table and say, 'You had twins, mate! You had three kids actually – the other one is me. You are a United fan. You saw the Busby Babes. You married Elsie. She's the best woman on the planet.'

I would feel at times very, very patronising. I was always somehow waiting for him to go, 'I beg your pardon. Are you talking to me? Who's put me in here? I'm not having this.'

There was a total awareness of talking down to him, the tone of voice you might adopt with a child. There was part of me that wouldn't have been at all surprised if he'd got up – 'Come on, Elsie! This is bloody stupid. I'm off.'

Mum was going to the home all the time, barely a day went by without her visiting Dad, even though it meant two buses there and two buses back, well into her eighties. Sometimes, Alan, Keith or I would join her. When I was with her, I could sense Elsie, forever selfless Elsie, thinking of not just Ronnie's emotions but mine as well. 'How's Chris going to handle this?'

I never wanted to disturb Mum and Dad's dynamic – don't ruffle too many emotional feathers. I was hugely sensitive to what Mum and Dad had, so often just sitting with them was enough. I've never been to a Quaker meeting, but the notion that they just sit down and don't necessarily speak has always been attractive to me. That is what I found myself doing.

Mum's visits, by their very nature, would generally be

formulaic. She'd sit and talk to Dad, sometimes getting a reaction, other times receiving very little at all. They were, however, not always predictable. After all, no one on the outside can ever know exactly what is going on in a mind affected by dementia, what connections are being made, what barriers raised and lowered, what echoes of the past rattling and resonating. I love the story about him trying to kiss her in his room. She wasn't to know, but in his head, he was thinking, *I'm in here!* It was still there, fancying her. I love what he, they, shared in those fleeting few seconds. A glimpse of a life snuffed out, and yet somehow ever flickering.

'Ronnie, do you know who I am?' Elsie asked him one day.

'I don't,' he told her, 'but I love you.'

There is another moment of great tenderness that will forever stay with me. Three months after Dad went into the home, Albert was born in Saint Mary's Hospital, south Manchester – I was in the city working on a TV job. I wanted Dad to see Albert and so picked him and Mum up and took them to the hospital. I sat Dad down and handed Albert to him. As ever with dementia, it was a bittersweet moment. He didn't know who I was; he didn't know who Albert was. But I was happy that one day I could now say to Albert, 'You met him.'

Dad held this tiny baby close, looking into his eyes. It brought about a calmness in him for a moment.

'What a lovely boy.'

And for me the circle was complete.

23

THE END

'Daddy, I'm not going to celebrate any more birthdays, and I don't want you to celebrate any more because that means you're getting older and then you'll die.'

'Don't worry, Albert. I plan to get younger the older I get. I'm lucky. I have a job that means I never have to grow up. I play characters. I play.'

Children are right. Everything is as precious as they see it.

The fact I was now dealing with a son at the beginning of his life and a father at the end wasn't lost on me. Sometimes it felt almost mythical and biblical. Other days there was so much going on I couldn't feel anything. What was always apparent to me was that I was building a world with Albert while the one I occupied with Dad had long slipped away. Mum was facing the other end of the line. I had renewal in my life. She had prolonged loss. Dad's demise was always going to be long and drawn out because he was such a powerful spirit and also because he was physically powerful, which I think I've inherited, both being from generations and generations of workers, the same with being very strong-willed.

Dad's strength would trick Mum at times. After the cancer, he lost huge amounts of weight, but his physicality soon returned.

'I think your dad's getting a bit better,' Mum would say to me.

'What, from the cancer?'

'No, generally.'

She was asking for it to be true – that the dementia was in reverse.

'He's getting better physically, Mum,' I had to tell her. 'That's all.'

I'd argue that his body was kept going far too long. My mum would challenge that. She'd say, 'No, it was his life and he had to live it.'

Dad's resolve to carry on, I believe, only truly left him once he entered the care home. The eagle was still in there, but its eyes lacked the spark. It was an animal stripped of reflex and instinct. With Elsie no longer always by his side, Dad lost his will.

Early one morning, I got a call. Dad had got up in the night, fallen, and broken his hip. I put the phone down. I had only one thought. *This man has woken up, got out of bed to try to reach the toilet, doesn't really know who he is, where he is, and he's fallen over and broken his hip – and none of us were there with him.* For Mum, the sense that she had abandoned him to his fate was overpowering. The rest of us felt it too, a terrible guilt that we were all comfortable sleeping in our beds while he was lying prone on the floor like an animal. I wanted to look after my mum, to say to her, 'Look, you had no choice, you had to put him in the home.' But it wasn't that easy. The spike to the conscience was felt deeply by us all. An overriding emotion of 'I should have been there'.

The fall meant surgery, a hip replacement. Dad was

eighty-three, incontinent, and had no idea what was going on. After the operation, he was being stood up, put through rehab, and didn't even know he'd broken his hip in the first place. He was demented, in pain, and knocked about mentally, as he had been after the cancer surgery, by the anaesthetic.

In the wake of the operation, Dad contracted pneumonia. I woke one morning a few days later to find eighteen missed calls on my phone, mostly from Alan. I was working in London and looking after Albert at the time. The phone rang again.

'Hello, Chris.'

'Hi, Alan.'

And he just started crying. At that stage, I wasn't sure whether he was upset about Mum or Dad. Eventually, he got it out that my dad had died. My first instinct, as would Alan's have been had he not been at the fierce end, was to ask him if he was OK and thank him for telling me, because that's not an easy job for anybody. I felt very close to him at that point.

I did that thing we all do – 'Listen, I'll be fine. Don't worry about me. You've got enough on your plate.' Which is exactly what my dad would have told us in any similar circumstance. I then rang Mum. As much as she could, I knew she had readied herself. Just as death was a release for Dad, we'd said good-bye to the person we knew a long time ago. It's true what they say, when it comes to someone with dementia, you say goodbye twice.

Keith worried me more. He and Dad were particularly close. There was a chemistry between them, a special bond. Later I discovered that, at the moment of death, Keith convinced himself that the death rattle was not the death rattle and that my dad was coming back.

He put Dad's glasses back on his face. 'Come on,' he said, 'you're Ronnie Ecc. You're Ronnie Ecc.'

He took it very hard, and bottled it up more. While from the minute in 2001 when the doctors said the word dementia, we'd all started steeling ourselves, and there were then a lot of little steeling ourselves all along the way, the shock of the actual event remains. Somebody in your family is going mad. Your father is going mad. And the full stop will be his death. That finality still has to be met.

Dad was laid out in a funeral parlour in Little Hulton, about 200 yards from The Vulcan where I used to go with him on a Friday night. We'd have a pint and then go and get fish and chips and take them home for my mum.

'You know you can see him, cock, if you want,' she told me.

'Do you think I should?' With me being an atheist, I wasn't sure.

'Yes.' She was quite firm.

I went up to the parlour and was shown into the small room where Dad was being kept. Immediately I started behaving like an actor in a film. Acting, definitely acting, maybe to protect myself from the fear – it was the first corpse I'd ever seen.

Dad was covered up to his chest. He was wearing a shirt and tie. My mum would have chosen it, as ever. She had always turned him out beautifully when he could no longer look after himself and this was no different.

I looked at the body before me and thought how there was only a vague resemblance to Ronnie Eccleston. He looked so gaunt. There was no life in the face, and it was the life that made the man. But there'd been very little life in that face for a good few years. It had been replaced by fear and confusion. Ronnie had died spiritually almost completely before he died physically.

Like in the bad film that was being projected in my brain, I kissed his forehead. It was the coldest thing I'd ever touched in my life. And yet I also felt a huge sense of relief. I realised my dad was not his body; he was his personality, and how I received his personality and held it in my heart.

He was no longer suffering.

Later, I had a glass of wine with Mum. I asked her why she thought I should go to the funeral parlour.

'I thought if you went,' she told me, 'you wouldn't in later life say, "I wish I'd seen my dad." There's just a chance in ten years' time you might have thought *I could have seen him one more time.*'

You've always been a brilliant mother, I thought.

All three of us brothers were pallbearers at the funeral, along with Keith's son Peter and Alan's son Joe. I was determined to speak at the service. It was a situation not unfamiliar to me. I do generally get asked to say something at funerals back home because of my acting. I find that touching, while also liking the northern practicality of it – 'He'll know how to do it.' But, having attended many funerals, I also knew I wanted Dad's, for me at least, to be different.

Other than always taking a hard-backed chair in a café and making a joke about it being because I'm a Protestant, I've no real interest in religion, and that can be traced back to my early days. As a child, Mum took me with her to church, but I was bored. There was nothing there that interested me. I'd just sit and play with the umbrella stand at the end of the pew. The only part of it I liked was getting an ice cream on the way back. Unlike the twins, I was never confirmed. I'm glad. Even as a kid I'd have been questioning it.

My attitude echoed my dad's disinterest in the church. There was a Catholicism to him – his family on his mother's side are Irish – but his attachment had long lapsed. My mum, meanwhile, is very English, very C of E. I watched my dad closely when it came to religion. He always went through the motions when we attended a wedding or any church occasion. He would adopt the supplicant posture, sing the hymns, but I never bought it. I was suspicious of how he really felt. He wouldn't go to church with Mum on a Sunday morning, which I took as him expressing his views. The difference between me and him is I don't think a man of his time would assume he had the intellectual clout to go a step further and express atheism or agnosticism. He wouldn't have considered it his place, and even if he did, he wouldn't have wanted to detract from something that was clearly very important to my mum. Only when the dementia came would he actually go with her to church functions. I've a feeling, though, even then it was mainly for the beer.

As an atheist, I'd often been frustrated by the religious side of proceedings taking over at funerals, with the real person, at the very point they should be celebrated, somehow lost within. I truly believed that somebody should speak about Dad unclouded by religion. Rather than it be a religious occasion, if someone had delivered the lines from 'On Ilkley Moor Baht 'at', about the real nature of death, that someone is everywhere and yet nowhere, it would have made more sense to me.

I knew also that my mum, Keith and Alan are more

respectful of religion, and I was mindful of that. I wanted to be reflective of what we as a family would say, but I was conscious too that all of us had very different relationships with my dad. While my mum had her faith, and both her and Dad loved that particular church and spent a lot of time there, equally I thought there was a place for me there as Ronnie's atheist son. There will be some who'll read that and say, 'He just wanted to make it about himself.' But it wasn't that at all. This was my dad's send-off. The church, as in organised religion, weren't going to tell me about my father, my family, and so I delivered a eulogy that encapsulated Dad as I saw him. It wasn't an easy task, but I tried my best to sieve the words right down to the essentials of who my dad was.

Those words weren't just for the family and congregation; I was talking to him.

When Mum passes away, I will want to say something again, but I would never want to take Alan and Keith's space if they want to. We can all say something if we want. But then I get an image of my mum in my head, the coffin opening – 'Chris, Keith's already said something so you don't have to. Goodnight!'

I think the English can learn a lot from the Irish when it comes to death. A traditional Irish wake puts the focus right on the person who's gone, from the moment of death onwards. Stories, drinks, celebrations for two or three days. The attitude is very much, 'This is a massive event, so let's not draw the curtains and turn away from it.' I love that approach. It informed my desire to speak in a different way at my dad's funeral and it will at my mum's.

While the home was, quite clearly, the last stepping stone

before the grave, and I had been waiting for Dad to die, grief, actual physical grief, didn't afflict me at the funeral. I think mentally I was too consumed by events in my own life, particularly the arrival of my children. Three days before Dad died, Mischka had told me she was pregnant again – one in, one out – while Albert wasn't yet a year old. That whole synergy of arrivals and departures again.

Some days later, however, I went for a run on Hampstead Heath, a run that I knew was about my father's death, just as I had known other runs had been rehearsals for it. There, 2.5 miles in, on the heath, right in the depths of winter, I saw a tree, completely bare, except for a blackbird alone on a branch. I was struck immediately how it looked like my dad in the home. Underfed. Anxious. And then it flew off. It sounds like pretentious poetic thinking, but as an atheist my sense of otherness is in nature, and that order of life meant there was a connection between that bird and my father. If that's pretentious, then tough. Some people find comfort in the Bible, but all that stuff about 'he's just gone into another room' means nothing to me. We should be careful when foisting platitudes about death onto other people, especially children. When Auntie Annie died, I was told she was 'inside a star'. I thought the inside of a star looked like the *Star Trek* set. Somehow she'd fallen off the slab and ended up in there. No wonder I've ended up like I am.

The blackbird, though, did mean something to me – an expression of my love for my dad. Ronnie, real Ronnie, had flown. *He's Ronnie again now,* I thought. *He's been released.* Ronnie had himself back, and I definitely felt like I had Dad back. This interloper, wraith-like, thrashing, kicking his sons out the house, shadow Ron, demented Ron, had gone. That wasn't Dad. That was him trapped. Beirut hostage Brian Keenan spoke of an evil cradling, and that's what my dad experienced, imprisoned, kept captive, reduced to a subhuman state. I was angry about that and what it did to my dad's existence. I was watching a dance of death, and it's horrendous to see anyone in that state, let alone someone you love so deeply. You can pretty it up – 'The home's nice isn't it?' – you have to. But my dad, could he have seen himself, would have been angry too. His dignity, his sense of independence, hygiene – his basic sense of 'You don't bloody have to look after me' – was taken from him, stripped. He was, as Shakespeare calls it in *King Lear*, 'a poor, bare, forked animal'. I'm not ashamed of using that phrase because, if I'd said to Dad, 'Shakespeare called humanity a poor, bare, forked animal,' the first thing he'd have said to me is, 'Well, that is marvellous.'

When it's all over, you realise death is the eighth stage of dementia. It can come naturally, or, as in Dad's case, a person falls, they go for a hip operation, they get an infection, generally pneumonia, and they die. And yet somehow dying isn't the same as being dead. Some months later, I was in Los Angeles for reshoots on *Thor: The Dark World*. I was in a hire car at some lights when it suddenly occurred to me that, while my dad was physically dead, the love I felt from him and towards him was still coursing through me, informing my decisions and driving me onwards. It wasn't a moment of consolation; it was one of enlightenment – 'If there's been love, which there was, and is, it, he, can never die.'

He still exists today.

24

I HAVE THEE NOT, AND YET I SEE
THEE STILL

'Daddy,' Esme looked at me, 'I don't want to grow up. I just want to be a child and play with my toys.' I thought of myself on the living-room carpet playing with my Indians. I shouldn't be surprised if I had said those exact same words.

Writing this book has emphasised to me what I already suspected – my dad has shaped me in every way imaginable. Over the past months I have taken a metaphorical journey from Salford to Stratford and back again. It is a route I thought I knew well – the key junctions, the forks in the road. Truth is there have been waypoints and markers that have taken me down routes never previously explored. Waiting for me at the end, time and time again, was a single figure – Ronnie Eccleston.

All my choices in life, past and present, I can directly relate to him. Same with my career. Always acting for my dad, always trying to get his attention, reacting first and foremost to his frustrations, unhappiness and personal limitations. I ended up playing a succession of versions of him, characters he could have been had he been shown a different path in life. I've used everything I've absorbed and observed about my father to express Matt Jameson in *The Leftovers*, Nicky Hutchinson in *Our*

Friends in the North, Drew Mackenzie in *Hearts and Minds*, and countless others. Sometimes that worked, sometimes it didn't, but they were all a continuation of my lifelong attempt to work my dad out. I was all at sea in *Hamlet* because I could never see how me or my dad could have become a philosophy student.

Dad isn't alone. I've played versions of Alan, I've played versions of Keith, and I've played versions of Mum, too. All of them are very different people from one day to the next, but they were far easier to work out. My dad was forever an enigma, one who is following me through the generations, with me every step of the way, almost quite literally. I was getting ready to go on holiday recently when I heard '*pad, pad, pad*' on the stairs. I turned round and there he was. Or rather there was Albert, wearing my dad's scarf and coat, which I'd had hung up in my bedroom for years. Topping off the effect was my cap. Albert as Ronnie. He was laughing. So was I. It was as funny as it was moving.

To have such joy in my life is incredible. I am a man who, like the majority, has been held hostage by buried emotion. The ransom could never be paid because the required currency was personal openness and honesty. And yet now, finally, I feel freedom. I was thinking today about some of the major issues in my life, and, as I did so, I became conscious of my mental mechanism. But instead of sinking me into depression and negativity, as would previously happen, that mechanism was positively reinforcing my decisions and the way forward. It was almost as if I could feel the neurons firing in my brain – 'It will be fine,' they were telling me, 'you are doing a good job. It will work out.' I've never had a moment like that, ever, where I've felt I'm actively monitoring my own brain activity in a positive manner. Prior to my severe clinical depression, my motor was entirely the opposite. Actually, that's not entirely true. I am aware of a period of paradise pre-breakdown, but it boils down to a single afternoon when I was walking down Coniston Avenue on the grass verge on a warm summer's day. A car drove past with the windows down and I could hear 'Summer Breeze' by the Isley Brothers on the radio.

In that moment, I felt blissful – 'This is me, doing this, right now.' An awareness of presence, an awareness of happiness. I believe that was a moment of out-of-body euphoria where, for once, briefly, my mental processes emerged from the cloud. Otherwise my engagement with the world was permanently shadowed. I suspect 50 per cent of that is nature, the way I came into this world, my genetic predisposition. The other half is the separation I have talked about, being alone among two pairs, and the years prior to my dad's nervous breakdown when he moved from being a stacker truck driver to a foreman, years when, while I never thought it intellectually, his rages traumatised me to the point where I firmly believe there was part of me thinking I could die.

It is my breakdown that finally allowed me a release from the mindset of that terrified little boy, the most terrifying thing to have ever happened to me, and yet by far the most revelatory. But I am acutely aware that many, perhaps the majority, don't come through such an experience intact. I did, and to do so has given me so much understanding of myself. It's given me self-respect, and also confidence, because I saw myself through it. I was helped by chemicals, medication and brilliant people, but I went and sought that help.

A therapist once said to me, 'We don't ask to come into this life. We have no choice on the matter. We have no choice when and how we leave. We leave whether we want to or not. And in the middle of those two things is this tranche that we have to make sense of.' And it's true. That's why I drop what happened to my mental health into conversation very easily. I realise it's part of human experience, it informs every day of my life, and, having been such an extreme event, it was bound to. I was walking along late last year, the dog days of November, and the light was so murky it could have been eight in the morning or eight at night.

'Bloody hell,' I winced, 'this is miserable.'

And then I had another thought, *Hang on, actually this is great compared to how I once felt.*

That's a change in me that has been brought about by a near-death experience. The glass is always half full now. It was always half empty before. I faced my own death. I know what that's like – terrifying – but it has made me calmer. I feel weathered, experienced, happier. I face my problems now with fortitude, not fear. I have come to recognise that I was seeing my world, and my place in it, through an unorthodox prism. The shards that sprang from it included acting and adventure. They also included anorexia, self-loathing and, inexorably, breakdown.

I'm grateful for the body dysmorphia, grateful for the self-hatred, the combative approach to authority, the self-sabotage, because again, like the breakdown, they will inform my relationship with my children, allowing ongoing and mutual freedom of expression that I hope will help them tackle their own problems in life. I have taken what I learnt from my own father/son dynamic and taken it into that relationship. Dad loved me, could be incredibly tender, and proud, but those expressions of affection were hugely overshadowed by a chronic lack of communication. I internalised a lot of his moods and his frustrations and depressions and would be deeply upset were my children to do the same. Again, that is why I can thank a severe clinical suicidal depression. It was excruciating in its hurt, but it managed to break the chain. I'm at peace now, know where I am, know what I've got to do, know where I'm going. My children will surprise me and scare me but I'm ready for anything because I know how extreme and complex I myself was as a child and young person.

I know also that my mum and dad weren't afforded the luxury of such awareness. They didn't have the opportunity to ponder quirks of personality in themselves or anyone else. They were educated until they were fourteen and then kicked out into the workplace. They received one message and one message only – that they, and everyone like them, were worthless. That made the truth of my father difficult to find. When it comes to Albert and Esme, I hope their search for the truth of their dad will be rather easier to uncover, not hidden, shielded behind centuries of stultifying convention in which emotional honesty, by a perverse necessity, was smothered at birth. The truth of their dad will be plain to see. I don't want them to search online to find out about me, nor feel a need to analyse my performances down the years. Never must they peer hopelessly over a barrier of non-communication. There has been honesty from the start. The cycle of silence has been broken, scrapped, remoulded into something that screams openness.

Esme asked me the other day, 'Daddy, do you like Mummy?'

'Well,' I said, 'when me and Mummy met, we fell in love and had you. Having two children very quickly is hard on parents in a relationship and then Mummy and Daddy started to not like each other. Now, Esme, as you've seen, we are trying to be friends.'

As a child, I would have liked that level of honesty and can-didness with my parents, but it was no more part of Ronnie and Elsie than it had been their parents, and so on and so on before. I completely understand that the openness switch was neither at their fingertips nor was it socially reinforced. Emotion could hold a working-class child back, make them unready for what was to come – what they were for. I am thankful to have been given the opportunity to have a more grounded relationship with my children. Before Albert and Esme, playing football, wrestling, doing a crossword or mock-boxing with my own dad were the happiest things I could ever imagine in my life. They go right to the heart of me. Now, I have a new happiness with my own children. And it is a happiness born of honesty.

The blight on that happiness is that I don't live with them. I know I've yet to come to terms with that fact. This book will help, the increasing distance from the hospitalisation will help, but it's something that will always hurt inside. The legal system could certainly help deliver balance for parents and children involved in separation and divorce. Hopefully, we are in the dog days of the Victorian view of men and women and their role in their children's lives, which has led to institutional and historic bias. In the twenty-first century, an authentic emo-tional relationship can come from a man as much as a woman. I've tried very hard to achieve that with Albert and Esme. Even though there was a six-month hiatus in my relationship with them, it didn't feel like there was a barrier between us when we resumed because of how involved emotionally and in every other way I had always been in their lives. Until I had children, I was a selfish and self-obsessed man who'd been pursuing his career and taking care of himself and himself alone, but when they came I understood completely that the love comes from the drudgery – the nappies and the sleepless nights – and I was more than ready to put myself aside. I love that unseen side of parenting. If Albert or Esme had colic and I could put them on my shoulder for two or three hours and it went, that to me genuinely felt like a bigger achievement than playing Macbeth. It really did. Parenthood isn't about me; it's about them. I've spent my life trying to understand human motivation and what shapes us, and now here I am involved in shaping other human beings, my flesh and blood, given a wide-open window into how impressionable we are and how we receive the world. It's fascinating. And they're yours. Yours and your partner's. And if that relationship fails, it's for the legal system to help, equally, for you and your partner to rebuild and share.

Back in 1932, when Mum entered the world, equality wasn't even a pipe dream. Dad's imprint is all over this book, but I'll never let it be forgotten the huge role Mum has played in my life. While Dad's investment tended to depend on his mood, Elsie could never be so fickle. Her expectations for herself were secondary to those for her family. The sacrifices she made, conscious or otherwise, have given me a beautiful constancy. I never dream about my mum. Brothers, mates, my dad, are all there, but never my mum. That shows how utterly at peace with her I am. I always was, almost to the point of taking her for granted. Mum is the one I've always relied on to be there, and she always has been. Were she to enter my dreams, then that would fall into the realms of her not being there, which, of course, one day is inevitable. She will still, though, like my dad, be the epicentre of myself.

It says a lot about social conditioning that, even with such a strong female presence, I should have spent so much of my life trying to be like my dad and not trying to be like my dad. There is one element of Ronnie, however, on whose proximity to myself I am unable, at this stage at least, to deliver a verdict. Is dementia going to happen to me? It's an appropriate question, and one, inevitably, that looms larger as I get older, just as it did for my dad. When he watched Grandpa Pop go mad, it's unarguable that a thought would have been reverberating in his head – *Christ, I hope that doesn't happen to me.* And now I'm thinking the same. But why shouldn't it? I share so many characteristics with my dad, why should dementia be any different? Here I am, a bloke who's written this book about his dad and dementia, and there's almost an inevitability it will happen to me.

Am I living with that dread? Definitely, there's an inner fear. I don't want to be in his position. I felt unbelievable pity for him thrashing about that hospital bed, having this person, me, trying to keep his hand away from his penis to stop him pulling off the catheter. It could have been any human being and I'd have felt the same degree of pity. Could that be me one day? No one can honestly know. But I can't help but wonder. Certainly, I am more forgetful now than I've ever been, but as a parent, as a working person, that's unavoidable. Memory loss is part of the ageing process. Its little joke is to come just as you have so much to cram in.

In *Macbeth*, there was a scene where every night I would bang my head on the floor. I kept thinking, *I shouldn't be doing*

this – I'm inviting trouble down the line, but I know also that I've
given myself as good a chance as I can. I've kept myself fit all
my life, kept the weight off, clearly to extremes at times, and
when I have my heart and blood pressure tested, the professionals always tell me how good they are for a man my age.
In my mid-fifties, I was recently told I have the metabolic age
of a man of forty-two. Maybe, however, personality type will
override all that, which makes me think dementia is indeed
very likely to call. I've echoed my dad, in mind and body, all
my life. Is it realistic to expect our paths to diverge over the last
few miles? The probability we will remain entwined means I've
put together a healthcare package for myself in later life. I love
Albert and Esme so much. If the time comes when I'm swal-
lowed by dementia, I don't want them to have to go through
what I did with my dad. I don't want it to consume their lives.
I don't want it to scar again and again and again.

The difference in the end may be that, unlike Dad, I have
been allowed to live. He could have been an actor. He had all
the raw materials, intelligence, a mercurial emotional life, life
experience. But it was me who was given my freedom. I have
a job that I love and that stimulates me. As his soul was caged,
so mine has roamed. Maybe that will save me. If it does, there's
a chance I could find myself aged eighty playing King Lear and
acting dementia. That resonance isn't lost on me. If I do play
Lear, he will be based on that image of my dad, naked, trying to
pull the catheter out – that poor, bare, forked animal. Stripped
in every way. As with Macbeth, Dad will be right up there on
stage with me.

Let's face it, he already physically accompanies me in every
role. The resemblance is clear. A cursory glance at any photo

in this book will explain where I got that nose, those ears. What always struck me more, though, were his shoes. The left one would be perfect, the right looked older by a decade, smashed up on one side because of his gait. My shoes are a size bigger but exactly the same. Peter Bowker calls my walk the 'Margate pimp roll'. I have, without any conscious knowledge, quite literally followed in Dad's footsteps. Perhaps that, more than any mental analysis, any time in an armchair being quizzed by a cigar-puffing psychologist, reveals my essential obsession with Ronnie Ecc.

I was in two minds whether to write this book. Again and again, well into the process, I have woken in the night and asked myself a simple question, 'What am I trying to achieve?' I never drifted back off entirely sure, but I knew the last thing I ever wanted was for these pages to be a celebration of my Wikipedia entry. 'This is me – look what I've done!' There's always been a disconnect with me and celebrity. I've never embraced it. I'm not stupid, I see people recognise me, but from the first few minutes of it happening around Manchester in the early '90s, I saw it for what it was, dismissed it, and never engaged with it. That has been a very healthy thing in my life. Forget 'celebrity', 'the business'; I wanted this book to explore elements far more deep and elemental – the nature of father/son relationships, dementia, masculinity, mental health. I wanted it to show that to succeed is not always to keep your head down and try to fit in. And, most importantly of all, I wanted to throw a spotlight on the generations, the millions and millions, for whom 'success', defined as anything other than the basic survival of themselves and their family, was a concept of which they were denied to the extent that they were chained, leg, wrist and neck, to an institutionally blessed mindset of zero expectation. To those in charge of those institutions, the working class is as it describes. A production line of workers, nothing more, nothing less. People? With character, hope, intelligence, ambition? Forget it. Get back in your box and shut up.

I was asked a few years ago to go on the BBC genealogy show *Who Do You Think You Are?* I agreed and they started looking into my family tree. It says everything that the project went nowhere. They tugged aside the leaves on those branches and concluded, 'Nothing to see here.' Generations of working-class people dismissed. Individuals with their own hopes, dreams and stories. Not army generals, industrialists, vaudeville singers, but factory workers, farm labourers, cleaners, nothing in any way 'sexy' enough for TV.

No doubt if someone like me had popped up in the dim and distant, all would have been good. But why? My father had all my abilities, linguistically, physically, and then some. So, no doubt, did generations before him. I get that my life has been far more fulfilled than my father's and those before him, but for me that makes him the far more interesting story. What do I know of life? I'm not driving stacker trucks all day at Colgate-Palmolive and then going to Bulmers and driving stacker trucks there all night. I'm not cleaning floors in a launderette like Mum. And yet how often is the story of the working class ever told on TV? I don't mean the dross that is soaps. I mean properly told? The answer is less and less. Working-class stories don't fit in boxsets. They don't make money. They don't fit the business model of selling to global TV. And yet they are the lives that talk to me, define me. They are the lives I find endlessly fascinating. I would like one day to make a series about dementia, play the role of someone in a home, and that same person on his route to getting there. The person he is, was, and everything in between. That person will, of course, intentional or otherwise, be my dad. Until I die, every role I play will be my dialogue with my dad continued.

There is something inside me that dislikes intensely the fact that we live in a world where only the stories of people like myself 'matter'. But if readers of this book see I was anorexic, had a nervous breakdown, was wracked with self-doubt, and harboured a rollcall of other issues, and draw something from it, then its writing has been justified. I hope it helps to see that someone, a reasonably successful actor, was actually dodging, and occasionally plunging headfirst, into mental crevasses so sadly familiar to us all. That, like so many others, my life is a 1,000-piece jigsaw tipped daily onto the floor.

When I read *The Boy Who Was Afraid* as a child, it was an early indication of how I have spent a lifetime thinking about myself, same as my dad, and his family before him. My mum and dad's lives were ruled by fear — fear of money, fear of unemployment, fear of illness, fear of saying the wrong thing, fear of not using the right cutlery in a hotel. That parcel was passed along and ended up with me. And yet I wanted to play Macbeth at the RSC, and I did it. I wanted to play a lead at the Olivier Theatre, and I did it. I'm not bigging myself up; I'm saying that anybody else who feels they are The Boy Who Was Afraid can do it too. I want to tell my story because I hope it's universal. I've never felt good enough, always felt afraid, never quite trusted my head, but somehow . . .

Now I have a book on a shelf too. Again, though, its meaning goes way beyond simple achievement. As soon as the first seed of this idea was sown, I had a single thought, *Of all the things my dad could have done, he would have loved to have written a book.* It was, I think, my dad's great unexpressed unconscious desire. His passion for language, his love of crosswords, was where we always connected. If my dad had walked into a bookshop and seen 'by Christopher Eccleston', I know he'd have found it incredible. He knew I played Hamlet and countless other significant roles, but if I told him there was going to be a book with our name on it, that would have been a different level. If he was still here to see it, I'd remind him of one thing – all this started with his dictionary.

Dad's chair remains in the same position. My mum, the twins and I still feel a bit self-conscious when we sit in it. The memories it harbours aren't cushioned; they're strong, hard, vivid. It's why, no matter how old I am, however distant the memory, there will forever be a part of me on the carpet with my toy Indians looking up at him in it. We moved to that home when I was seven months old, and Dad only left it for the last year of his life. Every time I go into that house, I am accessing memories, but now instead of the past I am thinking of the present. I think of Dad sitting in his chair, but instead of picking up his dictionary he is picking up this book. What Dad, I hope, would find when he opened these pages is an open and honest letter to himself. I wanted to express not only the complexity of our love but its truth. I have said throughout that the writers who captivate me, take me to areas that both fascinate and inform, are those who present life in its most absolute form. Sometimes they leave a kiss, sometimes they leave a bruise. But always they leave something. I wanted this book to be the same, sometimes bathed, sometimes shadowed, in reality. Relationships are complex. You can, if you want, present a key connection in terms of two people skipping hand in hand through a sun-dappled meadow with a butterfly net, but surely there can be few for whom that picture is realistic. To be truthful has a worth. A value. Honesty is not to heap criticism on someone, it is not to present life as a spaghetti western, one person a goodie, another a baddie; it is to explore, emotionally, environmentally and historically, the dynamics of interplay, character and personality. Cause and effect. Effect and cause. Me and Dad. Dad and me.

My dad died in 2012. His self went some years previously. What writing this book has allowed me to do is have a conversation with him the like I've never had before. The same bloke who, in my head, sighed wearily at my travails in Macbeth – 'What? You fell off the stage?' – is there trawling through the pages of this book. 'You think it happened like that do you, Chris? Aye, well, I might have to have a word about that!'

Dad, I'm sorry if there are elements misremembered. And, Mum, I'm sorry about the glitter on the box-room carpet.

I love the bones of you.

Eulogy

I would like to say more than a few words about Joseph Ronald Eccleston Esq – a gentleman and a scholar.

Mum, Keith, Alan – I am very sorry for your loss. I would never assume to speak for you. We all had our own very specific relationship with Dad. He wasn't just the Two Ronnies, as my mum used to call him, he was lots of Ronnies. But I hope I can reflect some of your feelings about the man as well as my own.

In 2004, Dad was in the Hope Hospital having his life saved. He was recovering from a massive operation. My mum and a nurse were linking him as he walked — shuffled really — along the corridor. He was in a lot of pain and was confused both by the anaesthetic and his dementia. But from somewhere within himself, as he approached the swing doors, he remembered to step aside to let my mum and the nurse go first. The only problem was they were holding him up. He had impeccable, impeccable manners — he insisted on it with us three lads — so the first thing he would want to say to you is thank you. Thank you for coming out for him and thank you for supporting his family — we won't forget it.

To use one of his favourite expressions, he would 'drop cork-legged' to see how many of you are here. He would not have expected it. He was modest. He would have counted you though — just as he would count our Christmas cards every year and numerous other things. He would have counted you and then said to me, 'How many people do you think are in this church?'

'I don't know, Dad. How many?'

'Eighty-six! Eighty-six! I can't stand it.'

Whenever we drove past a churchyard, my dad would be guaranteed to say, 'How many people do you think are dead in that cemetery?'

'I don't know, Dad — how many?'

'All of 'em!'

He had a volcanic temper. He could be fierce and uncompromising and he lacked patience. I got on the wrong side of him and most of the time I deserved it. There may be a few other people who felt the blaze. There are certainly some in the upper echelons of Colgate-Palmolive on Ordsall Lane. 'Upper echelons' is an important detail. Dad was never going to advance his career options by being nice to the bosses. He was a man who put principle, as he saw it, before self-interest. If you were wrong, you were wrong, and you were told.

Anybody would have thought he was born in Salford.

He was born in Salford and my mum's grandmother remembered a little boy running around James Street shouting, 'Vote Labour! Vote Labour!'

He voted Labour all his life. He also voted for Pat Eddery, Willie Carson, Lester Piggott and Jonjo O'Neill at the bookies at the top of Coniston Avenue. He liked a bet. Money had always been tight, especially when he was a child, and having a bet was a lovely bit of defiance. Two fingers to a false idol.

My dad read me Black Beauty *and* The Adventures of Tom Sawyer. *My mum was working night shifts at Westerns and he was suddenly in charge of my bedtimes. I was amazed. As far as I knew, Mum did all the soft stuff, the lullabies and the comforting. It was magical hearing him read. He had a very strong reading voice, a deep love of language, and he read with feeling and skill. It brought us closer.*

Sometimes he would fall asleep before I did, and I would just look at him – my dad.

If I had to distil mine and my dad's relationship down to one period, it would be those nights in the early '70s in that bedroom on Coniston Avenue, because, though my dad was very male and protective and fierce and a great footballer, I loved him most for his tenderness – we all did.

He was really very, very vulnerable, my dad (perhaps we all are). But his class, his era, his gender, meant he had to keep it hidden.

Before I went to bed, I'd wash my face and brush my teeth and then he'd say, 'Part your hair.' I was puzzled by this. My mum didn't make me part my hair, and anyway, I didn't have a parting, so I'd say, 'Why, Dad? I'm going to bed. Nobody will see me.'

'Never mind,' he'd say. 'Part your hair.'

I went to bed looking like Alan Ladd.

Somebody once said to him, 'You must be very proud of your Chris on the telly.'

And he said, 'I'm proud of all my three sons. One's a builder, one's an upholsterer, and one's an actor.'

If Keith was building an extension, he would turn up just to look at it. If Alan was upholstering a Chesterfield, he would deliver it with him, brimming with pride. And if I was on the telly or in a play, he would say to me, 'You took off a very good part.'

Me, Alan and Keith went out into the world with the absolute certainty that he loved us and that if we needed him he would be there – it may sound banal or clichéd, but many people don't have it.

He believed in loyalty. It was the centre of him. It was how he made sense of life and the world. If he said he would do a thing, he did it. And if you then returned that loyalty, he was in your corner for life. He wasn't interested in money or possessions (apart from his dictionary – he loved his dictionary) or status. He believed in an exchange of trust. He believed in – and it's an old-fashioned phrase this, from his era – 'good fellowship'. 'All for one and one for all.'

I'm going to shut up now, but I can hear him in my ear saying, 'I enjoyed it, but you left out the most important thing. You haven't said anything about my wife, Elsie.' And I really am saying it because it's what he would want me to say – and this is a direct quote, which I heard many, many times.

'Marrying Elsie was the best thing I ever did.'

Dad, from the bottom of my heart – thank you.

ACKNOWLEDGEMENTS

I would like to thank the countless millions who each day provide care, unseen, unacknowledged, for those they love afflicted by the terrible illness of dementia. They are the ones who truly deserve our respect and accolades. I would like also to recognise the pain, strength and dignity of those who experience mental illness, and the work of those committed to helping them. For facilitating my own desire to make the socially reflective drama so pertinent to the family I grew up in, I thank the incredible writers who shared that same belief, determined to highlight the institutionalised blight of injustice and inequality that has treated generations with disdain, when, in fact, they were remarkable, individual, irreplaceable.

For allowing me to shine the spotlight on one such family, I'd like to thank Simon & Schuster UK, my publisher Iain MacGregor and my editor Melissa Bond. I was given the opportunity to reveal the man and woman who made me – Ronnie and Elsie Eccleston – and I am sure their tireless love and dedication will resonate with many. My agent, Claire Maroussas, I would like to recognise for all her hard work in bringing this book to fruition. I would also like to thank my literary agent Paul Stevens, my former agent Lorraine Hamilton, and my great friend Davey Jones, who was there for me in my time of need. Thanks also to Larry Taube and friend-through-the-ages Pooky Quesnel. John Woodhouse, many thanks for your diligence in seeking to understand me and transforming my mind into the written word. Anthony Venditti, thanks for your great help and comprehension as an existential psychotherapist.

The city of Salford is also deserving of mention. Those remarkable square miles shaped me, and still do, for which I am eternally grateful. You can take the boy out of Salford . . .

More than anything, I would like to thank four people: Elsie and Ronnie Eccleston and my children – all you have ever given me is love. Albert and Esme, if I can give you what my mum and dad gave me, then I'll be happy. Thank you for your love. The future is yours.